CRITICAL ELECTIONS AND CONGRESSIONAL POLICY MAKING

STANFORD STUDIES IN THE NEW POLITICAL HISTORY

Allan Bogue, David W. Brady, Nelson W. Polsby, and
Joel H. Silbey, Editors

Critical Elections and Congressional Policy Making

DAVID W. BRADY

STANFORD UNIVERSITY PRESS
Stanford, California

Stanford University Press
Stanford, California

© 1988 by the Board of Trustees of the
Leland Stanford Junior University
Printed in the United States of America
Original printing 1988
Last figure below indicates year of this printing:
00   99   98   97   96   95   94   93   92   91

CIP data appear at the end of the book

To my mother, who taught me at an early age that politics matter

Preface

THE CONTEMPORARY CONGRESS is viewed as an institution whose structure and policy are essentially shaped by incumbent members' reelection desires. The dominance of the reelection motive has had, it is believed, an adverse effect on public policy. In light of this, Richard Fenno once observed that we need a book on Congress when its major goal is to make good public policy. In one sense this is such a book. I analyze the House of Representatives during critical periods when it has legislated major policy changes. The Congresses of the Civil War, 1890's, and New Deal eras were responsible, in part, for outpourings of new comprehensive public policies.

In showing how critical elections affect both the institution and the policies it passes I do not refute the consensus on how the contemporary House works. Rather, the argument is that certain elections are national in focus, and that the newly elected majority party has both comprehensive policy goals and the unity required to pass its policy shifts. In this sense, then, the book is about Congress when its goal is to make good public policy. Moreover, it should be added that in each of these critical periods the policy changes legislated by the Congress established a new equilibrium in American politics.

In the process of writing this book I have picked up obligations— intellectual, institutional, and other. My primary institutional obligations are to Rice University, which generously supported this work, and to the Center for Advanced Study in the Behavioral Sciences, Stanford, California. While at the Center my work was supported by the National Science Foundation (grant number BNS8011494). I owe Gardner Lindzey a special thanks for his support, both personal and institutional. I also received a Project 87 grant in 1979 that allowed me to start this project. My primary intellectual debt is to my colleagues in the History of Congress Group: Nelson Polsby, Allan Bogue, and Joel Silbey. I am equally indebted to Joseph Cooper, John Ferejohn, and

Morris Fiorina. At one point or another each of them forced me to reach for better explanations, and without them this book would not have come to fruition.

I am also indebted to other scholars who have in various ways made contributions to this work: John Alford, James Anderson, Rick Wilson, Richard Fenno, Ken Shepsle, Charles Bullock, Sam Patterson, Paul Joskow, Robert Bates, Peter Mieszkowski, Bob Stein, Harold Hyman, Roger Noll, Lance Davis, and Bernie Grofman, among others. I was fortunate enough to have two editors, Muriel Bell and Barbara Mnookin, whose careful work caught and thus saved me from errors of both style and substance.

Last, but certainly not least, I thank my wife Carolyn and our daughters Emily, Elizabeth, and Anna, who put up with having their lives disrupted for a year so that I might finish.

D.W.B.

Contents

Tables

Figures

CRITICAL ELECTIONS AND CONGRESSIONAL POLICY MAKING

CHAPTER ONE

Introduction

★ THE FOUNDING FATHERS created a constitutional system designed to keep majorities from enacting public policy of a broad, decisive nature with unreasonable haste. Some 200 years later, it is clear they succeeded: scholars and observers of the U.S. Congress attest to its inability to legislate major policy changes. To cite a particularly trenchant comment: "Congressional decision making sometimes resembles a meat slicer, reducing large public problems to a series of discrete, unrelated, and often contradictory tidbits of policy." And another: "After viewing recent events in Washington, more than a few skeptics maintain that the U.S. House of Representatives has already joined the ranks of the dead."[1] Looking at the present Congress, the founding fathers might well be pleased to see that it does not hastily enact public policies. They would, however, be puzzled by the House of Representatives' role in the policy process. The House of Representatives was created as *the* democratic institution. "Here, sir, the people govern," Alexander Hamilton announced. "Here they act by their immediate representatives."[2] But the authors of the Constitution feared that as the people's branch, the House would act quickly and chaotically. Therefore, they created an indirectly elected upper chamber, which they hoped would use reason and judgment to temper the House's passions. The founding fathers would indeed be surprised by the continuity, stability, and policy incrementalism that characterize the modern House.

Criticism of the House is not restricted to the post–World War II period, to be sure. As early as 1831 Alexis de Tocqueville found the House "remarkable for its vulgarity and its poverty of talent." He believed that it might even cause the country to "perish . . . miserably on the shoals of democracy."[3] Davy Crockett wrote that he and his fellow House members "generally lounge or squabble the greater part of the session."[4] And in a famous speech in 1925, House Speaker Nicholas

Longworth said, "I find that we [the House] did not start being un-popular when I became a Congressman. We were unpopular before that time. We were unpopular when Lincoln was a Congressman. We were unpopular even when John Quincy Adams was a Congressman. We were unpopular even when Henry Clay was a Congressman. We have always been unpopular."[5] One of the major causes of the House's unpopularity has been its inability to legislate broad public policies.

Samuel Huntington argued that the intensity of criticism of Con-gress "varies inversely with the degree and dispatch with which Con-gress approves the President's legislative proposals."[6] The House's power, he wrote, is the power to obstruct legislation. And certainly in an era of executive governments, the U.S. Congress has retained greater obstructionist power than other Western parliaments. Indeed, it sometimes seems that one could make an even larger claim than Huntington's: that the House's power lies in its ability to obstruct broadly purposeful public policies.

Yet for all these long-standing criticisms of the House, we know that at certain critical points it *has* legislated major public policy changes. As recently as 1965 the second session of the 89th Congress was hailed as "the most productive congressional session ever held" and "the Congress of realized dreams"; polls indicated that "fully 71 per-cent of the American electorate [gave] a favorable rating to the job done by Congress in 1965."[7] Certainly the Congresses of the New Deal, Civil War, and 1890's eras, like the 89th Congress, were respon-sible, in part, for outpourings of new, comprehensive public policies.

This book confines itself to the House of Representatives. Its pur-pose is to account for such outpourings in the Houses of those eras. How and under what conditions does the House—noted for obstruc-tionism—create majorities capable of governing? The answer put for-ward is that critical elections create conditions in the House that en-able the majority party to legislate significant policy changes.

How do critical elections create conditions for major shifts in public policy? Any answer depends on our view of the way the House nor-mally operates. The assumption of this study is that "motivational, in-stitutional, and environmental features hang together in a sort of equilibrium, with changes in one affecting and constraining adaptive responses in the other."[8] This assumption is best understood in the light of a problem set forth by William Riker in *Liberalism Against Populism*. Loosely stated, the problem is that whereas the deductive models of social choice theorists show that political instability is en-demic,[9] the observations of behavioral scholars indicate a substantial degree of political stability. And in the case of the House, students of that body find almost nothing but stability: "Congress equals continuity plus stability."[10]

How do these "motivational, institutional, and environmental features" hang together in the contemporary House? To begin with, the primary motive of House members is election and reelection, and one assumes that members rationally pursue this goal. In most parliamentary democracies, members' election bids are heavily dependent on the party loyalty of the voters and on the party as organization.[11] That is, the electorate is divided into two or more groups who express a preference for candidates bearing the appropriate party label. Candidates are nominated and funded via the party organization, and withdrawal of party support is normally tantamount to electoral defeat. Thus members' motivations are tied to their environment through the party organization of the electorate. In addition, the structure of the legislature itself reflects the importance of party as a linkage between environment, motives, and institutional arrangements. In the United States political parties are, and have been, weaker than their counterparts elsewhere. Members of Congress today seek nomination and election by and large on their own. Candidates win nomination via a primary election within the party, which means that they must create their own campaign organization. Funds, workers, schedules, contacts, and so forth are arranged by candidates, not parties. In the general election the party may be of peripheral help, but members rely primarily on their own organization to appeal to voters.[12] Add this organizational schema to a system that features weak party preferences and local and regional diversity, and you have a system in which members of the House have relatively greater individual control over their electoral fate than their counterparts in other representative democracies.

House members in the United States engage in neutral political activities like voter contacting and constituent service because such activities increase their chances for reelection.[13] Once elected they choose, within limits, committee assignments that enable them to serve constituents, thereby furthering their reelection prospects. Overall, this process results in a committee system characterized by Riker as a set of congealed preferences.[14] Members of the Agriculture, Commerce, Interior, and Appropriations committees, for example, all have related preferences, and since policy is largely made in committees, stable policy is the result. Members not on a particular committee do not seriously challenge its bills on the floor since they know that their own committee's policies could be similarly challenged. Shepsle and Weingast demonstrate the universalism of this norm, and the attendant logrolling that results.[15] Under these conditions, policy is clearly stable and change thus incremental.

Given this theoretical approach, anyone interested in explaining nonincremental change must necessarily be concerned with both the exogenous electoral conditions and the internal structural arrangements that account for stability. For major changes in policy to occur, either electoral conditions or the structural arrangements that support incrementalism, or both, must change. This, of course, assumes that the members' reelection or election motive is constant.[16] In the sections that follow, both the structural factors and the environmental factors that promote stability are examined in greater detail, since without an understanding of those factors, we cannot know how certain elections change conditions such that they result in new public policies.

In answering the question why policy incrementalism prevails under normal conditions, I shall focus first on the ways federalism, separation of powers, checks and balances, and single-member plurality elections limit the possibility of strong majority government. Second, I turn to an analysis of how these factors affect the three parts of a party system—party in the electorate, party as organization, and party as government.[17] Third, I analyze the ways the internal structure of the House reflects these institutional and party arrangements. At this point it becomes possible to hypothesize that realigning or critical elections create conditions under which majorities are capable of legislating clusters of policy changes. The rest of the book tests the thesis.

It is important to point out that I am not claiming that major policy shifts can only occur during critical election periods. It is simply that my emphasis is on periods when major policy change is most clearly linked to elections and institutions. It is, of course, a central feature of representative democracy that elections, institutions, and policy be linked together in some systematic fashion. Moreover, it has become increasingly clear that in the history of each nation-state, there are critical periods that define and shape the politics and policies of that state for a generation or longer. In one sense, this is a book about three such periods in American political history.

★ Historical Background

The U.S. Constitution was to a large extent a response to problems that the Articles of Confederation proved unable to solve. It reflects the founding fathers' recognition of the fact that any viable government must be organized to deal with the existing problems in the society and their attempt to deal with what they saw as the dominant political problems of their day. The first defining feature of the House's environment is that the American system of government is federal. The Articles of Confederation had proved unable to pull together the various and diverse state and sectional interests. Shay's Rebellion and other localized flare-ups attest to the sectional diversity of the United States.[18] Thus a critical problem for the drafters who gathered in Philadelphia in 1787 was that of creating a centralized government that would be effective but at the same time not so centralized that it would be repudiated by the various sectional interests. There was never any serious question of creating a uniform national government. Not only would the idea have been repugnant to many of those gathered in Philadelphia, but no practical possibility of creating such a government existed. Delegates to the Constitutional Convention were selected by each state, voting was by state, the various governmental proposals such as the Virginia and New Jersey plans were proposed by and named after states, and ratification was by state. Before, during, and after the Constitutional Convention, states' interests were an accepted fact of political life.

The federal nature of the system reflected the social, economic, and religious differences between states and sections. Indeed, many have argued that sectionalism has been and remains the mainspring to an understanding of American history.[19] Whether or not that thesis is correct, my purpose here is to show how the federal system of government promotes policy incrementalism in the House of Representatives. The most obvious effect is that to the extent that a federal system reflects and recognizes in government organization the social, economic, and religious differences between states, it demonstrates a "numerous and diverse population."[20] The father of the Constitution, James Madison, argued that such a population constituted a real check on the formation of a majority capable of acting in haste. From Alexander Hamilton's use of the Treasury Department to boost industrial and monied interests to the present competing claims of the sun- and snowbelts, different sectional interests have pressured Congress to pass legislation viewed as beneficial to one and inimical to others.[21] The Civil War, the 1896 realignment, and countless other events in American history all testify to the effects of sectional diversity on the American system of government. As a focal point for those differences, the House has had not only to deal with issues in a policy sense, but also to temper sectional demands by integrating sectional divisiveness. And of course, as Madison anticipated, such divisiveness made it difficult to form "hasty" majorities—which is to say, majorities capable of enacting significant policy changes.

Diversity was not a sufficient roadblock to potentially tyrannical majorities for the drafters. On the assumption that the concentration of legislative, executive, and judicial powers in the same hands would invite tyranny, they wrote into the Constitution the doctrines of separation of powers and checks and balances. These doctrines have resulted in an American system of government that is characterized by "separate powers sharing functions."[22] Thus one distinguishing feature of the U.S. House is that, unlike the British House of Commons, it shares power with an upper body, a chief executive, the courts, and the bureaucracy. The most immediate effect of the separation of powers and checks and balances on the House is that even when it can build majorities for innovative policies, the Senate or the courts may thwart them. Richard Neustadt and others have shown that each of these institutions has different constituencies to please and therefore different policy solutions even when they agree on where the problem lies.[23] Policy makers in either chamber are likely to compromise or water down strong policy proposals made by the other branches of government. The 1977 Energy Act is a case in point. The Senate's version of the bill was very different from the House bill, and the final bill altered the status quo much less than the House bill would have.[24] Such compromises, whether anticipated or forced, are readily associable with incremental public policy.

In the American system opponents of policy changes have access to a large number of power points where a defeat for the majority position spells defeat until the next Congress forms.[25] The history of the Elementary and Secondary Education Act of 1965 corroborates the difficulty House leaders have in building coalitions capable of enacting major policy changes.[26] In the American system, having a policy majority does not readily translate into significant policy change. Those who seek to preserve the status quo always have a decided advantage. This contrasts with the way majorities are built in most other representative democracies.

The only popularly and directly elected body established by the Constitution is the U.S. House of Representatives. Each member of the House was to represent an approximately equal number of people, and more important, each was responsible to his constituents alone. There was no national party to supervise or control the nomination process. There was no mechanism to purge members who did not follow party principles. All this has nourished localized elections, as has an electoral method in which members win a district by a simple plurality.[27] Members elected on local issues by localized, limited constituencies owe little to House leaders and can behave as they choose as long as their constituency is happy.

An important policy consequence of localized elections is that an intense representation of local interests pervades the House across a broad range of issues. Representatives choose committees that will increase their reelection chances.[28] Members from agricultural districts serve on the relevant committees and subcommittees; members from other types of districts serve on committees and subcommittees relevant to their constituencies. Thus committees and policy outputs are dominated by local interests. This phenomenon has been called policy making or control by "little government," "the iron triangles" of interest-group liberalism, pork-barrel politics, and policy reciprocity.[29] The name matters little; what counts is that localized interests are recognized as congealed within the structure of the House's policy-making process. Forming majorities capable of enacting major policy changes against a backdrop of institutionally localized interests is a difficult task at best, impossible at worst.

Although many parameters of the doctrines of federalism, separation of powers, and checks and balances have changed to make the system more democratic and centralized, the American system of government remains fragmented and cumbersome. Shortly after the Constitution took effect, difficulties inherent in governing within its framework presented themselves. In response, Hamilton crossed executive boundaries and led pro-national factions in the Congress.[30] Over time these factions developed into political parties. Yet even though American parties were founded because the system was too cumbersome without them, the same system also inhibited their full development.

Perhaps the most distinguishing characteristic of American political parties is that their three roles—party in the electorate, party as organization, and party as government—are disjointed.[31] Certainly no one claims that American parties are mass parties in the European sense. Federalism, separation of powers, checks and balances, and single-member plurality districts are in no small way responsible for the fragmented nature of the American party system.

The most basic effect of a federal form of government on the American party system is that rather than a two-party system, we have a fifty-party system.[32] Each state's party system has demographic, ideological, structural, and electoral peculiarities. Thus the Democratic Party in the electorate and as organization in New York has been distinct from the Democratic Party in the electorate and as organization in Georgia. The same applies to the components of the Republican Party in these states. The heterogeneity of the state party systems means that at the level of party as government, *unlike*-minded men bearing the same party label will come together in the House of Representatives. Put another way, the federal system brings built-in differences between states and regions to the House. Although this may be useful in maintaining system equilibrium, it has most often been an extremely poor basis for building coherent congressional parties. The New Deal coalition of rural Southern and agricultural interests and urban Northern industrial interests is a case in point. Long after this coalition had passed its major policy changes, it served as an electoral base for the Democratic Party.[33] Such successful electoral coalitions, however, often are divided on major policy issues. In fact, on a number of major policy issues, such as civil rights and social welfare, the components of the New Deal coalition were poles apart.* American political history abounds with examples of successful electoral coalitions that cannot make major policy changes because of ideological differences. It is not difficult to surmise how such coalitions lead to static or incremental policy.

The separation of powers and the system of checks and balances contribute to the fragmentary, disjointed status of American parties. Parties formed out of numerous and diverse state party systems will emphasize electoral success and minimize policy cohesion (and thus policy success). When given the opportunity to compete for numerous offices (both appointive and electoral) in the various branches, national parties formed on the basis of a sectional coalition will be further fractionalized. Thus, for example, one faction of the party may be dominant in presidential politics, another in congressional politics; and since both have powers over the courts, an equal division of court appointments may result.[34] The Democratic Party from 1876 to 1976 was characterized by just such an arrangement. The Northern wing dominated presidential politics and elections, the Southern wing controlled congressional leadership posts, and both wings influenced court appointments. Such a system may help represent political differences, but it does little to elect House majorities capable of legislating public policy changes.

*Sinclair, "Party Realignment." This phenomenon is deeply rooted in the American federal system. The Republican Party was divided over the gold-silver question before 1896 and was divided over the questions of welfare and government management of the economy during the post–Franklin D. Roosevelt period. The Democrats were divided on questions of civil rights through a large part of the 20th century.

The constitutional arrangement of single-member plurality elections also helps to fragment the party system. House members elected on local issues by a localized party in the electorate build local party (or personal) organizations.[35] Once elected, owing little to national party leaders, representatives can behave in nonpartisan ways with little consequence for their congressional careers. That is, throughout most of the House's history, party leaders have been able only to persuade, not to force, members to vote "correctly." Party leadership without even the threat of sanctions is likely to be unsuccessful in building consistent partisan majorities. It should not be surprising that the highest level of voting along party lines in the history of the House occurred at a time when the Speaker's sanctions over members were greatest. Representatives elected by local majorities can in turn work and vote on behalf of those interests regardless of the national party position; House leaders do not "persuade" from a position of power.

The ways local and state diversity are institutionalized in the American system of government allow diversity to work its way up from party in the electorate through party organizations to the congressional parties almost unchanged. Thus at the top as at the bottom, the party system reflects the cumbersomeness and fractionalism of the American system of government. Whatever policy parties are able to enact under these conditions is bound to be incremental in nature, and changes in the status quo will be hard to come by.

★ House Organization

Like all organizations, the House of Representatives has adapted to societal change by creating internal structures designed both to meet the pressures or demands from its various constituencies and to perform its policy-making function.[36] Given the enormous range of interests in the United States and the concomitant pressures they generate, the House responded with a division of labor. The result is today a highly complicated committee system. When the country was in its infancy, and government limited, the House formed ad hoc committees; as early as the Jacksonian era, however, a standing committee system was in place.[37] As the country grew more industrial and complicated, the House responded by expanding and enlarging that system. Early in this process committees were established to deal with such domains as war, post offices and roads, and ways and means to raise revenues to support the government. These committees, the "little legislatures" of George Goodwin's recent study, were organized around governmental policy functions; they were and are decentralized decision-making structures. The making of Reconstruction policy after the Civil War and Woodrow Wilson's claim that "congressional government is committee government" testify that the power of committees is no new phenomenon.[38] Decentralizing power to committees was a necessary response to pressures for government action in certain policy areas; it meant, however, that to the extent the committees decided policy, party leaders were limited.

As decentralized decision-making mechanisms, committees are dominated by members elected to represent local interests. The fact that within limits members can choose the committees they serve on determines to a large extent the direction the committees' policy choices will take. This is essentially what Riker means by congealed preferences. The decentralized committee system that allows members to represent local interests has become a powerful force for policy stability. In the modern House, as Ralph Huitt and others have shown, committees are entities unto themselves—they are stable, with little membership turnover, and new members are socialized to committee norms that affect policy decisions.[39] Since turnover is slow and decision norms remain stable, committee leaders are often able to prevent House majorities from enacting major policy changes. It takes years for new members to acquire the degree of specialization and expertise needed to make their voices heard in committee, a fact that at once increases the committee's power and promotes policy stability.[40] For example, even though from the late 1930's on, majorities of both the American people and the House favored such policies as medical aid for the aged and federal aid to schools, committee leaders were able to obstruct enactment until the mid-1960's. Almost 30 years of obstructing majorities is proof of both the independence and the power of the committee system. It is reasonable to conclude that the decentralized House committee system constitutes an effective deterrent to building majorities capable of enacting major policy changes.

What the division of labor pulls apart in organizations, integrative mechanisms have to pull together.[41] In the House the major integrative mechanism is the majority congressional party. And as we have seen, congressional parties are limited by the governmental structure established by the Constitution and by the fact that members are elected by local parties (or groups) on the basis of local issues. Members responsible to and punishable only by local electorates tend to be responsive to those electorates, not parties. In these circumstances, party strength tends to be low. Even in those periods when party voting has been at its peak in the U.S. House of Representatives, it was low compared with the party discipline evident in other Western democracies.[42] If, under ideal conditions the congressional parties in the House have limited integrative capacity,[43] then clearly under normal conditions policy decisions are likely to reflect localized committee interests, thereby limiting the national party leaders' attempts to lead majorities toward forceful policy solutions to pressing problems. House voting patterns show different coalitions active on different policy issues.[44] Coalitions cut across regional party and social and economic lines, making party leaders' jobs a "ceaseless maneuvering to find coalitions capable of governing" in specific policy areas.[45]

A third factor affects the House's ability to legislate quickly. Not only is it a collegial body; it is a body whose operation has manifestly been influenced by the American cultural emphasis on equality. Because each member represents a separate and equal constituency, members receive the same pay, have the same rights to introduce bills and serve on committees, and so on. Under these circumstances, the House has a limited capacity to organize itself hierarchically, and since hierarchy is limited, the House has established elaborate procedural rules and precedents to control the passage of legislation from Speaker to committee to floor.[46] This procedural elaboration emphasizes the individual member's right to affect legislation at various decision points in the policy process. The effect is to slow down the policy process and to encourage compromise to avoid parliamentary snafus. Both slowness and compromise favor incremental solutions to policy problems.

The House is, then, a relatively nonhierarchical body, with power decentralized in committees operating under elaborate rules and lawmaking procedures. The weakness of the congressional parties is partly the result of factors external to the House (e.g. local elections, cultural stress on equality, separation of powers) and partly the result of the way the House is organized (members' preference for decentralized power and the lack of leadership sanctions). In short, in "normal" times committees are strong and the parties weak and divided. This is in part true because, as David Rhode and Kenneth Shepsle have argued, localism produces heterogeneous preferences that limit leaders' ability to enact policy shifts.[47]

Over time the relationship between committee power and party strength has waxed and waned, but the general rule has been that committees are strong and congressional parties weak, and House leaders thus become middlemen. The policy choices emanating from this system have normally been incremental in nature. Pressures for major change are hindered by the decentralized decision-making structure that has dominated in the House. The formation of the

Democratic Study Group (DSG) in 1958 was a response to this fact. The group was founded to press liberal policy alternatives in a House dominated by cross-party conservative interests. The founders of the DSG found the policy process in the House cumbersome to operate and weighted toward interests (minority or otherwise) that sought to block legislation, thus preserving the status quo.[48]

In sum, major public policy changes occur rarely in the House of Representatives for the following reasons: (1) members are normally elected by local interests on local issues; (2) once elected, members choose committee assignments (within limits) based on those local interests and issues, thus localizing and congealing rather than nationalizing policy alternatives; (3) the committee system is powerful in part because it is stable; (4) the congressional parties are normally weak and divided because members' preferences are heterogeneous and conflicting, and thus they cannot assemble coalitions to override the localism of committee decisions; and (5) the organization, rules, and procedures of the House serve those who wish to preserve the status quo. It should also be mentioned that there are many historical periods when inertia or incrementalism accords with what both the majority of the public and the majority of the House want. When this is the case the congressional system is in harmony with political pressures. However, as Walter Dean Burnham has argued, political systems must over time adjust to majority pressures for change.[49] How the U.S. House of Representatives has managed to overcome inertia and incrementalism at periods when the majority desires change is the subject of this book.

★ A Theory of Policy Change

For a century or more scholars and reformers (who are sometimes the same people) have bemoaned Congress's inability to act on a variety of issues with major social consequences. In the late nineteenth century, for example, Woodrow Wilson claimed that Congress exhibited a distressing paralysis in moments of emergency; in the 1940's George Galloway berated Congress for "working with the tools and techniques of the snuffbox era"; and as late as the 1960's James MacGregor Burns saw Congress as the "prime institutional reason for the lagging social progress of the 1950's."[50] Like many scholars and reformers, these critics cited most of the same reasons offered above to account for congressional inertia. Woodrow Wilson attributed it to the power and unrepresentativeness of the standing committees and the diverse local loyalties of representatives:

I know not better how to describe our form of government in a single phrase than by calling it a government by the Standing Committees of Congress. This *disintegrative* ministry, as it figures on the floor of the House of Representatives, has many peculiarities. In the first place it is made up of the elders of the assembly; . . . in the second place, it is constituted of selfish and warring elements; . . . in the third place, instead of being composed of the associated leaders of Congress, it consists of the disassociated heads of forty-eight "little legislatures."[51]

He went on to argue that in committees, national interests held by the President, the national parties, and the public were excluded.

Galloway attributed congressional inertia to Congress's lack of hierarchy, the dominance of local interests, and the absence of cohesion between parties and committees: "Its internal structure is dispersive and duplicating. It is a body without a head. Leadership is scattered among the chairmen of 81 little legislatures who compete with each other for jurisdiction and power. . . . Most of its time is consumed by petty local and private matters. . . . Its posts of power are held on the basis of political age, regardless of ability or agreement with party politics."[52] And Burns attributed congressional inertia to congressmen's lobbying for the "dominant economic interests" in their districts, interests that were not in the national interest.[53]

Congressmen themselves have been among the severest critics. From the beginning, reform-minded senators and representatives like Thomas Bracket Reed, Joseph Clark, and Richard Bolling have attempted to explain why Congress is not responsive. The essence of these criticisms is perhaps best summed up by Gary Orfield. Policy impasse, he writes, "reflects both the built-in difficulties of achieving decisive action from a constitutional system designed to prevent excessive governmental activity, and the close and indecisive ideological division of the country."[54]

There appears to be a consensus regarding the House's inability to legislate major policy changes. How, then, has it been able to overcome these obstacles to activity and generate important clusters of policy changes during certain critical periods?

It is obvious that critical elections do not generate changes in the basic structure of federalism, the separation of powers, the system of checks and balances, and single-member plurality elections. All are still with us; critical elections have not created a uniform hierarchical national government. Realigning elections can, however, create changes in policies that affect these structures. The movement from dual federalism to cooperative federalism occurred during the New Deal realignment; and increases in presidential power relative to the Congress occurred during the Civil War and New Deal realignments. To assert that these changes took place, however, does not answer the fundamental question: How do critical elections create conditions that enable a majority to legislate significant policy changes?

The answer begins with the way such elections affect the nature of results. House elections are normally determined by local factors (local interests, alignment, organization, and issues), thereby ensuring the dominance of localism in the politics and policy decisions of the House.[55] Certain elections, however, are dominated by national rather than local issues. Realignment scholars point to the cross-cutting nature of the issue or issues that dominate critical elections.[56] These issues do not fit within the framework of the party system, and they are too intensely held to be brushed aside. In the long run the major parties must respond to these national, cross-cutting issues. Responses to such issues vary from a change in the majority party to the replacement of both the majority and minority by new parties.[57] The major realignments dealt with in this book cover three of the four possible types of realignments. The Civil War realignment replaced the Whigs with a new party—the Republicans. In the 1890's realignment the Democratic Party adopted the policy positions of a third party—the Populists. The New Deal realignment saw the Democrats replace the Republicans as the majority party.

In each of these periods there was at least one intense, cross-cutting issue that dominated the election results. In each case the nationalization of issues *greatly reduced* the effect of localism on the House. Voting patterns showed national swings, with the result that the newly elected congressional majority felt it had a mandate to legislate. During each of these periods the national political parties took strong, opposing positions on the dominant issues. At such times the parties are less fragmented and disjointed than they are under normal conditions. The party in the electorate is choosing between clearly defined, opposing views articulated by the parties as organization, and the voters send congressional parties elected on national issues to the House. In the House this set of factors clearly reduces localism and results in increased party voting. The effect of a more cohesive majority congressional party is most obvious on the issues that dominated the election. Put another way, the gap between local constituency and national party positions is reduced. Huitt claimed that one of the major drawbacks to increased party voting in the House was the cross-pressuring of representatives by their constituents.[58] During critical eras such cross-pressuring is greatly reduced; thus party voting in the House should be appreciably higher. In sum, the nationalizing of issues during critical election periods creates majority parties that are relatively united on major policy issues. And the strengthened majority party legislates the clusters of policy changes associated with these eras.

Clubb, Flanigan, and Zingale, in their excellent study of electoral realignment (1980), argue that critical election results do not directly translate into policy changes. Thus, for example, voters choosing Franklin D. Roosevelt and Democratic representatives in the 1932 election were not directly voting for the Agricultural Adjustment Act, the National Industrial Recovery Act, the Civil Conservation Corps, or any specific policy associated with the New Deal. Rather, the voters' actions created the conditions under which the party leadership could legislate major policy changes. In part, as noted above, the election results send to the House members with relatively homogeneous preferences. Equally important for an understanding of how critical elections create conditions for policy change is the effect of such elections on the structural characteristics of the government. One important result in each of the periods examined here is that the new majority party controlled the House, Senate, and Presidency for at least a decade. Unified control of the government for a relatively lengthy period is necessary in order for the policy changes to be passed and then accepted and ratified by the electorate in subsequent elections.

Another major change effected by critical elections is in the House's committee system. Committees, as we have seen, are an important reason why the House's policy decisions are normally incremental. Power is decentralized in the House and committee turnover (especially on major committees) is slow, ensuring that preferences will remain congealed, and that committee norms and practices that promote incrementalism are passed along to new members. For committees to be strong, local interests must be represented, and on major committees so must ideological differences within and between parties.[59] This combination of factors—ideological representation, localism, stability of membership, and apprenticeship (seniority)—leads inexorably to policy incrementalism. The ability to change or make policy hinges on the representatives' expertise, acquired through years of experience on the committee, which further ensures that change will be slow. Critical elections change this pattern of decision making by inundating the committee system with new members and removing old ones. Moreover, as the new majority party takes over, not only does committee membership change, but so does leadership. These abrupt changes greatly reduce the committees' ability to slow down or compromise major policy innovations. In fact committee turnover is so rapid that the "new" committees strongly support and encourage the major policy changes associated with the realignment.

Critical elections create conditions for majority party government in the House of Representatives by uniting (or decreasing the fractionalization of) the three elements of parties. The effect of a united new majority party in the House is to increase the party's ability to legislate and to decrease the committee system's ability to thwart policy initiatives. The enactment of clusters of policy changes is thus the result of national elections determined by national issues.

Critical elections have not changed the fundamental nature of a "constitutional system designed to prevent excessive governmental activity." The constitutional system is perhaps the basic reason why the House does not have a responsible party system.[60] That is, in the American system, party government is limited for structural reasons to periods of intense stress. High levels of party voting in the House fade as issues become localized or as consensus on policy changes crystallizes and the minority party accepts their consequences. After the New Deal sputtered on court packing and the Fair Labor Standards Act, for example, the Republicans made significant gains in House seats, and voting patterns returned to normal as the conditions for party government and policy change disappeared. Policy outputs were again incremental in nature, committees dominated, and a cross-party coalition of Southern Democrats and Republicans emerged to thwart the policy agenda of New Dealers on civil rights and social welfare.

I shall show in these pages that party government in the House is a constant across all three critical election eras. Each of the eras, however, had unique features. Each fits a separate type in James Sundquist's typology. Two of the periods were the result of gradual changes in the American society and economy, whereas the third was more the result of a single monumental event. The policy changes resulting from these critical periods are bound to affect the policy process in different ways. Thus a second major purpose of this book is to tap the richness of critical elections by analyzing the differences between them.

Most students of critical periods have simply asserted the temporal relationship between party in the electorate and policy changes during critical elections. A notable exception is Barbara Sinclair, who has demonstrated how critical elections affected policy in the New Deal era.[61] Analyzing voting patterns in the House, she shows the increased importance of party strength in pushing the New Deal programs through Congress. Yet up to this point no one has dealt with policy changes except to show how major legislation such as Social Security was passed. This book undertakes to analyze how such elections affect committees' decisions, specifically appropriations decisions made by the House during the 1890's and 1930's. The analysis shows that during critical eras, the Appropriations Committee and the House legislate *nonincremental* money bills, and that what accounts for these decisions is increased party strength—both in organization and in voting patterns.

In sum, what I hope to achieve in this book is what political scientists call mid-level theory. I seek a specification of how critical elections usher in major policy change because of changed motivational, environmental, and institutional features that normally lead to policy incrementalism. To this end I need to demonstrate for each critical period the way electoral results affect the composition of the congressional parties, the structure of committees, the strength of the party system, and policy outputs. The strategy is to treat each critical election period in a separate chapter (Chapters Two–Four). Each of these chapters will briefly describe the historical milieu—the critical issues—and then present an analysis of election data demonstrating the nationalization of the election results and the effects of those results on voting patterns in the House. These sections will rely heavily on a technique devised by Aage Clausen to determine consistent issue domains. The purpose is to demonstrate that policy changes associated with critical elections were passed as a result of increased party strength in the House.

In Chapter Five the behavior of the Appropriations Committee during the 1890's and New Deal realignments is examined (the Civil War era is omitted because the committee did not exist until 1865). The thesis is that the Appropriations Committee will appropriate nonincremental amounts during realignments to fund new programs. The general pattern of turnover found in the House will also be found in Appropriations, for both committee leaders and members. Moreover, the new members make decisions in a highly partisan fashion. In short, it will be shown that committee behavior follows the pattern established in the House.

Chapter Six focuses on the role of electoral competition in determining House election results. That is, since the theory is electorally driven, it is important to ascertain how the distribution of electoral results relates to changes in the composition of congressional parties. Party systems characterized by strong, sharply divided partisan blocs with relatively little give in the electorate and no large group of uncommitted votes generate congressional parties significantly different from those observed in the contemporary House of Representatives.

Chapter Seven summarizes the results of this study and speculates on conditions for policy change outside critical election periods. This chapter draws on Morris Fiorina's theory of retrospective voting.

★ Summary

The American constitutional system of government sought to prohibit majorities from enacting major policy shifts with any dispatch. The separation of powers, the system of checks and balances, and the federalism set out in the Constitution together ensure that policy decisions will be incremental. These structural factors, combined with an electoral system that institutionalizes localism in a diverse population, severely limit the congressional leadership's ability to change public policy. Yet in at least three periods the political system responded with major shifts in public policy—the Civil War era, the 1890's, and the New Deal era. Each of these periods was associated with one or more major realigning elections.

The thesis of this book is that in each realignment American political parties were the primary integrative mechanism linking the electorate to the party in government. During realignments political parties perform three functions that are necessary for concerted, consistent, and responsible policy actions:

1. Aggregating and articulating interests

2. Translating these interests into effective demands

3. Providing a stable electoral base for the new policy directions

In short, during realigning periods the three levels of party—electorate, organization, and government—are relatively united. The interrelated elements of the realignments are that the voters intentionally remove the incumbent party in response to the tension of crosscutting issues. These shifts in the popular distribution of the vote create a "new" majority party, which has unified control of the government. The new majority party's policy changes alleviate the crisis and reinforce the new distribution of the popular vote.

The role of the U.S. House of Representatives in this process is the major focus of my analysis. The task therefore becomes to show how realignments create the conditions for majority party government in the House. This entails demonstrating that during realignments the House is elected on national, not local issues, thus giving a sense of mandate to the new majority party. Realigning elections are characterized by issue differences between the dominant parties. The election results change the constituent bases of the congressional parties. This combination creates a relatively coherent and unified new congressional majority party. The turnover in membership reduces party constituency cross-pressuring, which is one of the two major inhibitors of party government in the House. It also reduces the tendency for standing committees to inhibit policy change. That is, turnover on committees is so high that they are no longer fiefdoms, independent of the party leadership. The combination of an electoral mandate and greatly reduced committee importance creates the conditions for party government. Each congressional party will be especially unified and divided from its opponent on votes dealing with the dominant issues of the realignment. In sum, in order to prove the party government thesis it is necessary to show that in critical periods:

1. Elections are national rather than local
2. The constituent bases of the parties change
3. Turnover on committees is sharp and inclusive
4. Party voting increases rapidly
5. Party is especially determinative on the issues associated with the realignment

Although the expectation is that each of the three realignments under discussion will have all five of these characteristics, it is important to note that realignments differ. Each realignment had its own structural characteristics. The Civil War realignment was, in Sundquist's terms, "realignment through the replacement of a major party," whereas the 1890's realignment was via "absorption of a third party," and the 1930's "realignment of the two existing parties."[62] Clearly these differences are grounded in the nature of the cross-cutting issues and in the nature of the economy and society. The realignments will be compared to one another at various points in the analysis to capture the richness of these differences.

CHAPTER TWO

The Great Dilemma: Slavery and the Civil War Realignment

THE PERIOD FROM 1831 to 1877 was rich in significant events. It covered the rise and decline of the second
party system (i.e., the party system in effect from 1824 until
the 1850's), the formation of the third party system, the rise of the
slavery issue, the Civil War, and Reconstruction. The era is characterized by important elections, controversial issues, great leaders, and
significant public policy changes.[1] For my purposes, however, the relevant historical milieu encompasses the decline of the second party system, formation of the third party system, and the effects of issues on
political parties—in short, the conditions associated with the rise of
the Republican Party and the Civil War era realignment.

The second party system began with the presidential election of
1824, acquired its dominant characteristics by 1840, and began to
come apart in the 1850's. Like the systems that preceded and followed
it, the second party system was a two-party system. It was distinct from
the first party system in its competitiveness, sectional alignments,
breadth of appeal to potential participants, and potential for resolving conflict.[2] Under the second party system party organizations were
formed in each state, and voters developed a loyalty to party labels.
Thus, unlike the elitist first system, the second had all three components of a party system: party in the electorate, party as organization,
and party in government.[3] The Whigs and Democrats competed across
all regions of the country, and in national elections voter turnout and
interest were high. The parties sought to aggregate national interests;
each party embraced powerful Northern and Southern wings. The
parties differed on national issues. The Whigs favored Western expansion, homestead legislation, government activism in promoting
growth, and, in general, protective tariffs. The Democrats were less
enthusiastic about expansion, and governmental promotion of growth,
and against homestead legislation and protective tariffs. The ques-

tions of slavery and slave states versus free states were often resolved during the era by compromises. The Northern and Southern wings of both parties compromised on nullification, Texas, fugitive slave laws, and slave auctions in Washington, D.C., among other related issues. Thus the second system was indeed a full-blown party system, complete with national parties differing on issues and competing for electoral victory across regions. Yet despite the cross-sectional strength of the parties, it was a sectional issue that brought the system down.

With the first issue of the *Liberator* in 1831, William Lloyd Garrison began the movement that would ultimately destroy the second party system. The preeminent issue was, of course, slavery. The slavery question cut across Whig-Democrat divisions, both in elections and in Congress. As early as 1836 abolitionists were credited with having cost the Whigs the governorship of Ohio, and the congressional Whigs split over the gag-rule question in 1836. Although both parties had antislavery elements, the Whigs were always more divided on the question than the Democrats. The creation of the Liberty Party, the Hale revolt in New Hampshire, the Barnburners in New York, the Free Soil Party, and the "conscience Whigs" are all eloquent testimony to the electoral divisiveness of the slavery issue. Even the Compromise of 1850 could only buy a little time for the second party system. Prior to that agreement, the gag rule, the Texas question, and the Wilmot Proviso were prominent issues before the House; after it, the Kansas-Nebraska Act, secession, the abolition of slavery, and civil rights for blacks dominated the House's time. In short, the question of slavery would not go away, and the Whig-Democrat party system could not in the long run accommodate it.

The rise of the slavery issue as a divisive force is complicated. The simple view that the Republican Party was formed to eliminate slavery has long since been discounted.[4] Many of the abolitionists were, by any standard, racist.[5] David Wilmot introduced his famous Proviso to exclude slavery from territory acquired from Mexico by assuring the Congress that he was concerned about the rights of free white men, not about black slaves. The Free Soil movement was less antislavery than antiblack. The Know Nothings were concerned about the rising tide of liquor-loving Catholic immigrants from Ireland and Germany. Democrats, it was said, "pandered to the lowest class of foreign citizens, . . . combining the forces of Jesuitism and Slavery, of the Pope and the Devil."[6] Thus the antislavery movements and parties of this era were not only antislave, they were also antiforeigner and antiliquor. In this chapter I shall focus on the slavery issue, leaving the discussion of the nativist issue to Chapter Seven.

By the mid-1850's nativism and temperance had declined as independent political forces. The issues of race, slavery, slavery expansion, and slave power were the ascendant issues. By 1856 the Republican Party had become the party with the most liberal views on race. Although it is true that some Republicans, like Lyman Trumball of Illinois, were out-and-out racists, and that the Republican position tied emancipation to the elimination of slave power and the rights of free white men to jobs, the Republicans were clearly distinguishable from the antiblack Democrats.

The single issue that united most of the various antislavery elements into the Republican Party was the Kansas-Nebraska Act. The passage of the act effectively repealed the Compromise of 1820. Senator Stephen Douglas's doctrine of free choice applied to unorganized territories and included the territories recently acquired in the Mexican-American War. The result was civil disruptions in the Kansas and Nebraska territories as slave interests fought antislave interests, with the anti–Kansas-Nebraska forces ultimately unifying to defeat the proslave Le Compton Constitution. As Richard Sewall notes, "Before the tempest [over the Kansas-Nebraska Act] subsided it had splintered the Democratic Party, smashed the last remnants of organized Whiggery, and crystallized anti-slavery elements from all parties into a formidable new political coalition [the Republican Party]."[7] Thus, by the mid-1850's the second party system was gone, the Republicans had made their entrance, and slavery had become the dominant cross-cutting issue.

Although slavery was the dominant issue underlying the Civil War realignment, the Republican Party also brought nationalistic economic policy views to the Congress. The Republicans, "like the Whigs, stood for aggressive action by the national government to develop manufacturing and commerce through a protective tariff, expansionist banking policies, and internal improvements—logically extended to include a transcontinental railroad and homestead legislation . . . to promote settlement of the West."[8]

★ Partisan Differences

Benjamin Ginsberg has carried out content analyses of party platforms from 1844 to 1968 in an attempt to determine both the salience and the partisan divergence of conflict.[9] He concludes that realigning elections are characterized by intense partisan conflict. His figures for the Civil War realignment are revealing. With regard to the slavery issue, he shows that whereas in 1844 and 1848 the salience of the slav-

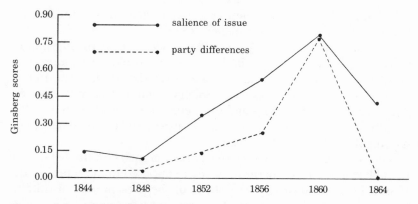

Fig. 2.1. Salience of the slavery issue, 1844–1864. Source: Benjamin Ginsberg, "Critical Elections and the Substance of Party Conflict: 1844–1968," *Midwest Journal of Political Science*, Aug. 1972, pp. 603–25.

ery (or universalism) issue was only 0.13 and 0.09, the figure rises steeply thereafter, to 0.42 in 1852, 0.48 in 1856, and 0.71 in 1860.[10] His analysis of the salience of issues dealing with the exercise of power by the federal government in regard to the states reveals the same general pattern. That is, in the 1852–60 period, the issue was more prominent than it was in the latter years of the second party system, 1844–51.

Ginsberg also measures the extent of partisan conflict for the 1844–1968 period. Here his analysis shows that in regard to both slavery and federal-state power questions the parties differed greatly during the Civil War realignment. Figure 2.1 dramatically documents both the increased salience of slavery as an issue of concern to the parties and their polarization on the issue after 1844.

Useful as Ginsberg's analysis of platforms is to demonstrate the importance of the slavery issue in a quantitative fashion, the text of the party platforms adds a qualitative dimension worth investigating. At the Whig and Democratic conventions of 1844 and 1848, there was little if any difference between the parties on the issue. In 1844 the Democrats passed a states' rights resolution that spoke of the dire consequences if Congress followed the abolitionists' lead to ban slavery. The Whigs did not mention the issue in their short platform. In 1848 the Democrats defeated a plank on slavery (216 to 36) that would have prevented interference with the rights of slaveholders. The Whigs again were silent, choosing to focus instead on the qualifications of Zachary Taylor for the Presidency. In short, both parties accepted the Missouri Compromise and thereby avoided a North-South split. Specific planks on slavery were left to minor parties such as the Liberty Party in 1844 and the Free Soilers in 1848.

The major party platforms in 1852 reflected the growing importance of the issue. Although both parties supported the Compromise of 1850, the Whigs were more divided over slavery than the Democrats. The Free Democrats (Free Soilers) came out against any new slave territories. The Whigs and the Democrats continued to disagree over the role of the federal government in internal improvements, the settling of the West, and protective tariffs.

The conventions of 1856 were still farther apart on the issue. The Republicans called for all those "who are opposed to the repeal of the Missouri Compromise; to the policies of the present administration; to the extension of slavery into Free Territory; in favor of the admission of Kansas as a Free State" to join with them in electing John C. Fremont.[11] The Democrats, by contrast, adopted the following convoluted statement: "Resolved, that claiming fellowship with, and desiring the cooperation of all who regard the preservation of the Union under the Constitution as the paramount issue—and repudiating all sectional parties and platforms concerning domestic slavery, which seek to embroil the States and incite to treason and armed resistance to law in the Territories; and whose avowed purposes, if consummated, must end in civil war and disunion, the American Democracy recognize and adopt the principles contained in the organic laws, establishing the Territories of Kansas and Nebraska as embodying the only sound and safe solution of the 'slavery question' upon which the great national idea of the people of this whole country can repose in its determined conservation of the Union—*Non Interference By Congress With Slavery in State And Territory, Or In The District of Columbia.*" Thus, by 1856 there had emerged a clear difference between the two major parties on slavery.

The tumultuous Democratic convention of 1860 was testimony enough to the divisiveness of the slavery question. The adoption of a moderate proslavery plank sent the Southern delegates to Richmond, Virginia, to nominate John C. Breckenridge for the Presidency on a strong proslavery platform. The Republicans, meeting in Chicago, adopted an even stronger antislavery plank than they had in 1856: "The normal condition of all the territory of the United States is that of freedom; . . . we deny the authority of Congress, of a territorial legislature, or of any individuals, to give legal existence to slavery in any territory of the United States." Clearly, the lines were drawn—Republicans were the party of antislavery forces, Democrats the proslavery party. The election results would tell the tale.

★ Electoral Change

If the realignment in the electorate was precipitated by the cross-cutting issue of slavery and the secondary economic issues mentioned above, then the congressional election results should reveal national, not local, forces at work. Demonstrating the nationalization of election results entails calculating the variance across all House elections from 1852 to 1876 and within districts over time. The argument is that when elections are determined by local factors, the variance around the mean party vote will be high, whereas when elections are determined by national forces, the variance will be smaller because the same forces are affecting all districts. David Butler and Donald Stokes use this argument to show how national factors are more important in Britain than they are in America.[12] Their point is that variance around the mean swing in pairs of elections measures the uniformity of change; that is, the extent to which national forces are at work.

My strategy for analyzing electoral change in each of the three critical periods discussed in this book is first to show the mean swing in the vote and standard deviation for the following time periods: 1848–74, 1884–1902, 1924–40. (In Chapters Five, Six, and Seven, however, my purposes change, and the time series will, depending on need, be extended to cover longer periods.) An additional measure of change to be used is the coefficient of variation—$V = S/X$, where S is the standard deviation and X is the mean. I want to take into account both the mean swing for or against a party and the variance around that mean. The argument is that as the standard deviation increases relative to the mean, local variation is greater in relation to the national trend; and that as the mean swing increases relative to the standard deviation, national trends eclipse local factors. In short, the lower the value of the coefficient of variation, the greater the likelihood that an election reflects national rather than local factors. With regard to critical elections, the specific argument is that as one approaches the critical election(s), the coefficient of variation should decrease. This is so because the cross-cutting issues of realignment are national in nature and voters respond by electing a "new" majority party.

In order to test this hypothesis for the Civil War realignment, electoral data from congressional districts were collected for the period from 1848 (31st House) through 1874 (44th House). However, the demise of the Whigs as a party, the rise of the Republican Party, the secession of the eleven Southern states, and their readmission to the Union during this period complicate a time-series analysis of electoral results. Ideally, such a time series should be run on both major parties for all points in the set.[13] Obviously, this is not possible for the 1848–74 time period; thus, the analysis that follows focuses on the Democratic percentage of the vote in each national election. The Democratic Party contested elections throughout the era, including the period of secession. Joel Silbey's work demonstrates the party's strength throughout the era.[14] During the Civil War era the Democrats almost controlled the House in the 1862 elections, and lost the Presidency in 1864 by an extremely narrow margin. Thus, we can test the hypotheses concerning national versus local factors because the Democrats were stable and competitive over the entire period. Table 2.1 shows the mean Democratic percentage of the vote and the standard deviation of the vote in all House elections from 1848 through 1874.

The results show a drop in the standard deviation of the Democratic vote in the 34th House. The elections for that House show Democrats losing 5.4 percent from the previous congressional elections, indicating a swing away from the Democrats nationally. The standard deviation of the vote drops below 20.0 for the first time and falls even farther in the elections for the 36th and 37th Houses. The drops in the standard deviation of the vote indicate that national electoral forces continued to be at work. In the two Houses elected during the war years, the Democrats gained votes in the 1862 elections but dropped by over 5 percent in the next election. After the war ended, the Democrats' percentage of the vote rose for five consecutive elections until they controlled the House in the 44th Congress. The rise in the 44th House was largely the result of the readmission of the Southern states to the Union. The lowest standard deviation occurs in the elections for the 43rd House, and results from the readmission of a block of Southern states that voted strongly Democratic.

Overall, these results show a somewhat mixed pattern. The pre-1862 results reflect the emergence of the Republican Party and its rise

TABLE 2.1

Mean Democratic Vote and Standard Deviation in House Elections, 1848–1874

House	Election year	Mean vote (percent)	Standard deviation	House	Election year	Mean vote (percent)	Standard deviation
31	1848	45.2%	20.4	38	1862	46.9%	15.6
32	1850	48.6	20.8	39	1864	40.6	16.7
33	1852	49.6	20.8	40	1866	43.1	15.7
34	1854	44.2	19.6	41	1868	44.1	18.0
35	1856	50.0	18.7	42	1870	45.8	16.7
36	1858	50.8	18.5	43	1872	46.3	12.0
37	1860	43.0	17.9	44	1874	50.1	19.4

NOTE: In this table and those that follow, the principal election year is given.

TABLE 2.2

Mean Swing in Democratic Vote and Standard Deviation of Swing in Paired House Elections, 1848–1874

Houses	Election years	Mean swing (percent)	Standard deviation
31–32	1848–1850	3.7%	25.3
32–33	1850–1852	3.0	26.6
33–34	1852–1854	−7.4	20.7
34–35	1854–1856	6.3	18.4
35–36	1856–1858	−1.7	15.2
36–37	1858–1860	−6.1	17.6
37–38	1860–1862	3.0	16.3
38–39	1862–1864	−3.2	13.3
39–40	1864–1866	4.9	17.8
40–41	1866–1868	3.8	8.4
41–42	1868–1870	1.6	13.6
42–43	1870–1872	0.6	17.5
43–44	1872–1874	3.9	17.2

to majority status, whereas the later results reflect first the secession of the Southern states, and then, their gradual readmission to the Union. There is, however, no change in the variance around the mean Democratic vote of the magnitude one would have expected.

This anomaly can be explained by examining what Flanigan and Zingale have identified as compensating change versus across-the-board change.[15] If, in a critical election, parties gain votes in some regions but lose votes in others, the change is compensating. If, on the other hand, they gain votes across all regions, then the change is across the board. To ascertain the nature of change in the Civil War era realignment, we need to analyze voting changes within congressional districts over pairs of successive elections. Summing such changes obtains both a mean swing in pairs of elections and the variance around the swing. Table 2.2 shows the results of this analysis.

The table indicates that the elections of the 34th and 37th Houses were the two showing the greatest swing away from the Democrats. In the elections for the 34th House, the Democrats lost an average of 7.4 percent across all districts; however, the 20.7 standard deviation of the swing indicates that the swing was not consistent across all districts. This result is not surprising, given the sectional nature of the realignment. The national elections that brought the Republicans control of the Presidency and the House look very similar to the results obtained for the 34th House. That is, in 1860 the Democrats lost an average of 6.1 across districts, with a standard deviation of change at 17.6. These figures again indicate a regional explanation of the re-

TABLE 2.3
Mean Party Vote in House Elections by Region, 1848–1874
(Percent)

Year	New England and Northeast			East and West North Central			South and Border		
	Democrat	Whig	Republican	Democrat	Whig	Republican	Democrat	Whig	Republican
1848	25.3%	68.4%	0	68.6%	27.5%	0	66.7%	33.3%	0
1850	52.6	45.3	0	56.9	37.3	0	50.0	31.0	0
1852	59.1	38.7	0	67.3	27.3	0	65.4	22.2	0
1854	25.1	54.8	5.4%	15.8	10.5	71.9%	65.4	1.2	0
1856	35.5	0	55.9	44.1	0	52.5	63.0	0	0
1858	17.5	0	66.7	33.9	0	61.0	63.0	0	0
1860	20.4	0	75.3	36.7	0	61.7	28.0	0	20.0%
1862	42.0	0	58.0	51.4	0	41.9	5.9	0	41.2
1864	25.0	0	75.0	12.2	0	87.8	8.0	0	24.0
1866	25.0	0	72.7	13.3	0	86.7	48.0	4.0	48.0
1868	29.5	0	70.5	25.3	0	74.7	44.9	0	40.6
1870	37.5	0	62.5	32.0	0	66.7	48.7	0	32.9
1872	16.7	0	83.3	25.0	0	75.0	55.2	0	44.8
1874	51.0	0	47.9	48.0	0	44.9	83.1	0	15.7

NOTE: The region code is as follows: *New England* = Conn., Maine, Mass., N.H., R.I., Vt.; *Northeast* = Del., N.J., N.Y., Pa.; *East North Central* = Ill., Ind., Mich., Ohio, Wis.; *West North Central* = Iowa, Kans., Minn., Mo., Neb.; *South* = Ala., Ark., Fla., Ga., La., Miss., N.C., S.C., Tenn., Tex., Va.; *Border* = Ky., Md., W. Va. Columns may not total 100% because of third-party voting.

alignment. The Democrats' gains in the 39th–40th and 43rd–44th election pairs are the result, first, of their recouping their losses in the elections for the 38th House and, second, of the readmission of all Southern states to the Union by 1874.

The Civil War realignment was highly sectional in nature, and thus one should expect the electoral changes to occur on a region-by-region basis. The primary factor accounting for such changes is the formation of the Republican Party as the alternative to the Democrats. The drop below 20 in the standard deviation of the swing (Table 2.1) occurs at the time the Republicans gained a plurality of seats in the House of Representatives. Since Republican Party strength was regional in nature, a reanalysis of Table 2.1 by region might elucidate the matter. Table 2.3 shows the results of such an analysis. The Western states are excluded because of the small numbers of voters in the early period.

The election of 1854 marks a clear turning point for the Northeastern states.* In the previous two elections the Democrats won a majority of the vote, whereas for the next eighteen years they averaged less than 30 percent. After the 1856 election, the Republicans were the majority party in congressional elections, maintaining a better than two-thirds average over the next sixteen years. Thus, in terms of establishing a new majority party preference, the election of 1856 established the Republicans as an important party, and by 1860 they were the dominant party. The one exception during the 1856–74 period was the election of 1862, where Union Democrats took 42 percent of the vote. These gains were the result of Northern dissatisfaction with the war effort.

The pattern for the Midwest differs from the Northeastern pattern only in that the Republicans established their dominance some years earlier, in 1854. From then until 1874 they averaged over two-thirds of the vote. The single exception was the election of 1862, in which Union Democrats took slightly over one-half the vote. Thus, as in the Northeast, Republicans established their dominance of Midwestern congressional elections before the war and maintained it through Reconstruction. However, the Republican congressional vote was more susceptible to swings in the Midwest than in the Northeast. The range for Northeastern states was 55.9 to 83.3, compared with 41.9 to 87.8 for Midwestern states.

---

*Generally in discussing the Civil War–era elections I refer to the year in which most states voted, ignoring the fact that some voted in the following year (e.g., I speak of the 1854 election, actually held in both 1854 and 1855). In Chapter Seven I shall have cause to preserve the distinction, but it is unimportant in most contexts.

TABLE 2.4
Mean Swing in Anti-Democratic Vote and Standard Deviation of Swing in Paired House Elections by Region, 1848–1874

Houses	Election years	New England Mean swing (pct.)	New England Std. dev.	Northeast Mean swing (pct.)	Northeast Std. dev.	Central Mean swing (pct.)	Central Std. dev.	South Mean swing (pct.)	South Std. dev.	Border Mean swing (pct.)	Border Std. dev.
31–32	1848–1850	5.5%	15.7	13.5%	15.3	-1.7%	12.6	1.0%	40.6	1.2%	21.3
32–33	1850–1852	1.1	16.0	0.4	13.7	1.9	17.2	14.3	40.6	6.2	32.8
33–34	1852–1854	-13.5	19.5	4.5	16.9	-9.7	9.5	2.0	21.6	11.5	26.4
34–35	1854–1856	2.0	23.4	-7.6	19.7	-4.7	6.4	7.9	23.0	7.0	12.5
35–36	1856–1858	-11.3	18.7	0.7	13.9	0.9	3.7	1.4	21.1	1.9	6.5
36–37	1858–1860	2.9	9.8	-4.6	11.7	-1.4	3.9	0.9	19.7	27.7	34.9
37–38	1860–1862	7.9	22.9	3.7	10.1	4.4	8.4	secession			
38–39	1862–1864	-6.9	18.7	-4.0	7.8	-6.9	7.5	secession			
39–40	1864–1866	1.9	5.6	0.8	8.7	0.6	4.2	military rule, secession			
40–41	1866–1868	4.4	7.7	-2.5	8.9	3.0	2.9	military rule		9.7	14.5
41–42	1868–1870	1.5	6.3	0.9	6.1	0.6	7.6	0.9	14.8	8.5	31.4
42–43	1870–1872	-1.2	6.1	4.4	8.6	1.3	10.2	14.7	28.3	6.2	19.4
43–44	1872–1874	7.2	9.8	-2.8	9.7	2.9	15.3	12.6	17.4	7.8	21.4

The election of 1854 changed the partisan distribution of seats in the Southern and Border states. In 1854 only one Whig was elected from those regions, and no Republicans were elected there in the prewar period. The Civil War and Reconstruction eras were characterized by manipulated voter returns, and until 1874 Republicans controlled an average of 40 percent of these seats. The election of 1872 restored the Democrats as the majority party, and in the 1874 elections over 80 percent of the Southern and Border vote was Democratic.

The cross-cutting issue of slavery was indeed a national issue, one that realigned political parties, and the congressional parties reflect these circumstances. The Republicans became the dominant party at the congressional level in the Northeast by 1860 and in the Midwest by 1854, and the Democrats were by 1856 the only national party in Southern congressional elections.

The analysis of voting by region would not be complete without analyzing the vote swing within districts across pairs of elections, as in Table 2.2. Thus, Table 2.4 shows the regional breakdown of the national results shown in Table 2.2. Readers not interested in the technical details of regional vote patterns should skip to the electoral summary section.

Analysis of the standard deviation of the swing shows that the Central state elections were affected across the board by the slavery issue in 1854 (a drop from 17.2 in 1852 to 9.5—Table 2.4). The New England and Northeastern states were affected by this phenomenon in 1856 and 1858, respectively. The Border states were uniformly affected in the 1854 and 1856 elections. The Southern states had relatively high standard deviations during the entire prewar period. This was the result of local secessionist parties in the Southern states. The West North Central states (included in Central) were, of course, consumed by the Kansas-Nebraska question, and pro- and antislave forces battled it out in congressional elections. It should not be forgotten, however, that though local factors did affect Southern congressional elections throughout the prewar period, the overall electoral results made the Democrats the only national party in the South.

The critical elections in the New England states occurred in 1854 and 1856. In 1854 the Democrats lost over 13 percent on average from the previous election. The Whig Party held a majority of the vote, but the Republican Party made its first appearance (Table 2.3). In 1856 the Republicans became the dominant party and remained so through the election of 1876. The standard deviation of the within-district swings shows compensating change in those elections, with values of 19.5 and 23.4. The Democrats actually gained 2.0 percent on average between 1854 and 1856, but the Republicans replaced the Whigs as the new majority party; thus the high value of the standard deviation. With the election of 1860, the standard deviation of the swing falls below 10 for the first time. In the next two elections the vote swung first to the Union Democrats because the Union war effort was faltering, and then to the Republicans, as the war effort took hold. After the war the region exhibits a steady pro-Republican voting pattern until 1874—that is, with few dramatic swings in the mean vote and low standard deviations. In sum, the election of 1856 both eliminated the Whig Party and established the Republicans as the majority party.

The Mid-Atlantic states follow essentially the same pattern except that the Republicans replaced the Whigs as the majority party in 1858 rather than 1856. The high variance in the vote is determined in the prewar period by the Republicans replacing the Whigs and the decline of the Democrats. In the election of 1860 the variance drops to below 12 and remains at or below 10.1 for the rest of the period. In short, the Mid-Atlantic states became Republican in the 36th House and remained so through the period.

The East North Central states were the first to realign to the Republicans. The Democrats lost almost 10 percent within districts between 1852 and 1854; the standard deviation of the change falls below 10 and remains there until the Southern states began to gain readmission. The Republicans held a majority of votes until the elections of 1862, when the Union Democrats captured a majority of seats; however, in subsequent elections the Republicans were the dominant party until 1874, when the reintroduction of the Southern states made these competitive two-party states once again. The Democrats, in comparison to their showing in the Eastern states, were more competitive throughout the entire period, largely owing to Democratic strength in the southern portions of Illinois, Indiana, and Ohio. Thus, while the East North Central states were the first to vote for Republicans, they were never as heavily Republican as the New England and Mid-Atlantic states.

The Southern states posted an increased Democratic vote of over 14 points in 1852, and in 1854 the Whigs were reduced to less than 3 percent of the vote. In 1856 the Democrats gained almost 8 points over the 1854 figures. In some of the elections preceding the Civil War, the Democrats were challenged by various proslavery or prosecession parties. The result was Democratic percentages of the vote varying from slightly over 50 percent to over 80 percent, depending on the extent and strength of minor parties. The important point is that in 1854 the Whigs were eliminated as an opposition party in the deep South. The high standard deviation of the swing vote in the pre–Civil War era is the result first, in 1848–52, of the demise of the Whigs and the rise of separatist parties, and second, from 1854 on, of the rise and fall of third parties. When both factors were at work the standard deviation of the change was over 40; when only major parties were relevant, the score was around 20. In the period after the Civil War, the Democrats and Republicans were competitive in 1866 and 1868, owing of course to Reconstruction policies and the enfranchisement of blacks. After 1868 the region returned to its strong Democratic preference.

The Border states follow essentially the same pattern as the Southern states. In 1852 and 1854 the Whigs remained a competitive minority party (barely so in 1854); however, in the 1856 elections, they disappeared as a factor and were replaced by the Republicans, although voter support for Republicans was limited. The standard deviation of change is high in the 1848–54 period owing to the demise of the Whigs; in the 1854–56 and 1856–58 pairs, the standard deviation of change drops as the Democrats become the dominant party. In the 1860 elections the mean change is high and so, too, is the standard deviation. This is the result of the breakup of the national Democratic Party and divided feelings in the Border states. From 1860 to 1866 the status of the Border states prohibits meaningful analysis. In the postwar period the Border states follow the Southern pattern of gradually increasing strength for Democratic congressional candidates.

★ Electoral Summary

A summary analysis of swing voting across pairs of congressional elections during the Civil War period reveals that national electoral forces came into play during the 1854–60 elections (Table 2.5). Dividing the elections into precritical (1846–52), critical (1854–60), and postcritical (1862–76) periods, we find that during the precritical pe-

TABLE 2.5

Aggregate Democratic Vote Swings and Coefficients of Variation, 1846–1876

Period	Mean swing (percent)	Coefficient of variation
Precritical period, 1846–52	3.26%	8.09
Critical period, 1854–60	−5.31	−4.34
Postcritical period, 1862–76	2.87	8.15
Controlling election, 1860	−6.07%	−2.81

riod the mean swing is 3.26 toward the Democrats, and the average V coefficient 8.09, which indicates a relatively low swing and considerable variation in voting patterns. The critical period, in contrast, has a mean swing of −5.31 away from the Democrats and an average V coefficient of −4.34, indicating national electoral factors at work. The postcritical period has a mean swing of only 2.87 and an average V coefficient of 8.15. These data, in general, support the hypothesis of an increased nationalization of electoral results during the Civil War era. The data for the 1860 (or controlling) election are the most telling of all, with a mean swing vote of −6.07 away from the Democrats and a low V of 2.81.

This is not to deny that there was a regional overtone to these results. As Michael Holt has argued, in a varying pattern regions first abandoned the Whigs for the Republicans and other parties, and then, over time, Republicans came to dominate Northern state elections while the South turned strongly to the Democrats.[16] The fading of the nativism issue resulted in the Republicans becoming the major anti-Democratic party by late 1856.[17] The end of the Civil War and the readmission of the Southern states brought about solid Democratic Party gains throughout the country, such that by 1874 the Democrats were the majority party in the 44th House.

The most sophisticated and accurate measure of electoral change is that developed by Flanigan and Zingale. Their measure of change combines temporary and permanent change with uniform and compensating change, allowing them to determine if the electoral change was an across-the-board surge or interactive or compensating change. Realigning surges occur when the new majority party receives support from all elements of the electorate, whereas compensating changes occur when the majority party gains new voters but loses some old voters. Their technique applies a two-way analysis-of-variance model with interaction and with one observation per cell.[18]

I duplicated the Flanigan and Zingale analysis using the congressional district as the unit of analysis rather than the county or state. This allows one to distinguish between temporary and permanent change. Because my interest here is only in realigning change (either across-the-board or compensating), the following tabulation shows only results that can be interpreted as critical:

Election year	Across-the-board realignment	Compensating realignment
1854	−3.6	—
1856	1.9	2.7
1860	−2.8	1.8

The figures for across-the-board change can be interpreted straight-forwardly as a percentage point change. For example, the across-the-board change of −3.6 for the Democrats in 1854 means that the sub-units moved an average of 3.6 units away from the Democrats, and the change was not temporary. The compensating change figures mean that congressional districts moved in different directions from their own expected vote and from the nation as a whole. Because the fig-ures for compensating change represent increases in some districts and decreases in others, no sign is attached to them. Following Flani-gan and Zingale, I use the moving cross-sections of four elections.

The tabulation shows a 3.6 across-the-board shift away from the Democrats in the 1854 election, the result of Democrats' being re-placed in many Northern congressional districts. The 1856 election showed a slight shift (1.9) back toward the Democrats and a compen-sating change of 2.7. The election of 1860, which brought the Repub-licans to control of the government, resulted in a 2.8 percent across-the-board loss to Democrats and a 1.8 percent compensating shift. These results closely follow those of Clubb, Flanigan, and Zingale.

The rise of the Republican Party in the mid-1850's appears as an across-the-board realignment in the North.[19] Although the Republi-cans became the dominant party, by 1860 their success varied over time and by region within the North. The Republicans gained uni-formly in the North and compensating change was small. In the Southern states the espousal of antislavery views in the North precipi-tated an increase in the Democratic vote as early as 1852. In that year the Democrats increased their share of the vote by 16.3 percent. The standard deviation of the vote remained high, owing first to the rise of secessionist parties and candidates, and second to pockets of Whig strength, which persisted until the election of 1856. The electoral swings for the rest of the period appear to be the result of the seces-sion of the Southern states, the success or failure of the Union war effort, and the readmission of the Southern states. While the electoral results may be less dramatic than one would have wished, the pattern of Republican dominance of House elections is dramatic. The Repub-licans first contested elections in 1854, and by 1860 they were the ma-jority party in the House. Moreover, the Republicans retained unified control over the House, Senate, and Presidency for fourteen con-secutive years. Thus, in terms of seats in the House, the 1850's realign-ment is a clear demarcation from the preceding era. And of course, the contention is that the newly elected congressional majority party legislated the clusters of policy changes associated with the Civil War realignment.

★ Votes-to-Seats Ratios

Although there is evidence of a nationalizing of electoral forces during the critical Civil War era, the results are somewhat less impressive than one might have expected. Two factors seem to account for the electoral shifts noted above, namely structural changes and regional effects. The replacement of the Whig Party by the Republicans and the secession of the Southern states and their readmission are the major structural changes. The shift away from the Democrats occurred first in the New England and East North Central states between 1852 and 1854, followed by the Mid-Atlantic states in 1856; and in the post-1856 period the swing was to the Republican Party. The most important overall effect was that beginning in 1860, the Republicans controlled the Presidency and both branches of the Congress until 1874. How the Republicans were able to dominate the federal government is somewhat difficult to understand, since there was no massive shift of voters to the Republican Party during the critical period. The answer to this puzzle requires an analysis of the votes-to-seats ratio and the use of the so-called Cube Law.[20]

Demonstrating the effect of the vote change on the seat ratio in the House will show how relatively small swings in the vote can effectively create a "new" congressional majority party. The Cube Law is the most often used measure of the distortion of seats to votes. The law states that the ratio of seats to votes is

$$\frac{SR}{SD} = \frac{VR^3}{VD^3}$$

where SR = actual Whig or Republican seats; SD = actual Democratic seats; VR^3 = Whig or Republican percent of vote cubed; and VD^3 = Democratic percent of vote cubed.

My hypothesis is that the Republicans will have a greater seat-to-vote ratio than the Cube Law (which is a significant distortion to begin with) predicts. Moreover, the greatest distortion should occur in the election of 1860, the first in which Republicans have unified control of the government. Table 2.6 shows the ratio of Republican seats predicted by the Cube Law, the actual ratio, and the direction of the difference for the 1854–66 elections.

The results show a decided bias in favor of the Republican Party. The election of 1860 is the most clearly biased, with a +1.45 to the Republicans. In fact, in the 36th House by the Cube Law the Republicans should have been a minority rather than the plurality party. There are only two elections (1856 and 1864) where the Republicans

TABLE 2.6

Ratio of Whig and Republican House Seats to Democratic Seats Compared with Cube Law Predictions, 1854–1866

Election year	Cube Law prediction	Actual ratio	Difference
1854	0.80	1.30	0.50
1856	0.77	0.72	−0.05
1858	0.59	1.12	0.53
1860	1.07	2.52	1.45
1862	1.18	1.29	0.11
1864	3.21	3.15	−0.06
1866	2.09	2.92	0.83

do worse than the Cube Law predictions, and in both of these the difference is insignificant: −0.05 and −0.06, respectively. Thus, although the elections do not shift extremely large numbers of voters, the vote changes result in the creation of significant differences in congressional party strength. By 1860 the swing to Republicans had occurred across all the Northern states; the result was the creation of a larger number of Republican seats, a pattern that lasted for fourteen years. In short, party systems characterized by strong, highly divided partisan blocs with relatively little give in the electorate and no large group of uncommitted voters can yield significant shifts in congressional power with only minor shifts in election results.

★ Constituency Bases of the Congressional Parties

If the realignment in the party in the electorate demonstrated above was reflected in the composition of the congressional parties, then the constituency bases of the parties should show drastic shifts during the realignment period on a regional basis. Specifically, the competitive national party system should be converted into a highly sectional system with Republicans being the party of the North and Democrats the party of the Southern and Border states. Table 2.7 shows the ratio of Whig (1852–54) and Republican (1856 on) seats to Democratic seats by region for the period.

The results reveal the extent of change occurring during the Civil War realignment. In the Southern and Border states, as the Whigs faded from the political scene, the Democrats increased their share of seats in both regions, with the Whig-Republican ratio decreasing from 0.27 to 0.06 in the South and from 0.92 to 0.03 in the Border states over the period. In contrast, in the New England, Mid-Atlantic, and East North Central states, the rise of the Republican Party signaled

TABLE 2.7

Ratio of Whig and Republican House Seats to Democratic Seats by Region,
33rd–39th Houses, 1852–1864

Election year	New England	Northeast	North Central		South	Border
			East	West		
1852	1.2	0.4	0.4	1.4	0.3	0.9
1854	1.4	2.8	0.8	3.0	0.2	1.0
1856	11.0	0.4	1.1	0.2	0.0	0.1
1858	21.5	3.7	1.9	1.2	0.1	0.2
1860	9.1	2.2	1.6	1.0	0.1	0.0
1862	8.1	2.5	0.9	0.9	*secession and*	
1864	11.6	3.7	1.7	1.5	*military rule*	

NOTE: The first two rows show Whig ratios; the others Republican ratios.

both the end of the Whigs as a force in Congress and the demise of Democratic strength in these regions. In New England the Democrats were competitive with the Whigs in 1852 and 1854, with ratios of 1.15 and 1.42, respectively, but with the election of 1856 the Republicans had an advantage of 11 to 1 over Democrats, and the area remained heavily Republican throughout the period. In the Mid-Atlantic and East North Central states, by 1858 the Republicans had advantages of 3.67 and 1.94 to 1, respectively. In these regions the competitive second party system was transformed into a one-party dominant system by 1858. It is interesting to note that the major effects of the realignment in the electorate were clearly present in regard to the composition of the congressional parties by 1856. Although the policy changes associated with the Civil War realignment were not passed until after 1860, the constituent base of the new majority party that passed the clusters of policy changes was set by 1856–58. Clubb, Flanigan, and Zingale have concluded that seat switches in Congress also precede realigning change in presidential elections.[21]

★ Congressional Turnover

It has been shown that the cross-cutting issue of slavery polarized the two major parties, and that election results during the realignment were decided on a national rather than local basis. One very important effect of these elections was to cause a high rate of turnover in House membership. In terms of our thesis it is important to document the high turnover levels because the new members were elected on national issues rather than local ones, thus reducing constituency-party cross-pressuring. Turnover on House committees was also high during this period. Dramatic turnover on a committee reduces its ability to pass along norms and decision strategies that lead to incremental policies. If both constituency-party cross-pressuring and committee influence relative to party are reduced, then voting in the House should be structured by party. This is especially so with regard to the dominant issues of the realignment.

The founding fathers recognized clearly the relationship between member turnover and policy changes. James Madison, arguing for longer terms and the indirect election of Senators, said: "The mutability in the public councils arising from a rapid succession of new members, however qualified they may be, points out in the strongest manner the necessity of some stable institution in the government." He went on to argue that the change of men in legislatures "must proceed a change of opinions; and from a change of opinions, a change of members."[22] Madison, to be sure, was arguing against such changes; our point, however, is that, as he maintained, rapid turnover (under critical conditions) effects changes in public policy.

Congressional elections between 1850 and 1860 were characterized by the changing party affiliations of members and high turnover in membership. The election of 1854 (the 34th Congress) gave rise to the Republican Party in the House of Representatives. In the 34th House the Republicans held 108 of 234 seats. Their number decreased to 92 in the 35th House, but from the 36th House to the 43rd, they held a majority of seats. In short, Republicans dominated the politics and policy of the House for sixteen uninterrupted years. Such periods of majority are one of the conditions that Clubb, Flanigan, and Zingale cite as an electoral condition that supports major policy changes.[23] Moreover, the turnover rates in elections during the realignment era were such that over 95 percent of the House members seated in the 32nd House had not served more than two consecutive terms. The greatest turnover occurred between the 1852 and 1856 elections. By the last of these three elections, which represent the end of the old Whig-Democrat party division and the first two elections of the transition to the third party system, 82 percent of all seats in the House were filled by new representatives. Of the incumbents managing to be contenders in all three House elections, 50 percent were Democrats from the Deep South and approximately 35 percent were Northeastern representatives who switched from either Whig or Democrat to Republican. Thus it seems clear that the turnover in House membership during this era was predicated on the growing differences between North and South—Republican and Democrat—over the slavery question. And the newly elected members were not cross-pressured between constituency and party.

TABLE 2.8

Turnover on Ways and Means Committee, 32nd–40th Houses, 1851–1869

(Percent new members)

House	Years	New members	House	Years	New members
32	1851–53	44%	37	1861–63	44%
33	1853–55	33	38	1863–65	78
34	1855–57	78	39	1865–67	56
35	1857–59	67	40	1867–69	56
36	1859–61	56			

In the contemporary House, committees have a life of their own. Committee norms and strategies are passed along to new members, and this in turn affects committee decisions.[24] When turnover on committees is high, norms and strategies cannot be passed along and conditions are ripe for major policy innovations. Committees in the House of the 1850's were not as stable as they have been since the early twentieth century; however, the realignment of the 1850's saw a greater turnover than there had been during the stable second party system. The case of the most important committee, Ways and Means, is illustrative. In Table 2.8 the percentage of Ways and Means members who had not served on the committee in previous Congresses is given from the 32nd House (1851–53) to the 40th (1867–69). Our expectation is that during the 34th and 35th Congresses, the turnover should be greatest. These Houses were elected in 1854 and 1856, the transition elections from the second to the third party system. In addition, membership should be more stable in the period after 1863 because once the Republicans become the dominant party, stability should be reestablished.

The results are fairly clear. Turnover on Ways and Means was high during the 34th and 35th Congresses. These were the first two Houses to which the newly formed Republican Party elected members, and this turnover reflects the results of those elections. In general, turnover on the committee is higher during the realignment and Civil War eras than in the last of the second party–system Houses. The high turnover figure for the 38th Congress, of course, reflects the secession of the eleven Southern states. That is, when the Democrats left the House, new non-Southern replacements had to be found, which increased the turnover figure.

One other example of committee turnover worth noting is the percentage of new members on other committees in the 34th and 35th Houses (1855–59). In those Houses the Republicans had come on the scene, and both major parties were in transition. Many Northern

TABLE 2.9

Turnover on Four Selected Committees, 34th–35th Houses, 1855–1859

(Percent new members)

Committee	House 34	House 35
Public Lands	78%	78%
Public Expenditures	78	89
Agriculture	100	100
Roads and Canals	100	89

Democrats and Whigs had not yet become Republican, and many Southern Democrats were still seeking compromise. In the 35th House the Democratic majority was clearly proslavery, and the Republicans were clearly antislavery. Thus in both the 34th and the 35th House, the expectation is that turnover would be high.

Table 2.9 shows that this was indeed the case. The lowest percentage of new members is 78 percent, and in three cases the new member total reaches 100 percent. This is in contrast to the post–Civil War Houses, where the percentage of experienced committee members was higher. For example, in the 40th House (1867–69) only 22 percent of the members of Public Lands were new to the committee, and on Public Expenditures only 44 percent. Thus the hypothesis that electoral forces dramatically impact committee turnover appears to be true.[25]

★ Voting Patterns

The argument offered in this book is that cross-cutting issues polarize public opinion and political parties reflect this polarization in their issue stances. Those elections that establish one party's dominance reduce the effects of the two major drawbacks to party government in the House—constituency-party cross-pressuring and the continuity of committees' decision strategies. It has been established that the congressional elections of 1854–60 meet the criteria for establishing the possibility of party government in the House. It remains to analyze voting patterns in the House.[26]

Since the 1860's realignment is so clearly associated with regional differences on slavery and economic issues, we would expect to find such issues dominating the House's policy agenda. And indeed such is the case: the issues before the Congress reflect the concerns of the nation as a whole. In the following section we determine the dominant issue dimensions and analyze voting on these dimensions.

The technique used to determine issue dimensions and members' scale scores on the dimensions is essentially the same technique developed by Clausen and Sinclair. That is, roll calls are subjectively classified by issue content into issue areas such as slavery or government management. These roll calls are then run against each other using Yule's Q to determine their relatedness to each other. All roll calls in an area with a Yule's Q, or .60 or greater, are then hierarchically clustered to arrive at a scale for the dimension. Individual members' scores on the resulting scale are used to determine their support for or opposition to the content of the dimension. (See the Appendix for details on this technique and its application.)

The era's dominant set of issues turned on slavery, secession, civil rights, and Reconstruction. Over the entire twenty years from 1853 to 1873, the House had repeated roll call votes on these issues. In the 33rd (1853–55) and 34th (1855–57) Houses the slavery scale was dominated by votes on the Kansas–Nebraska controversy, mixed with votes on the fugitive slave law and on foreign relations questions related to the slavery issue. In the 35th House (1857–59) a shift occurred, and the content of roll calls switched to secession and abolition. The most prominent votes dealt with the abolition of slavery, and after 1861, the use of black soldiers and their treatment in relation to white soldiers. In the 37th House (1861–63) and all subsequent Houses in the era, the roll calls in the scale reflected a more radical and egalitarian position. Typical of votes in the House were those on the general abolition of slavery, equal opportunity for blacks in the postal service, the funding of the Freedmen's Bureau, and with the end of the war (39th and subsequent Houses), civil rights and Reconstruction issues. Especially important were votes on the 13th, 14th, and 15th amendments and the maintenance of federal troops in the South. The policy questions at issue were how blacks should be treated, and what the federal role should be in ensuring fair treatment. In short, over the entire twenty-year period there is a single civil rights dimension that encompasses the changing policies toward blacks. The early period is dominated by the slavery question, the war period by secession-related issues, and finally, the postwar period, by civil rights and Reconstruction issues. Thus, even though the specific issues change, there is an objectively determinable black civil rights dimension that encompasses all the above issues throughout the period. The intercorrelation between roll calls on this issue dimension is .87 (Yule's Q) with no single correlation below .70. Thus the dimension meets the criterion for stability. All the issue dimensions that follow meet at least a .70 criterion for stability.

A second salient policy domain in this period was government expansion. Roll calls on procurement and the construction of public facilities, such as canals and roads, as well as legislation dealing with railroad and telegraph construction, are included in this category. In addition, legislation dealing with the Homestead Act and subsequent attempts to secure homesteads are also placed in this category. However, the existence of roll calls in the government expansion domain does not guarantee the existence of a government expansion dimension. In fact the Yule's Q analysis showed the existence of three separate dimensions relating to expansionism. Reanalysis of the roll calls revealed that each had a common context for which the minimum Yule's Q was .60. The first and dominant dimension was public works, the second was railroad construction, and the third and least in terms of longevity was homestead expansion. The public works dimension is composed of roll calls dealing with internal improvements, such as rivers and harbors legislation and canal and road construction. Questions dealing with the extent to which the federal government would fund public improvements are prominent in each House from the 33rd through the 42nd, with the exception of the 37th (1861–63), which was understandably not concerned with business as usual. It is not surprising to find a public works dimension in this era. The disposition of government funds for public works determined which states, regions, and communities got the roads, harbors, and other infrastructure that determined economic fates. The policy concept underlying this dimension is the extent of federal involvement in procuring and constructing internal improvements.

The railroad and telegraph construction dimension is present in each Congress over the twenty years. The underlying policy dimension is the distribution of public lands to states and communities for this purpose. The victors in these struggles could then promote railroad and telegraph construction. A slight drop in the stability of the dimension occurs in the 37th and 38th Houses (1861–65), a fact explained by the tendency during the Civil War to debate the issue in terms of the national interest. There is, however, no reason to presume that the issue was not continuous over the twenty-year period. The homestead dimension is scattered through only ten of these years, and as a result its stability is subject to different interpretations. Thus, this analysis excludes it from consideration.

Tariff policy constitutes another policy domain. The results of the unidimensionality analysis showed it to be a stable policy dimension over the entire twenty years. The dimension includes roll calls to reduce or raise tariffs across the board, votes for tariffs on specific commodities, and votes on resolutions holding that protective tariffs are unconstitutional. The policy question underlying this dimension is whether the government should adopt protective tariffs for certain industries and farm products or opt for relatively free trade and reduced tariffs.

Another category of roll calls, present in each of the Congresses, consists of votes on housekeeping functions, such as procedural votes, contempt citations, contested elections, and committee size. These votes formed a dimension that masked party disputes over who would control the House by what margin and in what manner. Nelson Polsby has already shown how, in the pre-institutionalized House, partisan particularism dominated institutional maintenance questions.[27] Thus, it is not surprising to find such a dimension present in each Congress in the era.

A final scale involves an issue dimension dealing with the federal government's control over the nation's banking and currency. This issue appears in the 36th House (1859–61) and all succeeding Houses. Roll calls on this issue dimension deal with such questions as the Treasury Department's attempts to control loans and the national debt, as well as votes on gold currency and the question of expanding currency supply. The policy dimension underlying the issue is the extent of federal control over money and banking.

The Civil War era was indeed a benchmark in American political history. The challenge of slavery and economic differences resulted in the birth of the Republican Party and the transformation of the nation's political agenda. The new Republican majority party abolished slavery, and constitutional guarantees of civil rights were extended to blacks. In addition, the electoral realignment resulted in major policy changes in the scope of federal power over the individual states and in the expansion of the federal role in the economy. These major policy changes were enacted by the newly formed Republican congressional party. It is clear that Congresses during this era legislated major public policy changes. What was the role of the congressional majority party in the transformation? As we have seen, the election of 1856 resulted in major changes in the composition of the congressional parties, and of course the election of 1858 completed the takeover of the House by the Republicans.

We would expect, then, to find party clearly structuring voting on dominant issue dimensions beginning with the 35th House (elected 1856), and continuing to do so through the 42nd House (1871–73). In order to test this hypothesis, members' party identification was cor-

TABLE 2.10

Product-Moment Correlations Between Party Identification and Issue Voting,
33rd–42nd Houses, 1853–1873

House	Slavery, secession, and civil rights	Public works	Railroad and telegraph construction	House-keeping	Money and banking	Tariff
33	.51	.65	.14	.27	—	.55
34	.41	.59	.22	.47	—	.02
35	.89	.89	.89	.96	—	.71
36	.87	.78	.67	.90	.86	.85
37	.88	—	.32	.64	.79	.74
38	.92	.67	.58	.92	.94	.92
39	.91	.78	.52	.79	.41	.71
40	.96	.64	.15	.84	.78	.58
41	.98	.91	.38	.97	.83	.79
42	.97	.91	.47	.94	.94	.59

NOTE: The dotted line indicates the cut-point in the rise of party identification with issue dimensions.

related (r) with each issue dimension in each Congress during the era. Table 2.10 shows the results.

In general the results support the hypothesis, and in the dominant issue area—slavery—the results are impressive. In the 33rd and 34th Houses the correlation between party and the slavery dimension is .51 and .41, respectively, whereas in the 35th House the correlation rises to .89; throughout the era the figure never falls below .87, and it peaks at .98 in the 41st House (1869–71). Clearly, policy changes regarding blacks were adopted by partisan majorities.

The pattern of partisan voting replacing relatively nonpartisan voting holds across the tariff and housekeeping dimensions. In each case the correlation coefficient remains strong throughout the period. On the new issue dimension of federal control over money and banking, partisan voting is apparent from the inception, in the 36th House (1859–61), and is characteristic of all but the 39th House. Thus policy changes aimed at expanding the economy via a protective tariff and favorable money and banking laws are passed on partisan grounds.

Unlike the other dimensions, the public works dimension was relatively partisan even before realignment. This result is not surprising, given that American realignments are dominated by certain issues, which become partisan when compromise is no longer feasible. The advantage of using Clausen's technique to determine issue dimensions is that it shows us which issues are transformed by the electoral results of realignments, and in this case, public works policy was not affected.

The overall results of Table 2.10 clearly show the 35th House as the cut-point where partisan voting rises, to inaugurate a sixteen-year period in which partisanship in general dominates issue dimension voting. It is thus fair to conclude that the "clusters of policy changes" passed in this era are the result of cohesive and partisan voting behavior on the part of the Republican majority. Moreover, the rise in such voting corresponds exactly to the first House in which the effects of the electoral realignment are clearly manifested—the 35th.

Additional support for this view is found by looking at aggregate levels of party voting in the House. From the 35th to the 42nd House (1857–73) an average of 74.7 percent of votes was divided along party lines as measured by a 50 percent–50 percent criterion; in the 32nd–34th Houses (1851–57) the figure was 68.2 percent. A more stringent criterion (90 percent of one party vs. 90 percent of the other) results in even stronger evidence for the increase of party strength. In the 1851–57 period only 8.9 percent of all votes met that criterion for party voting. But in the 1857–73 period no House fell below 8.9 percent and the average was 20.9. Thus, both party identification as a predictor of individual voting behavior and party voting in the aggregate increase in strength over the Civil War realignment. This increase in party strength in the House is associated with the shift in the constituency bases of the congressional parties between 1856 and 1860.

★ The Changing Shape of Voting on Issues, 1851–1873

In the 32nd House (1851–53) party structuring of voting was generally low. Democrats and Whigs were able to achieve 70 percent intraparty cohesion on only about a third of all roll calls. Aggregate levels of party voting were also low, with a majority of Democrats opposing a majority of Whigs on only one-quarter of all roll calls. With the introduction of the Kansas-Nebraska Act in 1854, the second party system began to crumble. Voting patterns in both the 33rd and the 34th House reflected the breakup of the parties along sectional lines. My slavery, secession, and civil rights scale (SSCR) shows only Southern Democrats united in their support for the Kansas-Nebraska Act and related matters. But only eight Democrats were strongly opposed to the Kansas-Nebraska Act in the 33rd House, and all were from New England and upstate New York. Thomas Hart Benton of Missouri was the only Border state Democrat scaling in an antislavery position. Mid-Atlantic and East North Central Democrats tended toward mid-range scale scores on this dimension.

Whig members of the House were badly split as early as 1854. Every Northern Whig in both the 33rd and the 34th House scores in the two strongest antislavery positions, whereas a majority of the Southern Whigs scale in the lowest two scale scores (proslavery). The divisiveness of the slavery issue is very evident in the 34th House. It required 133 votes to determine a Speaker, and the winner (Nathaniel Banks of Massachusetts) won by a plurality. The Republicans won 108 seats in the 1854 election, and they were cohesive from the beginning. Democratic party cohesion also rose in the House as the slavery issue came to dominate the agenda.

With the election of the 35th House (1857–59), both slavery and public works became highly partisan issues. Over 70 percent of the roll calls pitted a majority of Republicans against a majority of Democrats, and on both issues, over 90 percent of the roll calls were partisan. On the SSCR scale almost two-thirds of the Democrats scaled in the strongest proslavery position. Republicans occupied the strongest antislavery scale position in equal numbers. The election of the 36th House exacerbated the partisan structuring of roll calls. The shadow of John Brown's raid at Harper's Ferry lay over the opening of the House. The salience of slavery as an issue was such that a freshman representative (William Pennington of New Jersey) was elected Speaker.

The election of Abraham Lincoln in 1860 cemented the tie between region and party. The 37th House (1861–63) was dominated by the secession and war questions. Union Democrats were a force in the House, and in the 1864 election they gained strength—winning a majority of seats in the East North Central region. Union Democrats opposed Lincoln and the Republicans on secession and on economic issues. Joel Silbey has shown in his book on the Democratic Party during the Civil War era that they were a responsible and important opposition to the Republicans.[28] The voting patterns on the SSCR and the economic issue dimensions corroborate this view. Republicans scale at the strong antisecession points on the SSCR scale; most Democrats scale at points indicating conciliatory policies.

In the 38th House (1863–65) a split between radical and moderate Republicans developed; by the 39th House, however, the Radical Republicans were ascendant, and the legislation favoring a radical restructuring of Southern society was passed by a cohesive Republican Party in the 40th House. The Freedmen's Bureau Bill and the Civil Rights Act were passed over President Andrew Johnson's veto. Further, the Radical Republicans passed the 14th and 15th Amendments in an attempt to ensure national citizenship for blacks, and to guarantee their rights against state action. The extent of party voting on these issues is impressive. The 14th Amendment in June 1866 was passed on a straight party vote. The 15th Amendment, the Freedmen's Bureau Bill, the Civil Rights Act of 1866, and the Supplementary Reconstruction Act of 1867 were passed on almost pure party votes, with 95 percent of Republicans voting against 95 percent of Democrats. Throughout this period, 1865–69, Republicans are in the two most pro–civil rights scale positions, and over 80 percent of the Democrats are in the lower two scale positions. In general, party structuring of voting on SSCR-related issues continued until 1873.

Although the pattern on economic issue dimensions was somewhat less partisan during the 1863–73 period, party may still be said to structure voting on most of these dimensions. The money and banking (MB) and public works (PW) issue dimensions are dominated by partisan voting patterns. Most Republican representatives were for governmental-sponsored industrial development, whereas Democrats were opposed. On these two dimensions, however, as was not the case on the SSCR dimension, some Republicans and Democrats occupy midpoints on these scales. The railroad and telegraph construction (RTC) dimension is another story. On this issue dimension a majority of Democrats and Republicans are located toward the middle of the scale, with distinct minorities of each party at the end points. It should be noted, however, that even on the RTC dimension, party structuring of voting accounted for the passage of policies favoring economic development. It is not until after the 1874 election that a trend in the declining importance of party across issue dimensions becomes discernible. The readmittance of Southern states, President Ulysses Grant's lenient views toward the South and states' rights, the decline of Radical Republicanism, the end of abolitionist societies, and the economic compromise of 1876 all contributed to the decline of partisanship in the 1870's.[29]

In summary, the cross-cutting issue of slavery resulted in the demise of the Whigs and the formation of the Republican Party. The election of 1856 (35th House) gave rise to the Republican Party as the voice of opposition to slavery. Although the Republicans did not take over control from the Democrats until 1860, the division between parties was clear-cut in the 35th House. Throughout the Civil War era, the Republicans were opposed by Border and Northern Democrats— a fact often forgotten is that Lincoln barely won the presidential election of 1864 over the Democrat, George McClellan. The partisan division in the House was testimony to an ongoing competitive two-party system. It was not until the 37th House (1861–63) that the Republican majority was able to begin to pass the clusters of policy changes associated with the Civil War realignment, and even then they were passed over the opposition of the congressional Democratic Party. Thus, the electoral realignment resulted in a new two-party system characterized by a cohesive new party committed to changing the shape of the American political landscape. The Republican Party was especially united on the basic realignment issues of slavery, secession, and civil rights. In addition, the new majority party supported aggressive national action through tariffs, expansionist banking policies, and internal improvements—mainly a transcontinental railroad and homestead legislation. The Civil War realignment resulted not only in the end of slavery, but also in a commitment to an industrial future for America. And all these policy changes were attributable to a new cohesive majority party.

CHAPTER THREE

Assuring America's Industrial Future:
The 1890's Realignment

★ IN THE 30 YEARS following the end of the Civil War, the United States became a major industrial and world power. Rapid industrialization left in its wake the potential for an agrarian political movement. The movement that developed—Populism—was opposed not only to industrialism as such, but also to the kind of society it created.

Comparing the three major indicators of industrial production—pig iron, bituminous coal, and railroad construction—for the decades 1850–60 and 1865–75 shows the extent to which the Civil War contributed to the industrialization of the United States. Between 1850 and 1860 pig iron production increased 50 percent, and bituminous coal about 95 percent; 20,000 miles of track were laid down. For 1865–75 the comparable figures were 100 percent, 150 percent, and 40,000 miles of track. Clearly, Louis Hacker's conclusion that industrial capitalism benefited from the Civil War is correct.[1] The continued growth of the American economy from 1875 until the 1890's realignment has been well documented elsewhere.[2] The growth of heavy industry brought with it the beginning of a modern urban society—complex and interdependent.

The rise to industrialization not only changed the economics of farming, but in Charles Beard's words, signaled the end of the Jeffersonian ideal of an agrarian democracy. Not surprisingly, these pressures provoked resentment in rural America. The Reverend William A. Drew summed up the impact of these changes:

I confess, when I have witnessed, as we are annually seeing, the constant drain that is being made upon the young and working classes of our population—the very "bone and muscle" of our great state—when I have beheld, in vast numbers, the hardy sons of an honest yeomanry, discouraged with home, leaving the plow and the threshing floor of their fathers, to fill the workshops of Massachusetts, and people the Prairies of the Great West, the question has come upon my very heart . . . What, if anything, can be done to put a stop to this everlasting tide of emigration, and retain our people at home?[3]

The postwar dominance of the Radical Republicans in Congress resulted in changes in economic policy as well as in civil rights legislation. Under Radical leadership the Republican Party pushed legislation that advanced industrial interests. More land was given to those who were willing to move West from 1865 to 1873 than all the land previously given since 1789. In addition, railroad construction, which kept Eastern steel mills working, flourished under government land grants, and immigration was encouraged to supply Eastern industrialists with labor. States' rights issues and other objections raised by Democrats in opposing pro-industrial policies were brushed aside.[4]

The decline of Radical Republicanism in Congress, along with the readmission of the Southern states, rekindled the Democratic Party's hopes of attaining power. By 1874 the Democrats had a majority in the House of Representatives, and their prospects for winning the Senate and the Presidency looked good in 1876. The election of 1876 was sharply contested; the results of the presidential balloting were ambiguous. The ultimate winner would be determined by which sets of ballots from Southern states were accepted as legitimate. C. Vann Woodward's book on the "compromise of 1876" clearly shows the economic nature of that pact.[5] In effect the Republican and Democratic national parties both accepted an industrial future for the United States. Some Southern Democrats agreed not to support Governor Samuel Tilden's candidacy in return for the end of Reconstruction and the creation of the Southern Pacific Railroad, which would help industrialize the South. Woodward has shown that the key Democratic votes necessary for the compromise came from former Southern Whigs;[6] and as was shown in the last chapter, Whigs favored government involvement in expanding industrialization and Western development.

The point is that by 1876 both major political parties favored pro-industrial policies. The results of this development were manifest by 1881. Benjamin Ginsberg's analysis of U.S. statutes from 1799 to 1960 shows a peak in policy change accruing in 1881, with a buildup of changes beginning in 1877. He summarizes these changes as "positive changes in the Capitalism category and negative changes in the . . . Ruralism category from 1875 to 1885."[7] The increase in procapitalist legislation was accompanied by a decrease in legislation that favored the interests of the single-family subsistence farm. In short, the federal government aided industrial interests by encouraging railroad and telegraph development making generous land grants to industrial interests, adopting protective tariffs, and keeping states dominated by rural interests from regulating business interests.

One obvious result of these policies was the rapid acceleration of the urbanization of the United States. The logical concomitant to this development was what Richard Wiebe called "the search for order"; or what Samuel P. Hays has identified as the change from community to society. The dislocations that the transition from an essentially rural agrarian economy to a modern industrial urban economy caused in the society were apparent by the mid-1880's. Moreover, a strong majority of both parties in Congress favored policies that would accelerate the development of a modern economy and society.

The takeoff phase of industrialization has been harsh and exploitative wherever it has occurred. Nineteenth-century America was no exception. Those hardest hit by rapid industrialization were cash-crop farmers in the South and ethnic workers in the urban North. In the aftermath of the compromise of 1876, farm and labor interests were not successfully articulated and aggregated by either of the major parties. Agrarian and labor unrest were first expressed in the formation of farmer and labor groups. Ultimately, the agrarian interests expressed their opposition to the two-party consensus by forming the Populist Party. In some states Populist interests tried to combine with labor interests. In Illinois such a coalition elected John Peter Altgeld as governor. But the social changes wrought by industrialization worked against such a coalition, by threatening Jefferson's agrarian democratic ideal and challenging pietistic Protestant views. Nevertheless, a coalition of those dispossessed by the rise of industrialization seemed within reach, and the rise of the Populist Party signified discontent with the effects of American industrialization. The economic crisis of 1893 crystallized opposition to the industrial revolution and led directly to the critical period of the 1890's (1894–96). The Democratic Party was split between a pro-industrial faction led by President Grover Cleveland and an anti-industrial, pro-Populist faction. Although the Republicans were also split between pro-industrial forces led by Thomas B. Reed and William McKinley in the House, and pro-silver forces led by Richard P. Bland of Missouri in the House and Edward Teller of Colorado in the Senate, they were not as badly divided as the Democrats.

The fundamental cross-cutting issue that precipitated the realignment of the 1890's was the future for America—industrial or agricultural? The specific issues the realignment was fought over were the coinage of silver at sixteen-to-one parity with gold, protective vs. free tariffs, and America's role in world affairs. Underlying these issues was the moral question of the potential end of rural, communitarian life.

These critical issues were resolved in favor of America's industrial future. Thus, in a sense the 1890's realignment reaffirmed the post–Civil War move to industrialization. Over the longer period some of the Populist issues were adopted by the Progressives and eventually became public policy. For my purposes, however, the policy significance of the 1890's realignment lies in the passage of the gold standard, the enactment of the Dingley Tariff, and U.S. expansionism in foreign policy. In sum, these policies were a clear answer to the question of what direction the country's future would take.

★ Partisan Differences

Most students regard the period from 1877 to the late 1890's as a benchmark in the development of the American economy. During this period trusts were at their peak, and the survival of corporate structures depended on favorable treatment from the federal government. Especially relevant to these interests was the maintenance of selectively high tariffs and the gold standard. Over time the agrarian and silver interests of the Southern, North Central, and Western regions arrayed themselves against the industrial interests. The Populist interests felt they were exploited by the trusts and the Wall Street bankers.

The Panic of 1893 brought the long-smoldering division to a head, and by 1895 prosilver inflationists had captured control of the Democratic Party. Big business would have suffered severely at the hands of the silver advocates had they been victorious in 1896. Most evidence suggests that they would have split up corporations, lowered tariffs, disavowed extensive colonial activities, and of course inflated the economy by coining silver at sixteen to one. The key to the campaign of 1896 is the Panic of 1893, which ignited party divisions on economic policy. The question was whether America was to be a major industrial-urban world power, or whether (like France before World War II) it was to be partly industrial with large petit-bourgeois and agricultural sectors. The Republican and Democratic parties were the primary vehicles for carrying into operation the two differing formulas, as the platforms they adopted at their national conventions testify.

After the standard patriotic opening remarks, the Democratic Party platform of 1896 turns immediately to the gold-silver issue:

Recognizing that the money question is paramount to all others at this time, we invite attention to the fact that the Federal Constitution named silver and gold together as the money metals of the United States. . . . We declare that the act of 1873 demonetizing silver without the knowledge or approval of the American people has resulted in the appreciation of gold and a corresponding fall in the prices of commodities produced by the people; a heavy increase in the burdens of taxation and of all debts, public and private; the enrichment of the money-lending class at home and abroad; the prostration of industry and impoverishment of the people.[8]

This lead-off position clearly established the importance of the issue for the Democratic Party. Moreover, the Democrats focused on the gold standard as the basis for the "people's" plight. Their solution: "We demand the free and unlimited coinage of both silver and gold at 16 to 1 without waiting for the consent of any other nation."

On the gold-silver dispute the Republican platform of 1896 was "unreservedly for sound money. [The Republican Party] caused the enactment of a law providing for the redemption [resumption] of specie payments in 1879. Since then every dollar has been as good as gold." On the question of free coinage of silver, the Republicans' money plank read: "We are unalterably opposed to every measure calculated to debase our currency or impair the credit of our country. We are therefore opposed to the free coinage of silver, except by international agreement with the leading commercial nations of the earth. . . . All of our silver and paper currency must be maintained at parity with gold."

The lines could not have been more sharply drawn. The Democrats saw the gold standard as the personal creation of vested interests, which benefited "moneylenders" at the expense of the people of America. Their solution was to undercut the gold standard through the free coinage of silver, thereby solving the problem of vested interests. The Republicans strongly supported the gold standard, viewing the free coinage of silver as a radical attempt to stifle free enterprise. Their solution was to maintain the gold standard, and thus facilitate America's growth as a world economic power.

The partisan split over the second major issue, the tariff, was just as deep. At the time of the conventions the tariff in force was the Democratic tariff of President Cleveland, and the Democratic convention's tariff resolution was "opposed to any agitation for further changes in our tariff laws." The party's general stand on tariffs was embodied in one sentence: "We hold that tariff duties should be levied for purposes of revenue, such duties to be so adjusted as to operate equally throughout the country, and not discriminate between class or section." The McKinley protective tariff was denounced as a breeder of trusts and monopolies, which "enriched the few at the expense of the many, restricted trade, and deprived the producers of the great American staples of access to their natural markets."

The Republican convention countered by denouncing the Cleveland administration's fiscal policy and offering in its stead a return to the wisdom of Benjamin Harrison: "We renew and emphasize our allegiance to the policy of protection, as the bulwark of American industrial independence, and the foundation of American development and prosperity." This "true" tariff policy, according to the Republican platform, led to an American market for American producers, the upholding of the American workingman's wages, equity between business and farming, and a diffusion of general thrift, founding the strength of all on the strength of each. In a word, the Democrats favored freer trade, or tariffs for revenue only; the Republicans favored a protective tariff.

On the issue of foreign expansionism, as on the other pressing issues of the day, there existed clear-cut differences between the parties. Neither party questioned the right of the United States under the Monroe Doctrine to intervene in Latin America. The differences occurred on the extent and shape of that intervention. The Republican platform included strong statements favoring the annexation of Hawaii, the purchase of the Spanish islands, and an American-owned and -operated Nicaraguan canal, along with expansion of the U.S. Navy to protect America's foreign interests. The Democrats did not deal with these issues at Chicago in 1896; their main concern in the area of expansion was that the Alaskan forests and industries be placed under U.S. laws, thus limiting the possibility of industrial mayhem in that territory. But the parties' discord in this area is plain in their respective attitudes on Cuba. The Democrats simply extended their "sympathy to the people of Cuba in their heroic struggle for liberty and independence." The Republicans went much farther, stating: "The government of Spain, having lost control of Cuba, and being unable to protect the property or lives of resident American citizens, or to comply with its Treaty obligations, we believe that the government of the United States should actively use its influence and good offices to restore peace and give independence to the Island."

Ginsberg's content analysis of party platforms dramatically documents the rise of partisan differences during this realignment (Fig. 3.1). The data show the salience of the issues of "markets, monometalism, railroads, special interests, and utilities" over the 1876–96 period,[9] though it is not until 1892 that party differences are manifest. Before that, the measure of party conflict does not rise above .20 and

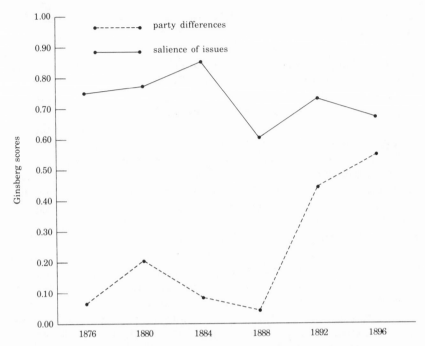

Fig. 3.1. Salience of the gold-silver issue and other economic issues, 1876–1896. Source: Benjamin Ginsberg, "Critical Elections and the Substance of Party Conflict: 1844–1968," *Midwest Journal of Political Science,* Aug. 1972, pp. 603–25.

averages less than .10. The value rises to .44 in 1892 and hits its all-time high of .55 in 1896. Thereafter it drops below .50 and does not rise significantly until the 1920's.

The partisan differences so clearly shown by Ginsberg are also visible in the behavior of the parties at their 1896 nominating conventions. The Democratic convention nominated William Jennings Bryan after his famous "Cross of Gold" speech and repudiated gold Democrats like President Cleveland by adopting the Populist Party planks on gold and silver, tariffs, and expansionism. In short, the Democrats purged the party of its pro-industrial interests.

When the Republicans convened in St. Louis, William McKinley's nomination seemed assured, but the Republican stand on the gold question uncertain. The two Ohioans, McKinley and his sponsor, Mark Hanna, had appeared to favor a two-metal standard in opposition to the Eastern Republicans, who were pushing a hard line on the gold issue. The actual author of the accepted plank may have been Senator Cabot Lodge of Massachusetts (a Reed backer); but Hanna appears to have feigned being sold on the gold standard to win points elsewhere. In any event, what is important here is that this was the crucial issue before the Republican convention. The adoption of the gold plank by a vote of 818½ to 105½ signaled the end of Republicanism for Senator Teller and his fellow Western Republican silverites. The Westerners, including Senator Frank J. Cannon of Utah, were exhorted by their former Republican comrades to leave: "Cries of Go! Go! swept the westerners from the chamber."[10] In short, the Republican and Democratic candidates who stood for election in 1896 offered the voters clear-cut policy alternatives on the critical issues.

Issues, candidates, and parties were fused, and as the campaign progressed, Americans perceived the consequences of the election as monumental. Representative James I. Doliver of Iowa said that the country was on the eve of changes that might upset "the very foundations of the social fabric."[11]

Republicans characterized Bryan, Altgeld, and "Pitchfork Ben" Tillman as demagogues who were intent on overthrowing "decency"; Senator Orville Platt of Connecticut went so far as to compare them to the bloodthirsty leaders of the French Revolution, Robespierre, Danton, and Marat. Bryan, on his side, charged the Republicans with being un-American. "You may go to New York or Boston," he said, "and find financiers who doubt the greatness of this country and proclaim the necessity for foreign aid, but the men who do that know more about Europe than they do about the United States." He promised when elected to "administer the law not for foreign syndicates but for the American people."[12]

On election day voter turnout was high throughout the country. McKinley won the Presidency with about 55 percent of the vote. The results were the most sectional since the Civil War. McKinley carried the Northeast and the industrial Midwest, while Bryan carried the Southern and Border states and most of the West.

★ Electoral Change

If the election was dominated by national issues, then congressional election results should reveal national, not local, electoral forces at work. Table 3.1 shows the means and standard deviations across all districts for congressional elections from 1884 to 1900. Since the Southern states had been heavily Democratic since 1876, the figures were also calculated without them.

The results for the entire nation indicate a competitive two-party system with the Democrats holding a slight advantage in mean percentage until 1894. The variance around the mean Democratic vote drops in the 1888 and 1892–96 elections. Excluding the Southern

TABLE 3.1

Mean Party Vote and Standard Deviation in House Elections Including and Excluding the South, 1884–1900

House	Election year	Democrat		Republican	
		Mean vote (pct.)	Std. dev.	Mean vote (pct.)	Std. dev.
		Entire Nation			
49	1884	53.2%	15.7	44.2%	17.6
50	1886	53.1	22.4	40.8	20.7
51	1888	51.7	14.6	46.1	14.6
52	1890	56.5	17.1	41.1	17.2
53	1892	51.6	14.4	40.1	17.1
54	1894	43.2	15.4	48.6	20.7
55	1896	46.7	16.3	52.1	19.4
56	1898	48.9	19.2	49.6	20.1
57	1900	46.8	19.4	50.9	18.1
		South Excluded			
49	1884	48.6%	12.0	46.8%	16.1
50	1886	46.1	17.3	46.8	14.6
51	1888	46.8	9.9	50.0	8.7
52	1890	50.5	11.7	47.0	11.2
53	1892	47.5	11.8	45.8	9.4
54	1894	37.9	11.3	52.5	10.9
55	1896	41.7	13.4	54.2	13.6
56	1898	44.7	12.6	51.3	11.8
57	1900	42.7	12.7	53.3	10.8

NOTE: Columns may not total 100% because of third-party voting.

states provides a more realistic characterization of the realignment because they were Democratic before, during, and after it. With the South excluded, we see an extremely competitive two-party system in the rest of the nation from 1884 to 1894. The variance around the mean vote is in general more stable, and the parties are never more than 5 percentage points apart. The Democratic mean for 1884–92 is 47.9 percent with a 12.5 standard deviation; the Republican mean is 47.3 percent with a 12.0 standard deviation. The 1894 election resulted in a difference of 14.6 percent between Democrats and Republicans. From 1894 on, the Republicans never fell below a 6.6 percent advantage, and the average was 11.0 percent. Thus the realignment of the 1890's was first felt in the House in the 1894 election, which introduced a lasting shift of more than 6 percent toward the Republicans. These results indicate that the realignment was regional, and in addition that the Democrats were affected by the Populist Party.

To see the extent to which the realignment was regional, refer to Table 3.2 showing the mean party vote and standard deviations for

TABLE 3.2

Mean Party Vote and Standard Deviation in House Elections by Region, 1884–1900

	Democrat		Republican		Democrat		Republican	
Election year	Mean vote (pct.)	Std. dev.	Mean vote (pct.)	Std. dev.	Mean vote (pct.)	Std. dev.	Mean vote (pct.)	Std. dev.
	New England				Northeast			
1884	40.0%	9.4	53.9%	7.9	49.8%	16.0	48.3%	16.0
1886	44.5	8.8	50.8	8.6	48.3	18.3	45.8	17.5
1888	44.0	7.5	53.5	7.4	46.9	14.1	50.1	17.8
1890	45.1	7.1	52.0	7.4	50.2	14.7	46.5	12.9
1892	45.8	6.8	51.0	7.3	48.9	12.1	47.4	11.2
1894	35.9	8.5	59.5	8.1	39.3	8.9	56.6	9.2
1896	30.4	10.5	66.7	9.1	36.4	12.4	59.2	14.6
1898	38.7	9.1	58.6	9.7	43.7	13.3	51.5	14.5
1900	37.6	9.6	59.1	8.9	41.0	12.6	55.9	11.6
	East North Central				West North Central			
1884	47.9%	6.7	50.0%	6.8	47.0%	7.7	36.0%	27.1
1886	44.8	11.4	49.2	10.2	37.4	26.4	46.4	17.2
1888	46.9	6.2	49.9	5.5	43.6	8.5	51.0	5.2
1890	48.9	8.3	47.0	8.5	53.2	7.0	42.8	6.1
1892	48.4	6.6	46.2	5.4	41.7	14.2	45.6	4.7
1894	38.8	9.0	52.9	6.6	33.7	15.4	50.6	5.4
1896	45.8	7.6	53.2	7.6	46.0	11.5	50.3	7.0
1898	45.4	7.2	53.0	8.6	45.1	10.6	51.6	5.4
1900	45.2	8.0	53.6	7.7	39.5	17.0	52.3	5.7
	South				Border			
1884	68.6%	17.1	30.7%	16.9	57.4%	13.8	42.3%	13.9
1886	76.6	21.5	17.0	21.8	56.9	13.8	39.6	17.1
1888	68.1	16.1	28.4	17.8	52.8	7.5	45.6	7.6
1890	76.8	17.0	18.6	17.1	58.4	16.6	38.8	17.1
1892	65.2	13.9	15.8	16.7	55.5	14.3	39.0	15.5
1894	61.2	13.8	14.7	19.1	46.1	10.6	45.1	18.9
1896	62.9	14.6	24.9	19.2	49.9	15.1	45.7	17.3
1898	76.2	17.7	16.3	18.5	54.6	14.2	43.3	14.5
1900	75.7	16.1	20.9	17.3	51.0	9.7	46.7	13.0
	West							
1884	46.4%	3.5	52.3%	3.7				
1886	46.8	3.0	48.6	2.1				
1888	46.3	3.8	51.3	3.3				
1890	45.7	3.6	51.6	2.8				
1892	45.3	9.1	47.9	2.9				
1894	31.4	8.7	42.2	5.2				
1896	39.6	12.1	46.7	8.6				
1898	35.8	20.9	51.3	3.5				
1900	40.2	4.6	53.8	2.9				

NOTE: The region code is as follows: *New England* = Conn., Maine, Mass., N.H., R.I., Vt.; *Northeast* = Del., N.J., N.Y., Pa.; *East North Central* = Ill., Ind., Mich., Ohio, Wis.; *West North Central* = Iowa, Kans., Minn., Mo., Neb., N. Dak., S. Dak.; *South* = Ala., Ark., Fla., Ga., La., Miss., N.C., S.C., Tenn., Tex., Va.; *Border* = Ky., Md., W. Va.; *West* = Calif., Colo., Mont., Nev., N. Mex., Ore., Utah, Wash., Wyo.

1884–1900 by region. (Readers not interested in all of the details of the regional analysis should skip ahead to the electoral summary section featuring Table 3.4.) The New England states were already Republican before 1894, but by relatively narrow margins. Democrats averaged around 45.0 percent of the vote, compared with 51–52 percent for the Republicans. With the election of 1894 New England became a bastion of Republicanism. From then on, the Democrats never received 40 percent of the vote, and the Republicans averaged about 60 percent over the next three elections.

In the Northeastern and East North Central states the two parties were extremely competitive until 1894. After that election both these populous areas became predominantly Republican, the Northeast slightly more so. In the East North Central states the Populist Party candidates hurt the Democrats, as is shown in the 1894 vote totals. In both regions the Democrats' share of the vote dropped during the 1894 realignment and in general remained low in the 1896 election. Although the results for the Northeast most clearly fit the national issues pattern of a shift in means and a drop in standard deviation, the timing of the shift in the East North Central states is the same.

In the West North Central states the results are complicated by the Populist vote. The Republicans seem to have been affected by national issues in 1888; that is, regardless of swings in the mean of up to 10 percent, the standard deviations remain low. The Democrats, however, were affected by contending Populist candidates. With the exception of 1884, 1888, and 1890, the variance around the vote fluctuates with the number of Populists contesting congressional elections. As in the other regions, however, 1894 marks a cut-point because it establishes the Republicans as the region's dominant party. The combining of Populist and Democratic forces beginning in 1896 allowed the Democrats to make sizable gains, but they remained the competitive second party.

The Southern states were heavily Democratic from 1884 to 1892, and were even more so in 1898 and 1900. The elections of 1894 and 1896 produced the lowest Democratic means in those states since 1876. The Republicans did not gain these disaffected votes unless, as in North Carolina, they combined with Populist interests. The Democratic losses in 1894 and 1896 resulted from a large Populist vote in many districts. After the electoral scare of 1896, Southern Democrats met in Jackson, Mississippi, to systematically dismantle a potential coalition of poor whites and blacks. The disenfranchisement of blacks decreased the vote totals in the South and made the region even more staunchly Democratic than it had been before the realignment. The variance around the mean Democratic vote dropped in 1892–96, reflecting a national anti-Democratic trend, although there was not a corresponding increase in Republican votes.

The Border states are an interesting counterpoint to the South. They were solidly Democratic before 1894. After the realignment this was a much more competitive two-party region. The Western states, in contrast, were Republican throughout the period and seem to have been little affected by national issues. This finding makes sense given the vast distances between the Western and Eastern states and the lack of modern communications.

In sum, a lasting realignment of parties in the U.S. House of Representatives occurred in the 1894 elections. Results of the realignment varied by region. The 1894 election converted competitive two-party states in the industrial East and Midwest into solid Republican regions and made the Border states into a competitive two-party region. Democrats, for their part, became even more dominant in the eleven Southern states. Only the Northeastern states fit the pattern of a dramatic shift in means and a decreased standard deviation. The other regions showed a shift in means in the 1894 elections, but the pattern of standard deviations differed.

Was the change compensating or across the board? If we compare differences in the vote across the same districts in pairs of elections, the answer becomes apparent. If the vote is compensating, variance around the mean change should be high; if the vote is across the board, the variance should be low. Given the results above, the expectation is that the two major parties will show different patterns. The Democratic vote should be compensating (high standard deviation of change) because the Democrats lost votes in the North while they gained in the South. The Republican vote should be across the board (low variance of change) because the Republicans gained in the North in every subregion and had little or nothing to lose in the South (Table 3.3).

The results for the entire nation show that in the paired elections of 1892 and 1894, the Democrats lose 7.6 percent and have a very high standard deviation of change—31.0. After the shift to the Republicans in 1894, the standard deviation stabilizes. The Republicans show gains of about 5 percent in the 1892–94 pair and no great change in the standard deviation. These results, however, are somewhat complicated by the Populist influence on both parties in the South.

The same analysis run without the South clarifies the pattern. The Democrats lose 5.1 percent in the 1892–94 pair and the standard deviation of change is 18.6, indicating a pattern of compensating or in-

TABLE 3.3

Mean Swing in Party Vote and Standard Deviation of Swing in Paired House
Elections Including and Excluding the South, 1884–1900

Houses	Election years	Democrat		Republican	
		Mean swing (pct.)	Std. dev.	Mean swing (pct.)	Std. dev.
		Entire Nation			
49–50	1884–1886	0.0%	16.6	−3.2%	17.4
50–51	1886–1888	−1.5	15.9	5.1	14.2
51–52	1888–1890	5.0	11.3	−5.5	11.8
52–53	1890–1892	−4.6	14.1	−0.6	12.5
53–54	1892–1894	−7.6	31.0	5.1	13.9
54–55	1894–1896	3.3	12.0	3.6	14.0
55–56	1896–1898	5.4	10.8	−4.2	13.3
56–57	1898–1900	−1.7	12.3	2.6	11.5
		South Excluded			
49–50	1884–1886	−2.5%	14.9	−0.1%	15.5
50–51	1886–1888	0.7	15.2	3.3	12.2
51–52	1888–1890	3.9	9.5	−4.3	8.5
52–53	1890–1892	−2.5	11.9	−0.1	8.9
53–54	1892–1894	−5.1	18.6	6.9	7.8
54–55	1894–1896	3.8	12.5	1.7	10.2
55–56	1896–1898	3.0	9.1	−2.9	10.9
56–57	1898–1900	−2.1	11.0	2.0	8.6

teractive change. The change in standard deviation is, as expected, lower when the South is removed. The Republicans show an increase of 6.9 percent, indicating a pattern of across-the-board change to the Republicans in 1894. From 1894 to 1896 both Democratic and Republican mean percentages of change increased. This is, of course, the result of decreased Populist strength once the Democrats adopted Populist principles. The standard deviation of change for the Democrats drops to 12.5 and does not approach 15.0 through the 1900 election. In sum, the analysis of change shows a Democratic pattern of interactive or compensating change, but an across-the-board Republican change in the North.

★ Electoral Summary

An analysis of the precritical, critical, and postcritical periods using the V coefficient shows a modified national trend at work (Table 3.4). In the 1894 and 1896 elections the Democrats lost 5.5 percent of the swing, and the Republicans gained 4.4 percent; the corresponding V's were below ±3.20 in each case. This contrasts sharply with the precritical period (1884–92), where the Democrats lost 1.8 percent of the swing and the Republicans lost 2.6 percent, with V's of −15.41 and −8.21, respectively. The postcritical period (1898–1900) is characterized by smaller swing votes and V's approximately twice as high as during the realignment. The election that shows the most dramatic effect is the 1894 election. That election gave the Republicans a large majority in the House as voters swung away from the Democrats (−7.6 percent) and to the Republicans (+5.5 percent). The election of 1896, normally considered the realigning election, produced at the Congressional level an increase for both Democrats and Republicans (+3.3 and +3.7 percent swings, respectively). The fact that both major parties gained in the 55th House elections (1896) over their totals for the 54th House is clearly the result of the Democratic merger with the Populist Party, just as the loss for both parties in the 53rd House reflects Populist gains in the 1892 elections. Thus, the election pair of 1892 and 1894 most clearly meets the criteria for a shift toward national electoral factors over local ones.

Turning, as before, to Flanigan and Zingale's modified analysis of variance technique, we find that they posit a 3.5 realigning loss for the Democrats in 1894, which was somewhat compensated for by a 1.2 gain in the 1896 election.[13] They do not find any national across-the-board realignment toward the Republicans between 1894 and 1900. However, when they turned to a regional analysis, they found Democrats losing across the board in the Midwest and West in 1894, with the Republicans gaining across the board in the East and Midwest. They conclude, "The congressional series suggests a shift away from the Democrats in most regions in 1894, presumably in response initially to the Depression of 1893 and perpetuated in subsequent elections by disaffection with the Populist alliance."[14] Their analysis of Congressional elections uses first the state and then the county as the unit of analysis.

TABLE 3.4

Aggregate Party Vote Swings and Coefficients of Variation, 1884–1900

Period	Mean swing (percent)		Coefficient of variation	
	Democrat	Republican	Democrat	Republican
Precritical period, 1884–92	−1.79%	−2.62%	−15.41	−8.21
Critical period, 1894–96	−5.45	4.39	−3.05	3.20
Postcritical period, 1898–1900	−3.13	−2.13	6.27	5.46
Controlling election, 1896	—	3.67%	—	3.90

Using their technique but applying it to congressional districts as the unit of analysis results in somewhat different values but essentially the same conclusion. In this case we find a slight across-the-board switch to the Republicans in the 1894 election—1.9 percent. The Democrats lost 3.9 percent in the 1894 election but posted a compensating 1.0 gain in 1896. Shifting the analysis to a North-South comparison clearly shows the regional effects noted above. The Republicans then show gains of 4.6 percent across the board in the 1894 elections and 1.8 in 1896. In sum, the Republicans gained votes in the North and Midwest during the 1894–96 period, while the Democrats lost votes there but gained in the South and Border states. The realignment was compensatory for the Democrats and across the board for Republicans, albeit with a shift of less than 6 percent even in Northern states. Again, these results concur with Clubb, Flanigan, and Zingale's conclusion that "while indications of lasting electoral results are clear, the realignment of 1896 appears substantially less impressive than might have been expected."[15]

★ Votes-to-Seats Ratios

If the electoral shifts are less impressive than we might have expected, the shift in congressional seats more than lives up to our expectations. As in the Civil War–era realignment, we would expect the votes-to-seats ratio during the critical period to exceed the Cube Law prediction. The argument is that the Cube Law distorts in favor of the majority party, and if the distortion is greater than the law predicts, then there is a truly significant advantage to the majority party. The realignment of the late 1890's was essentially an across-the-board surge to the Republicans. Thus, during the 1894 and 1896 elections, the votes-to-seats ratio should disproportionately advantage the Republicans. Table 3.5 shows the ratio of Republican seats to Democratic seats for 1884–1900. By our hypothesis, the greatest difference between the Cube Law predictions and the actual seat ratios should occur in the elections of 1894 and 1896, with the greatest difference in the 1894 election because the swing was greatest in that election.

The results for the entire nation show that the Cube Law underpredicts the ratio of Republican to Democratic seats generally, and most severely in 1894, with a predicted ratio of 1.05 to 1 against an actual ratio of 2.05 to 1. Moreover, in both 1896 and 1898 the Republicans had an advantage of +0.46 in actual seats. While these results corroborate the hypothesis, the inclusion of the South distorts the results somewhat toward the Democrats, since so few Republicans were elected from Southern states. Excluding the South from the analysis

TABLE 3.5

Ratio of Republican House Seats to Democratic Seats Compared with Cube Law Predictions Including and Excluding the South, 1884–1900

Election year	Entire nation			South excluded		
	Cube Law prediction	Actual ratio	Difference	Cube Law prediction	Actual ratio	Difference
1884	0.54	0.76	0.22	0.89	1.20	0.31
1886	0.42	0.88	0.46	1.05	1.38	0.33
1888	0.66	1.02	0.36	1.22	1.73	0.51
1890	0.35	0.36	0.01	0.76	0.51	−0.25
1892	0.42	0.55	0.13	0.89	0.83	−0.06
1894	1.05	2.05	1.00	2.66	5.70	3.04
1896	1.05	1.51	0.46	2.20	2.93	0.73
1898	0.58	1.04	0.46	1.52	1.83	0.31
1900	0.76	1.19	0.43	1.95	2.36	0.41

reveals an important seat advantage to the Republicans in the 1894 and 1896 elections. In 1894 the Cube Law predicts a 2.66 ratio of Republican to Democratic seats, where the actual ratio was 5.70 to 1. The results for 1896 show a 0.73 difference favoring the Republican Party.

In sum, the realignment of 1894–96 changed relatively few votes (less than 6 percent) toward the Republicans, but changed the ratio of Republican to Democratic seats dramatically. The electoral change may not have been as impressive as expected, but the seat change in the House is impressive indeed. And it was a change in the control of the House that lasted from 1894 until 1910—sixteen years of uninterrupted Republican control. Given Republican control of the Presidency and the Senate from 1896 to 1912, the Republican Party had undivided control of the government from 1896 to 1910. What was the composition of the now-dominant Republican Party?

★ Constituency Bases of the Congressional Parties

The realignment of the mid-1890's made the Republican Party dominant in congressional elections from 1894 to 1910. The Republicans were the majority party in the industrial, blue-collar urban East and in the more prosperous Midwestern agricultural regions. If realigning elections change the composition of preferences by party, then the constituency bases of the congressional parties should shift accordingly. The realignment of 1894–96 turned a competitive two-party system in most Northern states into a one-party-dominant system. Thus, the shift in the constituent bases of the congressional parties should be especially dramatic over the 1892–98 period. The hypothesis is that the Republican Party should shift to overrepresent industrial and Northern constituencies, while the Democrats should shift toward rural and Southern-Border states. Such a change in the constituency bases of the parties would corroborate our argument that the 1894–96 realignment was the result of the Democrats' absorbing Populist issues, thus forcing the Republicans to represent Northern and Eastern industrial interests and shifting House members' preferences accordingly.

Testing this hypothesis entailed extracting the number of farm operators and blue-collar workers from the county sections of the 1890 Census and mapping these figures onto congressional districts. Since the size of constituencies varied, these data were converted into percentages, arrayed and divided by mean, median, and quartile. The computation of district constituent characteristics was straightforward for districts composed of whole counties, as most of them were. Where there was more than one district per county (e.g. New York City), the city sections of the 1890 Census were used. This allowed us to locate the district's quartile ranking on the variables used—percent workers and farm operators. For those few districts that crossed county lines, estimates based on each county's share of the district were used. Analyses run with and without cross-county districts produced no significant differences. Table 3.6 shows the results.

The table demonstrates the striking shift that took place in the constituency bases of the parties with the 1896 realignment. In the 53rd House both parties were competitive across all district types. For example, Republicans captured 44 percent of the seats in heavily labor districts to the Democrats' 56 percent, the Democrats 64 percent of the heavily agricultural districts to the Republicans' 36 percent. But in the 55th House the Republicans won 79 percent of heavily labor districts and fell to 33 percent in heavily agricultural districts. The ratio of increase in seats shows that over the 1892 to 1896 period, the congressional Republican Party came to overrepresent labor and industrial districts, while the Democrats came to overrepresent rural districts located almost exclusively in the Southern and Border states. The critical elections of the 1890's yielded two relatively homogeneous congressional parties with distinct centers of gravity on both a sectional and an agricultural/industrial continuum. This pattern of representation would not have been possible without one of the parties' adopting Populist principles. Once the Democrats came forcefully down on the side of free silver and liberal tariffs and against expansionism, the Republicans took the opposite stands, thus drawing distinct ideological positions.[16]

TABLE 3.6

Shift in Constituency Bases Between 1892 and 1896

(Percent and absolute ratio of change in seats between 53rd and 55th Houses)

| Category | Percent | | | Absolute ratio of change |
	1892	1896	Difference	
District results				
Republican seats from labor districts				
Low	35%	31%	−4%	0.93
High	44	79	35	1.91
Republican seats from agri- cultural districts				
Low	40	71	31	1.78
High	36	33	−3	0.95
Regional results				
Democratic seats from South and Border states	47	64	17	—
Republican seats from New England, Northeast, and North Central states	62	76	14	—

SOURCE: 1890 Census data applied to 1892 and 1896 districts.
NOTE: Labor districts are based on number of blue-collar workers, agricultural districts on num-ber of farm operators. Low is defined as below the median, high as above the median. The polariza-tion evident in the 55th House persists until the election of 1910; David W. Brady and Phillip Althoff, "Party Voting in the U.S. House of Representatives, 1890–1910: Elements of a Responsible Party System," *Journal of Politics*, 36 (1974): 753–75.

Another way to document the change in the constituent bases of the congressional parties is to look at pairs of elections and determine which districts Republicans gained in over the 1892–96 elections. Having determined which districts Republicans gained in and the ex-tent of their gain, we can then ascertain the constituent characteristics of those districts in which the Republicans gained votes. Figure 3.2 shows the results of this analysis. The darkly shaded area of the illus-tration shows the percentage of districts above the median in laborers and below the median in farm operators (i.e. industrial districts). The results are clear and support the hypothesis. The Republicans' gains outnumber their losses by a sizable margin, and the gain side of the figure is heavily industrial and labor in composition. On the other hand, those districts where Republicans lost votes over the 1892–96 period are rural and agricultural. Further analyses show that these districts were almost entirely Southern and Border, those on the gain side almost entirely Eastern and Midwestern.

Both analyses clearly show that the shift of 5-to-7 percent of the vote to the Republicans in Northern states, plus the distortion of seats

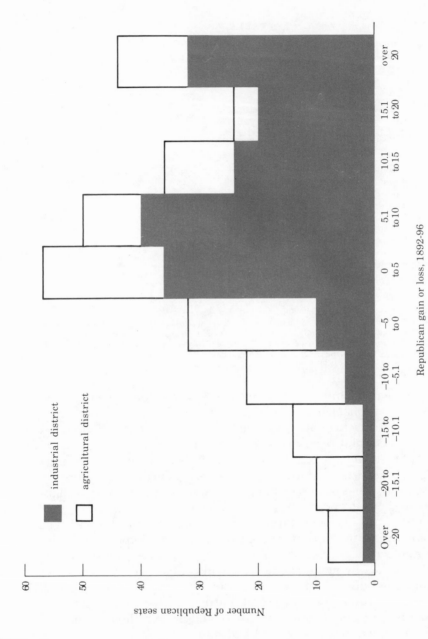

Fig. 3.2. Industrial constituent base of Republican seats during the 1890's realignment

to votes, resulted in two ideologically polarized parties in Congress representing distinct constituencies. The results of these differences should manifest themselves in congressional voting patterns.

★ Congressional Turnover

As we have seen, the cross-cutting issues associated with industrialization produced a national electoral result. A very important effect of the elections of 1894 and 1896 was a high rate of turnover in the House of Representatives. The argument put forward in this book is that high turnover in realigning elections results in a changed set of member preferences and a decrease in committees' ability to shape legislative results in an incremental fashion. If members' preferences are coherent and cohesive, and committee influence vis-à-vis party is reduced, then more consistent party voting should result.

Turnover in the House during the decade immediately preceding the realignment was high compared with the rate today. This was due primarily to retirements. As Nelson Polsby has shown, prior to the 1890's the House was not well differentiated from its environment.[17] That is, most members did not make a career of the House, but would serve a term or two and then retire to take local judgeships, to run for state office, or to follow some other pursuit. In those circumstances, we might expect the turnover rates in the House not to be markedly different during the 1890's. Nevertheless, the figures show a rise in turnover during the realignment. In the five Houses before the 1894 election, turnover averaged 38.5 percent; during the realignment the average rose to 43.3. More important, the turnover during the realignment was a result of the electorate's choice, not members' voluntary retirement, with about three-quarters due to the defeat of incumbents standing for reelection. Thus it seems safe to assert that the Republican members of the 55th and 56th Houses felt they owed their election in large part to their party and to the positions taken on the currency, tariff, and expansion issues, and that their Democratic counterparts felt similarly obligated to their party and its positions.

Anyone studying the 1890's is struck by the intensity with which House members held their policy views. Democrats viewed Republican policies as inspired by a conspiracy of Eastern and European banking interests intent on wreaking havoc on agricultural interests. Representative Curtis H. Castle of California summed up this view in a speech on the floor in 1897:

Rothschild and his American agents, Belmont, Morgan and Co., hold $200,000,000 in Spanish bonds. Should Cuba achieve her independence, the market value of these bonds would depreciate; hence, Rothschild favors Spain and will until he perceives that Cuban independence is inevitable. Then, provided he can persuade Cuba to issue bonds for his benefit, he will permit the U.S. Government to interfere. Rothschild controls Morgan, Morgan controls Hanna, and Hanna controls McKinley, the Supreme Court and this House. Hanna is America, America is Hanna.[18]

The Republicans, on their side, viewed Bryan and the Democrats as Western demagogues intent on overthrowing progress and decency. As they saw it, the Democrats posed a real threat to the nation's well-being and had to be stopped at all costs from enacting their legislative program; the Democrats sought to "array labor against capital, employer against employed," and if they succeeded in this, it would spell the end of industrial progress.[19] The intensity of opinion, the belief in conspiracies and in the moral rightness of their own cause, led naturally to victors interpreting their success as a signal to vote their beliefs. And since their beliefs were coterminous with their party's position, constituency-party cross-pressuring should have been greatly reduced.

Committees in the post–Civil War era were an important component of the decision-making process. As Woodrow Wilson observed in *Congressional Government* (1886):

The Leaders of the House are the chairmen of the principal Standing Committees. Indeed, to be exactly accurate, the House has as many leaders as there are subjects of legislation; for there are as many Standing Committees as there are leading classes of legislation, and in the consideration of every topic of business the House is guided by a special leader in the person of the chairman of the Standing Committee, charged with the superintendence of measures of the particular class to which that topic belongs.[20]

In fact, Wilson argued that congressional government was committee government, and that committee chairmen could determine policy outcomes. Given these conditions, a dramatic turnover in committee members and chairs could pave the way for innovative or nonincremental policies. If the 1890's was a true realignment, we ought to find a turnover in committee membership by 1896 massive enough to increase the new majority party's chances to push through major policy changes. Testing this hypothesis entailed collecting data to track the continuity of committee personnel. Table 3.7 shows the results. The argument is that committee continuity ensures gradual changes in leadership and the easy translation of committee norms to new members. As Richard Fenno puts it, "The tendency to rebellion increases as personnel turnover increases."[21] If turnover on House committees during realignments is high, and a substantial number of the commit-

TABLE 3.7

Total and Partisan Turnover on Thirteen Selected Committees, 55th House,
1897–1899

(Percent new members since 53rd House)

Committee	Total	Democrat	Republican
Agriculture	100.0%	100.0%	100.0%
Appropriations	64.7	66.6	50.0
Banking and Currency	76.5	88.9	62.5
Commerce	82.4	100.0	71.4
Education	100.0	100.0	100.0
Foreign Affairs	86.7	87.5	85.7
Judiciary	82.4	100.0	62.5
Labor	76.9	85.7	66.7
Merchant Marine	91.7	100.0	83.3
Mines and Mining	84.6	85.7	100.0
Public Lands	86.7	100.0	71.4
Rules[a]	80.0	100.0	50.0
Ways and Means	76.5	88.9	62.5

[a] During the 1890's realignment, the Rules Committee had only five members.

tee leaders are new, then committees will not be a stumbling block to innovative legislation.

The results of the committee turnover analysis are striking. The lowest rate of total turnover was 64.7 percent. If we exclude the Republicans on the Appropriations and Rules committees, the lowest turnover rate was 62.5 percent, and the average turnover was slightly over 80 percent. Comparing turnover during the realignment with the immediately preceding period reveals dramatically greater turnover during the realignment. Whereas the average turnover from the 52nd to the 53rd House was slightly over 30 percent, the turnover from the 53rd to the 55th House was over 80 percent. It seems clear that the 1894–96 elections effected drastic changes in committee composition.

Important components of the committee system, facilitating committee continuity and stability, are norms favoring seniority and specialization. Committee leadership positions become available with relative rarity; leaders are brought along slowly. A committee's leaders serve on the same committee for long periods of time, acquiring expertise and becoming custodians of committee norms and policy.

If in a very short time there are dramatic turnovers in membership, one would expect the norms of seniority and specialization to be affected—specifically, that committee turnover would be so drastic that many of the committee leaders in the realignment Houses would have little seniority. For the purposes of our analysis, any committee chairman in the 55th House who was either not on that committee in

TABLE 3.8

Low-Seniority Committee Chairmen, 55th House

Committee	Chairman
*Accounts	Odel (N.Y.)
*Agriculture	Wadsworth (N.Y.)
*Alcohol, Liquor, Traffic	Brewster (N.Y.)
Appropriations	Cannon (Ill.)
*Claims	Brumm (Penn.)
Commerce	Hepburn (Iowa)
District of Columbia	Babcock (Wis.)
*Education	Grow (Penn.)
*Election of President	Gorliss (Mich.)
*Expenditures, Agriculture	Gillet (N.Y.)
Expenditures, Interior	Curtiss (Kan.)
*Expenditures, Justice	Sullaway (N.H.)
*Expenditures, Navy	Stewart (N.J.)
*Expenditures, Post Office	Wanger (Penn.)
*Expenditures, Public Buildings	Colson (Ky.)
*Expenditures, State Department	Guigg (N.Y.)
*Expenditures, Treasury	Cousins (Iowa)
*Expenditures, War Department	Grout (Vt.)
*Immigration and Naturalization	Danford (Ohio)
Indian Affairs	Sherman (N.Y.)
*Invalid Pensions	Ray (N.Y.)
*Irrigation	Ellis (Ore.)
*Judiciary	Henderson (Iowa)
Labor	Gardner (N.J.)
*Levees on Mississippi	Bartholdt (Mo.)
*Manufactures	Faris (Ind.)
*Merchant Marine	Payne (N.Y.)
*Militia	Marsh (Ill.)
*Mines and Mining	Grosvenar (Ohio)
Pacific Railroads	Powers (Vt.)
Patents	Hicks (Penn.)
*Private Land Claims	Smith (Ill.)
Public Buildings	Mercer (Neb.)
Reform in Civil Service	Brosius (Penn.)
*Revision of Laws	Warner (Ill.)
*Rivers and Harbors	Burton (Ohio)
*Territories	Knox (Mass.)
War Claims	Mahon (Penn.)
Ways and Means	Dingley (Me.)

NOTE: An asterisk indicates the Chairman was not on the committee in the 53rd House. The other chairmen shown were below the median seniority on their committees in that House.

the 53rd House or was below the median rank of seniority on those committees, is considered a low-seniority committee leader. Obviously, a chairman in the realignment Houses who had not been on the committee for two or three terms could not have acquired either much seniority or much expertise in the intervening period.

During the period of the 1890's realignment, 49 House committees with more than five members were continuously in existence. In the 55th House, 27 of these 49 committees, or 55 percent, were chaired by men who were not even on the committee in the 53rd House. Another 11 had chairmen who were below the median seniority on that committee in the 53rd House. Thus, as a result of the 1896 election, the House ended up with 38 of its 49 committees, or about 80 percent, chaired by low-seniority men who were unlikely to be experts on their committee's business (Table 3.8). Since at this time the Speaker had the power to appoint committees and their chairmen, in theory at least the effect of the realignment was strengthened by the Speaker's power to jump members to committee chairmanships. But in fact most of these 38 low-seniority committee chairmen did not gain their positions through intervention.

Table 3.8 clearly shows that both important and unimportant committees in the realignment Houses had low-seniority chairmen. The most obvious effect of the discontinuities in committee leadership was that the committee system became more flexible or pliable in providing voting cues. Committee leaders and members had not acquired the norms and expertise necessary to provide the committee voting cues so prominent in the modern House of Representatives. The negative effect of committee continuity on party voting was thus diminished.

★ Voting Patterns

For the 1890's there are six issue dimensions that were present throughout the period and two dimensions that emerged during the realignment. The six continuous dimensions are currency, expansionism, tariffs, business, public works, and housekeeping. The emergent issues are taxation and immigration.

The currency dimension revolves around the coinage of silver at a sixteen-to-one parity with gold. Advocates of the free coinage of silver favored debtor and farm interests over industrial Eastern interests. Wall Street and industrial interests argued that if America was to compete with modern European nations, then the United States had to have the gold standard firmly in place. Almost all the roll calls on this dimension deal specifically with the question of bimetalism versus the gold standard. The only major exceptions are a series of bills proposed by the Democrats to tax the delivery of gold bullion in a way that made silver an attractive alternative to gold. The central issue underlying the currency question was whether America's monetary policy would favor Eastern-industrial interests or rural-agricultural interests.

The expansionism dimension consists of roll calls dealing with levels of funding for the armed services, the annexation of Hawaii, the takeover of Santo Domingo, and the opening of business markets in the Far East. From 1889 to 1896 the roll calls are dominated by questions of military preparedness and interdepartmental squabbles over who gets what; the roll calls after 1896 deal more exclusively with preparedness for the Spanish-American War and the expansion of American industrial interests. Prior to the realignment there is an underlying dimension of expansionism in arguments for having a strong Navy. The agenda changes abruptly in the 54th and 55th Houses (1895–99) as specific expansionist interests become dominant. The issue reflects a basic difference between those in favor of expanded American foreign interests and those opposed. Representative Henry Johnson of Indiana summed up the pro-expansionist position nicely when, in the debate over the annexation of Hawaii, he said, "Let us construct the Nicaragua Canal and annex the Hawaiian Republic freely offered us as a resting place in the Pacific for military and commercial considerations. These purposes accomplished, the future is bright almost beyond conception." [22] John Fitzgerald of Massachusetts summed up the opposite viewpoint in his response: the annexation of Hawaii was "nothing more than the alliance of the United States Government with a band of industrialists . . . who deliberately and willfully overthrew the legalized machinery of the Government of Hawaii and appropriated the government property of all the people to their own use." [23] Roll calls in this dimension average over .80 (Q) intercorrelation.

The tariff dimension comprises a series of roll calls dealing with the protection of American industry. The specific roll calls range from the passage of major bills such as the McKinley and Dingley tariffs to votes on such narrow concerns as commodity tariffs on Japanese armor plating. Those favoring protective tariffs saw them as a necessary condition for the growth of the American economy; those opposed saw them as merely another way for industrialists to fatten their wallets at the expense of "the people." Congressman Lewis Tillman of Tennessee, representing the antitariff view, said, "The country knows that the first chance you get you are going to rob them. It is not unnatural, therefore, that the owner of the premises should begin to bar the door when he knows a robber is coming." [24] In short, as with the gold-silver and expansionism dimensions, the issue was who would be favored, industrial or agricultural interests. The dimension disappears after the passage of the Dingley Tariff in the 55th House.

The business dimension consists of roll calls on a number of issues that deal with the proper role of big business in American society. One of the major issues concerned the Uniform Bankruptcy Bill (S. 105), the crux of the argument being whether or not it would favor businessmen. The agrarian interests opposed involuntary bankruptcy because that would enable federal judges to declare owners bankrupt, thereby giving business access to needed properties. Other roll calls deal with various aspects of monopoly legislation, such as the requirement that corporate officers list their holdings. Included in this category are roll calls on regulated railroad rates for farm products. In sum, the underlying issue taps the extent to which members favored the interests of big business as opposed to those of agriculture, which wished to limit industrial growth.

The public works dimension deals with the construction of railroads, canals, waterways, harbors, and other improvements. The content is strikingly similar to the same dimension in the Civil War era. In short, the question was who would get what share of internal improvements.

The housekeeping dimension is dominated by roll calls determining which party would occupy contested seats. Other roll calls have to do with general House control, (e.g. hiring and firing clerks). The underlying question was straightforward and needs no elaboration: Which party would control the operation and maintenance of the House of Representatives?

The taxation dimension, the first of the emergent issue dimensions of the realignment, deals with questions of income redistribution through a progressive income tax and the taxation of wealth, particularly industrial wealth. The Democratic-Populist platform had promised such a reform. The issue is broached in the 53rd House (1893–95) and surfaces again in the 55th and 56th Houses (1897–1901). The Democrats favored the income tax and, even more strongly, taxes on the wealth of industrial interests.

The immigration dimension, the other emergent issue dimension, is present in the 52nd House (1891–93) and in the 54th–57th Houses (1895–1903). The basic question was whether or not the federal government should have more restrictive immigration quotas. The issue is complicated by the fact that pietistic Protestants were opposed to the immigration of "liquor-loving Catholics," yet without the electoral support of both, Bryan had little chance for victory. Industrialists, while not personally fond of Catholic immigrants, sometimes argued that they were necessary for industrial growth. The roll call votes on this dimension vary from approval of specific quotas to overall policy objectives.

The policy consequences of the 1890's realignment represent another benchmark in American political history. The "crisis of vulnerability," in Walter Dean Burnham's term, was the agricultural-pietistic threat to America's new industrial order.[25] The combined Democratic-Populist threat to the industrial order focused on the currency, tariff, and expansionism issues, but the deeper issue was America's economic future. Had the Democratic-Populist coalition been victorious, U.S. history would have taken a significantly different turn. Thus, much of the significance of the 1890's realignment resides in the fact that the "threat from the West" was beaten back, ensuring an industrial future. Yet there was a "cluster of specific policy changes" enacted by the Republican Party. One of the most important policy changes was the currency bill establishing gold as the American monetary unit. The passage of the Dingley Tariff in 1897 established a protective shield for new American business in addition to protecting old interests. The rise of expansionism was clearly a marked change in policy. The Spanish-American War, the takeover of Santo Domingo, the annexation of Hawaii, the building of the Panama Canal—all are examples of the new expansionist policies enacted by the Republicans. Moreover, bankruptcy, taxation, and immigration policies favorable to an industrial order were all enacted by the new majority party.

The elections of 1894 and 1896 clearly established the Republicans as the majority party. The role of the congressional party in the transformation of policy should have been to pass these changes in a partisan fashion. To test this hypothesis, members' party identifications were correlated (r) with their scale scores on each of the issue dimensions outlined above. The expectation was that on the realignment-related issues, party would structure voting patterns. The strength of party structuring of the vote should be most evident in the 55th and 56th Houses (1897–1901). Table 3.9 shows the results.

On the three issues of currency, expansionism, and tariff, party

TABLE 3.9

Product-Moment Correlations Between Party Identification and Issue Voting,
52nd–57th Houses, 1891–1903

House	Currency	Expan-sionism	Tariff	Business	Public works	House-keeping	Immi-gration	Taxation
52	.02	.69	.97	.92	.31	.73	.26	—
53	.42	.19	.89	.78	.70	.93	—	.86
54	.71	.16	.20	.41	.26	.94	.47	—
55	.96	.89	.98	.92	.31	.88	.54	.92
56	.96	.93	—	.98	.31	.99	.81	.88
57	.91	.88	—	.97	.39	.93	.83	—

clearly structures voting by the 55th House (1897–99). The currency issue fits the predicted pattern quite well. Party does not structure voting in the early part of the era, but with the Republican victory in the 1894 elections, party structures voting at the r = .71 level. Following the 1896 party conventions, at which gold Democrats and silver Republicans were purged, party structures voting at very high levels—r = .96 in both the 55th and the 56th House. Thus the combined effects of the 1894 and 1896 elections result in party responsibility on the currency question.

The expansionism issue dimension presents a somewhat more complicated pattern. The correlation between party and position is relatively high in the 52nd House (.69) as Republicans oppose Democrats on funding for the Navy. In the next two Houses, however, the level of party structuring falls to below .20. After the parties took opposing positions in the 1896 platforms, the level of party structuring of the issues increases dramatically to about .90 and remains at that level through the 57th House. The major impetus for party differences was the campaign for the Spanish-American War and the fact that the President was a Republican favoring expansionist policies. The combination of Republican control of the government and the push for the Spanish-American War leads to a highly structured partisan determination of expansionist policy.

The tariff dimension is partisan throughout the era with the single exception of the 54th Congress. The tariff issue had divided Democrats representing rural Southern districts and Republicans representing industrial interests since at least 1874. The low correlation for the 54th House is the result of a badly divided Democratic party—President Cleveland and the gold Democrats favoring some protective tariffs—and a somewhat divided Republican Party. The Republicans split along the lines of those favoring a very strict protective tariff—the Reed/McKinley/Dingley faction—and the silver Republicans of the West, with Midwestern Republicans somewhere in between. Most of the votes on this dimension were concerned with the stringent Dingley Tariff. Once the parties had purged themselves of dissident elements, the 55th House quickly passed the Dingley Tariff, which had been written in the 54th House. In fact, the Dingley Tariff was passed in a special early session of the 55th House before the Speaker had even appointed committees.

The business dimension fits the same pattern. That is, it is highly partisan throughout the era with the exception of the 54th House. The period 1888–96 resulted in party structuring of votes on business matters but no resolution of the issue until the Republicans took control of the government. From the 52nd to the 54th House the same issues came up in each Congress, with most Democrats opposing and most Republicans favoring probusiness legislation. The election of 1896 resolved the issue in favor of business interests; the votes thereafter are essentially Democratic attempts to repeal the probusiness legislation passed in the 55th House.

The public works dimension, like its counterpart in the Civil War era, is dominated by regional and district interests. The correlation between party and issue dimension is below .40 in five of the six Houses. The dimension is structured by party only in the 53rd House (r = .70). In general, voting on this dimension was structured by whether or not representatives saw any benefits accruing to their district or region. The coalitions are not unlike those formed in the present-day House on such matters as water resources.[26]

In direct contrast, the housekeeping dimension is partisan throughout the period. The single largest block of roll calls in this dimension deals with contested election results, and as Polsby has shown, these were determined on a highly partisan basis.[27] Both parties viewed contested elections as a way to increase their congressional representation. The lowest correlation in the series was for the 52nd House, also the House with the most lopsided party majority. Thus in that House the Democrats let a Republican win a contested seat or two. However, when majorities were slim, the majority party viewed contested seats as crucial.

Both of the emergent dimensions of the realignment, taxation and immigration, are partisan. The taxation dimension is dominated by Democratic proposals for a progressive income tax, a taxation-of-wealth policy geared to hurt industrial rather than agricultural wealth. The issue first arises in the Democratic-controlled 53rd House and emerges again in the 55th and 56th Houses. In these two Republican-controlled Houses, the issue was brought to a floor vote by Populist-Democratic representatives from the Western North Central states. The voting pattern was heavily structured by party in all three Houses and, of course, the Republicans did not allow passage.

The immigration dimension arises first in the 52nd House, where the voting is essentially nonpartisan, r = .26. Beginning with the 54th House, the issue becomes steadily more partisan, reaching .83 by the 57th House.

Although party structured voting on the currency, expansionism, tariff, business, taxation, and immigration issue dimensions, the results are not as clear as for the Civil War realignment. Only currency and expansionism fit the pattern of nonpartisan structuring of voting prior to the realignment and party structuring of voting with the realignment. The most logical explanation for the ambiguous party structuring of voting before the 55th House (1897–99) is that the era preceding the 1896 election was one of divided government, or, in Burnham's phrase, "an era of no choice."[28] The President and Congress were of different parties, and thus the same bill was often presented to consecutive Congresses with no policy resolution owing to presidential vetoes or House-Senate disagreement. With the election of 1896 the Republicans took undivided control of the government, and on the crest of their victory, the 55th and 56th Congresses passed the legislation assuring America's industrial future: gold remained the basis of our monetary system until the New Deal; expansionism as a foreign policy was prevalent until after World War I; protective tariffs and probusiness legislation such as the involuntary bankruptcy law remained in effect until the 1930's. In short, the Republican House adopted pro-industrial policies during McKinley's first term in office, thus resolving the dominant issues of the realignment in a highly partisan fashion. Votes on these issue dimensions after 1900 were feeble Democratic attempts to reactivate the Populist positions of the late 1880's and early 1890's. It is therefore fair to conclude that the result of the 1894–96 realignment was the establishment of the Republicans as the dominant national party, which set about resolving the issues of the realignment in a party-responsible fashion.

One should not expect a uniform pattern across all dimensions of voting. Analyzing policy dimensions allows us to get at particular policy cleavages, some of which may not be affected by the new partisan realignment. The issues of protective tariffs and housekeeping, for example, had been partisan since 1856; they were not dramatically affected by the realignment. The same can be said of the local public works issue. Dimensional analysis, however, does demonstrate which issues are affected by the realignment, and such an analysis indicates that on the major realignment issues of currency and expansionism, party becomes a more salient determinant of voting and remains so in the post-realignment era.

Analysis of various aggregate measures of party voting further demonstrates the extent of partisan structuring of the vote in the 1894–96 realignment. Table 3.10 presents the following aggregate-level party voting measures: the average Party Cohesion score for each party in each House; the average Index of Party Likeness; and

TABLE 3.10

Party Unity and Party Voting, 52nd–57th Houses

House	Average Party Cohesion		Average Index of Likeness	Percentage of party votes	
	Republican	Democratic		90%–90%	50%–50%
52	79.6%	76.2%	61.0	4.2%	45.4%
53	86.1	85.1	59.6	6.1	44.8
54	82.2	86.9	46.1	24.8	68.5
55	93.2	89.3	30.8	50.2	79.8
56	94.2	89.5	31.0	49.8	77.2
57	93.4	87.2	42.6	38.9	67.0

the percentage of all roll calls where 50 percent and 90 percent of one party oppose 50 and 90 percent of the other party.* The expectation is that party voting as measured by the 50 vs. 50 and the 90 vs. 90 criteria will increase in the 54th and 55th Houses, and that the average Index of Likeness will decrease (more partisan voting).

The measures of party voting strongly corroborate the expectation. The stricter criterion of 90 percent moves from 4.2 percent and 6.1 percent in the 52nd and 53rd Houses to almost 25 percent in the 54th House (elected 1894) and to over 50 percent in the 55th House. The 50 percent criterion shows a similar pattern. The percent of ma-jority-vs.-majority roll calls jumps almost 24 points in the 54th House and then another ten in the 55th House. The party likeness measure drops about thirteen points in the 54th House and then over fifteen in the 55th. These results are all the more impressive considering that all roll-call votes (including unanimous ones) are included in the analysis. Clearly, party voting increases dramatically in the two Houses elected in 1894 and 1896.

The measure of party cohesion shows that it increased in the 55th House to over 90 percent for Republicans and to almost 90 percent for Democrats. This finding is consistent with the view that the election of 1894 resulted in large Republican majorities because the Democrats were held responsible for the depression of 1893. In the 54th House the Republicans were still somewhat divided, as were the Democrats, over the issues of bimetalism and expansionism; thus even though party voting increased, the increase was more dramatic after the 1896 conventions, when both parties purified their ranks by taking polar

*The Party Cohesion and Party Likeness measures are those developed by Stuart Rice (*Quantitative Methods in Politics*). The cohesion measure indicates the degree of party unity and runs from 0 (no unity, a 50–50 split) to 100 (all members of a party voting together). The Index of Likeness measure indicates the degree of interparty agreement. It runs from 0 (parties vote against each other unanimously) to 100 (parties vote together, no disagreement).

positions on the realignment issues. With voters offered a clear choice between the parties, the election of 1896 polarized the constituent bases of the two unified and opposed congressional parties. In the 55th House the "new" majority party passed the policies associated with the realignment in a highly partisan fashion.

★ The Changing Shape of Voting on Issues, 1891–1903

In the 52nd House (1891–93) the Democrats took over as the majority party, and Speaker Charles F. Crisp (D–Ga.) moved quickly to eliminate the rules imposed by former Speaker Thomas B. Reed (R–Maine) that allowed the majority to legislate.[29] Control of the government was divided, with the Republican Benjamin Harrison still President. In the 1892 election the Democrats held onto the House and gained control of the Presidency. However, in both Congresses the Democrats were divided on the currency, business, and expansionism dimensions. In general the division was regional. Southern and Western representatives favored the coinage of silver at sixteen to one and a noninterventionist foreign policy; they were pro-agricultural and thus anti-business. The Northern Democrats, led by President Cleveland, favored the gold standard, and in general were probusiness and expansionist. The split in the Democratic Party on these issues resulted in low party voting scores. Moreover, even if the Democrats could muster a majority for the coinage of silver or a business-limiting measure, they were faced with the threat of a presidential veto. Ideological differences, combined with the rescinding of the Reed rules, meant that very little was achieved by either the 52nd or the 53rd House. Drift rather than mastery was so evident that Speaker Crisp was forced to adopt Reed's rules midway through the 53rd House as his only hope of passing any legislation at all.

The minority Republican Party was also divided in the 52nd and 53rd Houses, though not as badly as the Democrats. Midwestern, Western, and Border state representatives often voted for legislation that favored agricultural interests, pitting them against their confreres on the issues of currency, expansionism, and business. Republicans representing Eastern industrial districts voted a straight pro-industrial position—for gold, expansionism, and business. This divisiveness carried over into the 54th House. Although Republican candidates all over the North swept to victory in 1894, the new majority party had not yet clarified its positions on the realignment issues. The Democrats were essentially reduced to their Southern wing in the 54th House; they were thus far more unified than the Republicans.

The internal split in the Republican Party, along with the fact that once again control of the government was divided, meant that little in the way of decisive policy legislation could be passed.

The 55th House met under entirely different conditions. The government was controlled by the Republicans, the splits in both parties were gone, and as a result both the 55th and 56th Houses acted decisively. In the first session of the 55th House, the Republicans passed the heavily protective Dingley Tariff. They beat back a recommittal motion with a 97.0 level of cohesion; the Index of Likeness was 2.0, indicating that 97 percent of Republicans voted against at least 97 percent of the Democrats. The Republicans also passed an amendment protecting certain industries even more than the original legislation had, with *every* Republican voting against over 90 percent of the Democrats. In addition, the House defeated a Democratic resolution to coin silver with *every* Republican voting against *every* Democrat. In the second and third sessions of the 55th House, the Republicans annexed Hawaii and supported the Spanish-American War by heavily partisan majorities. The average expansionist vote saw more than 80 percent of the Republicans opposing more than 90 percent of the Democrats.

The 56th House passed H.R. 1, the currency law that firmly established gold as the monetary standard. The two major votes on the issue saw over 90 percent of the Republicans voting for the bill, and over 80 percent of Democrats voting against. The only Democrats who voted for the currency bill were the fourteen Tammany Hall representatives and the Massachusetts and Pennsylvania delegations. The Republicans also passed legislation that brought raw goods from the recently acquired Caribbean countries into the United States at cheap prices, and sold American manufactured goods to them at high prices. These votes were also heavily partisan, with most of them reaching the 90 percent–90 percent level. War appropriations and laws expanding the Navy were passed by similar partisan votes. In short, the elections of 1894 and 1896 established the Republicans as the party of the industrial North. They responded by passing pro-industrial legislation, thus resolving the great issues of the 1890's realignment in favor of an industrial future for the United States.

Within the parties Republicans from New England, the Northeast, and the East North Central states were the most supportive of party positions across all issue dimensions, and those from the West North Central and Western states least supportive. Border state and Southern Democrats were most supportive of Democratic Party positions across issue areas. Northeastern Democratic representatives were least supportive of their party's position, particularly on the gold-silver question. Democrats from the Midwest occupied the middle ground. One should not conclude, however, that the congressional parties were seriously divided. On the contrary: the realignment created two relatively unified congressional parties—one Northern and industrial, the other Southern and agricultural. Within this framework there was regional variation in the support for various policies. But the fact of this framework was undeniable: the elections of 1894 and 1896 transformed a series of cross-party voting coalitions into two cohesive and opposed congressional parties.

CHAPTER FOUR

An Across-the-Board Realignment: The New Deal

- David Brady,
  *Critical Elections and
  Congressional Policy Making*
  (Stanford: Stanford University Press, 1988)

★ UNLIKE THE REALIGNMENTS of the 1860's and 1890's, the political revolution known as the New Deal was the product of a single event, the Great Depression. The realignment of 1894–96 led to fourteen uninterrupted years of Republican control and 34 years of Republican dominance. To be sure, the election of a Democratic House in 1910 heralded the election of Woodrow Wilson in 1912 and Democratic control of Congress through World War I. But in 1918 the Republicans recaptured the House, and the 1920 elections brought an overwhelming victory for the Republicans and a "return to normalcy."[1] Thereafter, through the administrations of Warren Harding, Calvin Coolidge, and Herbert Hoover, the Republicans stayed in power. For 24 of the 34 years between 1896 and 1930, then, they had undivided control of the government, compared with the Democrats' six. Clearly the first third of the twentieth century was a Republican era.

The Republicans maintained control of the House through their dominance of Northern congressional elections. The congressional Democratic party, for most of this era, consisted of representatives from the Southern and Border states. The decade 1920–30 was a solidly Republican period: Harding, Coolidge, and Hoover all won the Presidency by comfortable margins over James M. Cox, John W. Davis, and Alfred E. Smith; turnover averaged less than 20 percent per Congress; and Republicans controlled, on the average, 60 percent of House seats. The dominant congressional Republican party was relatively united in the House, with average cohesion scores (Rice Index of Cohesion) of over 60 percent. Comparable cohesion scores for the congressional Democrats were slightly under 60; and slightly over one-half the votes found a majority of one party voting against a majority of the other. The Republicans, in an era of prosperity and normalcy, were not interested in changing policy; rather, their concern was to keep the business of the nation—business—unfettered. Charles O. Jones has convincingly argued that this was a period of business as usual.[2] Thus, Republicans were able to keep the government from regulating business and agricultural affairs.[3] Democratic proposals to aid farm interests, regulate banking and currency, and make antibusiness changes were easily defeated in a series of Republican-controlled Houses.

All this was to change enduringly as a result of the Great Depression. The period 1919–29 was by most measures a prosperous one. Average weekly wages rose from $22.00 to $25.00; since the cost of living actually decreased by 1 percent, this represented an increase of 15 percent in real wages. Productivity rose 75 percent, and corporate taxes 33 percent over the decade. Despite the increased tax revenues, income taxes dropped from 20 percent of net income to 10 percent. Corporate profits were high, productivity was high, and although workers did not fully share these benefits, the average worker was better off in 1929 than he had been in 1919.

This is not to claim that the economy was problem-free. There were indeed problems, particularly for farmers. Net farm income dropped one-third from 1919 to 1929. The Southern farm economy was the most severely affected. For example, the number of rural Southerners resorting to sharecropping doubled. Nor was this a "black" problem—more whites than blacks were in fact forced into sharecropping in this decade. Per capita income in the South ranged from $270 in South Carolina to $521 in Florida, and even Florida was below the national average.

Moreover, disparities in income distribution were marked. The wealthiest 5 percent of the population had 33 percent of the income.[4] If one considers $2,000 the poverty level for a family of five in 1929, practically 60 percent of American families were below that level in the boom years of 1928–29.[5] Although the bloom of prosperity was on the land, there were areas of blight as well.

All sectors of the economy were severely shaken by the Great Depression. Between 1929 and 1932 GNP fell from $104 billion to $58 billion, corporate profits from $10 billion to $3 billion, and aggregate wages from $45 billion to $25 billion. Factory employment declined by a third, durable manufactures by 70 percent. Unemployment rose from 400,000 in 1929 to 12,000,000 in 1932. The industrial economy was a shambles, and the already less prosperous agricultural economy worsened, such that by 1932 the average farmer on 160 acres in Iowa would lose money.[6] A distraught farmer wrote President-elect Roosevelt, "With 61¢ a hundred lbs. of milk and 30¢ calves it's impossible to

live. If you don't help soon we will be homeless."[7] One-quarter of the
farmland in Mississippi was put on the block in sheriff's sales. Farmers
took over Davenport, Iowa, and only martial law restored order. In
short, in less than three years the nation moved from widespread prosperity to pervasive depression, with all the attendant human misery.

The fundamental issue underlying the New Deal realignment was
whether the government would actively deal with national economic
problems. Herbert Hoover and the Republican Party rejected active
government intervention. The Democrats, though not entirely clear
on which direction to move, had adopted an activist stance by 1932.
Unlike the two previous realignments, the New Deal realignment did
not polarize the country along regional or urban-rural lines.

★ Partisan Differences

The contrast between the two party platforms in 1932 is striking.
The Republican platform was long—a document of over thirteen
pages—and covered everything from unemployment to the Saint
Lawrence Seaway. The Democratic platform was very short—two
pages—and general. The Republican platform began with a long section praising President Hoover's leadership: "We have had in the
White House a leader—wise, courageous, patient, understanding, re-
sourceful, ever present in his post of duty, tireless in his efforts and
unswervingly faithful to American principles and ideals."[8] These
laudatory remarks were followed by the assertion that the depression
would have been far worse without Hoover and the Republicans:
"Throughout the depression unemployment has been limited by the
systematic use of part-time employment as a substitute for the general
discharge of employees. . . . As a result there have been fewer strikes
and less social disturbance than during any similar period of hard
times."

On the major issues of relief for labor, agriculture, banking, and
other sectors, the Republicans maintained that there was little the
government could do beyond what was being done. On unemployment, for example, the Republican platform said: "True to American
traditions and principles of government, the Administration has regarded the relief problem as one of State and local responsibility." On
agriculture the Republicans claimed that thanks to their measures (i.e.
the Smoot-Hawley Tariff), "it can truthfully be stated that the prices
received by the American farmer for his wheat, corn, rye, barley, oats,
flaxseed, cattle, butter, and other produce, cruelly low though they
are, are higher than the prices received by the farmers of any compet-

ing nation for the same product." They contrasted their own solid record of support for American traditions with the record of the Democratic controlled 72nd House (1931 – 32), pointing to the Democrats' action on "(1) the issuance of fiat currency; (2) instructions to the Federal Reserve Board and the Secretary of the Treasury to manipulate commodity prices; (3) the guarantee of bank deposits; [and] (4) the squandering of public resources and the unbalancing of the budget through pork-barrel appropriations." In sum, the Republicans eschewed an active federal role in alleviating the consequences of the depression.

In sharp contrast the Democratic platform of 1932 favored federal action to alleviate the human suffering caused by the depression. The Democrats advocated "the extension of federal credit to the states to provide unemployment relief wherever the diminishing resources of the states make it impossible for them to provide for the needy." In addition, they favored unemployment and old-age insurance under state laws. On agricultural issues the Democrats wanted to see "better financing of farm mortgages through recognized farm bank agencies at low rates of interest on an amortization plan, giving preference to credits for the redemption of farms and homes sold under foreclosure." Unlike the Republicans, the Democrats favored increased federal regulation of banking, payment of pensions to veterans, and repeal of the 18th (prohibition) Amendment. In short, there were important differences between the parties on the issue of the federal role in the economy and the society.

Ginsberg's content analysis of party platforms shows an abrupt rise in party conflict over "the aggregation and distribution of wealth by business, financial and mercantile elites."[9] Figure 4.1 shows the salience of what can be called, generally, the capitalism issues over the 1920 to 1940 period and the degree of party conflict. The issue is relatively salient over the entire period. The lowest value, 0.50, occurs in 1936, the highest, 0.67, in 1932, a difference of only 0.17. Critical party conflict ranges from 0.01 in 1920 to 0.64 in 1932, a difference of 0.63. The difference between the Democratic and Republican parties on the wealth issue is below .30 for the entire period, with the exception of 1932, when they took strikingly different positions on the control and distribution of wealth. Ginsberg's data clearly demonstrate the degree of partisan difference present in the 1932 election when, he concludes, "critical conflict [indicates] attempts by the parties involved to restructure the electorate by translating the dominant locus of interparty ideological conflict into a new system of electoral cleavage."[10]

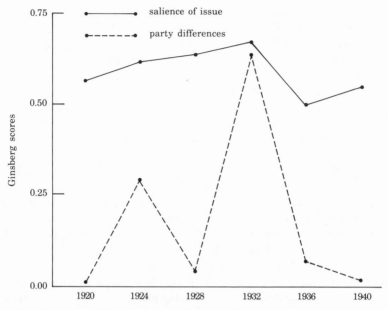

Fig. 4.1. Salience of the capitalism issue, 1920–1940. Source: Benjamin Ginsberg, "Critical Elections and the Substance of Party Conflict: 1844–1968," *Midwest Journal of Political Science*, Aug. 1972, pp. 603–25.

The partisan differences so clear in the platforms were also manifest in the conventions and electoral campaign of 1932. The Republicans met in Chicago in a subdued mood. Republican leaders knew that their electoral prospects were poor, but saw no realistic alternative to Hoover, who was renominated on the first ballot with 1,126½ of the 1,154 convention votes. The only threat, if it can be called that, to Hoover's renomination came when the former senator Joseph France of Maryland sought to take the podium to nominate Coolidge. He was denied access to the podium.

The Democrats also met in Chicago. Because party leaders were optimistic about their chances of winning the Presidency, the nomination was hotly contested. Roosevelt entered with a majority of the votes, but the rules required two-thirds for nomination. His principal opponent was the former governor of New York and the Democrats' 1928 presidential candidate, Al Smith. Roosevelt won nomination on the fourth ballot when supporters of House Speaker John Nance Garner went over to him. Roosevelt broke "the absurd tradition" of not personally accepting the nomination, and in his acceptance speech struck a liberal tone, including his now famous pledge of "a new deal for the American people."

Some scholars have argued that Roosevelt ran on conservative principles, offering no real ideological choice between himself and Hoover.[11] But though it is true that Roosevelt promised to balance the budget, he also favored "bold, persistent experimentation."[12] Before the campaign was over he had advocated government programs in transportation, utility regulation, poverty relief, and the regulation of the stock market. For this and other reasons, I agree with Frank Friedel's assessment of the Roosevelt campaign: "He shifted course from time to time in a fashion infuriating to his political opponents, and sometimes rather saddening to his supporters, but almost always with calculated intelligence and with profitable results. Though he tacked occasionally to the right, he customarily bore much harder to the left."[13] In short, in 1932 both the parties and the candidates offered voters a clear and consequential choice.

★ Electoral Change

If the elections of the early 1930's were dominated by national issues, congressional election results should reveal national rather than local electoral forces at work. Table 4.1 shows the mean party votes and standard deviations in House elections from 1924 to 1940, including and excluding the South.

Unlike the pre-1894 electoral system, that of the 1920's was dominated by the Republicans in the North and the Democrats in the South. Before 1932 the Democrats received only slightly over 40 percent of the vote outside the South; the Republicans averaged almost 57 percent. The Republicans had a majority of House seats from the 1918 elections until 1932. In 1930 the Democrats held the South and increased their share of non-Southern seats, but the Republicans maintained a slim majority. Even so, the Democrats were able to organize the 72nd House (1931–33) because death or illness had thinned the Republican ranks.

The 1932 election marks a clear cut-point: the Democrats increased their share of the vote by about 9 percent nationally and slightly over 9 percent in the North. The variance around the Democratic vote as measured by the standard deviation falls in both cases, notably so in the Northern states, where the figure drops from 23.8 to 14.9. Moreover, through the 1936 election, the variance remains relatively low. The 1932 election thus marked a strong national swing to the Democratic Party.

The literature on national factors in elections leads one to expect that the variance around the aggregated mean vote, Democratic or Republican, will drop during a critical election because there is a na-

TABLE 4.1

Mean Party Vote and Standard Deviation in House Elections Including and Excluding the South, 1924–1940

House	Election year	Democrat		Republican	
		Mean vote (pct.)	Std. dev.	Mean vote (pct.)	Std. dev.
		Entire Nation			
69	1924	47.4%	27.7	50.4%	25.4
70	1926	48.9	29.8	49.8	28.8
71	1928	47.8	26.2	51.1	25.7
72	1930	51.2	29.8	46.7	28.4
73	1932	59.8	20.6	38.6	20.3
74	1934	59.9	22.5	36.7	20.5
75	1936	60.6	18.9	36.7	18.4
76	1938	55.4	25.1	40.4	23.1
77	1940	56.2	24.2	40.1	22.8
		South Excluded			
69	1924	39.0%	20.5	56.3%	18.7
70	1926	40.1	22.9	57.8	22.2
71	1928	39.6	17.4	58.3	17.4
72	1930	42.7	23.8	54.6	22.7
73	1932	51.9	14.9	44.6	15.4
74	1934	52.3	15.3	42.7	16.8
75	1936	53.7	14.0	41.6	13.9
76	1938	48.6	16.7	47.4	15.7
77	1940	49.1	15.9	47.9	15.9

NOTE: Columns may not total 100% because of third-party voting.

tional swing favoring one party.[14] However, if there is a compensating effect, such as one region becoming more Democratic while another becomes more Republican, then the variance around the overall mean could rise. Analyzing electoral returns on the basis of change within districts across pairs of elections could show an increase in the variance even when national electoral forces are at work. Table 4.2 demonstrates this point. In Election 1, the pre-realignment election, the Republicans are the majority party. Three of the five districts, A, B, and D, are highly competitive; two are safe one-party districts, one Republican, one Democratic. In the critical election, 2, the standard deviation of the vote drops below ten just as one would have predicted. The Democrats move from two-to-three minority status to four-to-one majority status, which they retain in Election 3 even though their mean percentage of the vote drops. Calculating the standard deviation of change produces a figure of 1.64 from the precritical to the critical election (1 to 2) and 0.83 from Election 2 to Election 3. Thus the standard deviation in the precritical-critical election period is almost twice as high as the figure for the critical-postcritical period. In short, Table 4.2 shows that in an across-the-board realignment, the standard deviation of the change can be greater than that found in normal elections even though *critical* change has occurred.

Table 4.3 shows the results of the across-districts analysis both for the entire nation and with the South excluded. The analysis for the entire nation shows that the 1930–32 election pair has the greatest average swing for both Democrats (+7.19 percent) and Republicans (−8.03 percent). Moreover, the greatest variance around the vote swing occurs in the 1930–32 election pair for both parties, 15.1 for Democrats, 15.4 for Republicans. The shift to the Democrats in the 1932 election was of major proportions, and that shift occurred across almost all districts.

The Democrats had a high baseline vote in the South before the 1932 election; excluding the South from the analysis should show an even stronger swing to the Democrats. The results corroborate this expectation. The mean change to the Democrats was +8.95 percent, with a standard deviation of change of 15.8. The Republicans lost an average of 9.77 percent across districts; the standard deviation of change was 16.1. In sum Table 4.3 confirms 1932 as a critical election. The Democrats win across the board, with their highest gains coming in the non-Southern area, where they were weakest.

Our analysis of the Civil War and 1890's periods showed strong sectional and regional variations in the vote. The preliminary analysis

TABLE 4.2

Hypothetical Realignment in a Two-Party System Over Three Elections

(Percent of one party's vote)

Category	Election 1: Party X's vote	Election 2		Election 3	
		Party X's vote	Change	Party X's vote	Change
District					
A	47.0%	54.0%	7%	53.0%	−1%
B	45.0	53.0	8	53.0	0
C	40.0	45.0	5	43.0	−2
D	53.0	60.0	7	59.0	−1
E	67.0	71.0	4	69.0	−2
Mean	50.4%	56.6%	6.2%	55.4%	−1.2%
Standard deviation	10.4	9.7	1.64	9.5	0.83

NOTE: There is no provision for third-party voting. Thus, in District A in Election 1, the other party's vote would be 53%.

TABLE 4.3

Mean Swing in Party Vote and Standard Deviation of Swing in Paired House Elections Including and Excluding the South, 1924–1940

Houses	Election years	Democrat		Republican	
		Mean swing (pct.)	Std. dev.	Mean swing (pct.)	Std. dev.
		Entire Nation			
69–70	1924–1926	1.92%	12.7	0.38%	14.2
70–71	1926–1928	−1.06	14.4	1.26	14.1
71–72	1928–1930	3.37	14.3	−3.97	14.0
72–73	1930–1932	7.19	15.1	−8.03	15.4
73–74	1932–1934	0.81	12.8	−1.46	13.1
74–75	1934–1936	1.01	10.4	−0.13	11.4
75–76	1936–1938	−3.23	9.6	3.79	9.2
76–77	1938–1940	−0.46	9.2	0.38	9.6
		South Excluded			
69–70	1924–1926	1.42%	13.5	1.48%	15.1
70–71	1926–1928	−0.27	15.0	0.53	14.8
71–72	1928–1930	3.08	15.0	−3.82	14.6
72–73	1930–1932	8.95	15.8	−9.77	16.1
73–74	1932–1934	0.38	14.6	−1.50	14.4
74–75	1934–1936	1.37	10.4	−1.03	11.5
75–76	1936–1938	−5.14	7.9	5.76	7.6
76–77	1938–1940	0.50	8.9	0.47	8.0

of the New Deal period indicates a decided difference, namely, that the swing to the Democrats was less sectional in nature. Nevertheless, the expectation is that there will be regional variation in the results. Table 4.4 shows the mean change across districts by region. The reader not interested in the details of the regional analysis should skip to the electoral summary section.

In the mid-1920's, except for the Southern and Border states, the country was solidly Republican. From 1924 to 1928 New England, the Northeast, and the Midwest (East and West North Central states) voted about three-to-two Republican in the House races.* The lowest vote for Republican congressional candidates in that four-year period was 55.8 percent in the West North Central states in 1924; the highest Republican vote was 63.3 percent in the East North Central states. The vote swung slightly to the Democrats in 1930, but less than one

---

*The Western states had so few representatives that the variance tends to be unstable. Accordingly, the region is not discussed in the following analysis. The data are included in the table simply to show the strong movement of the Democrats in 1932–36. Although the Democrats attained a majority in only two years—1936 and 1938—there was clearly a significant move toward them in the New Deal realignment.

TABLE 4.4
Mean Party Vote and Standard Deviation in House Elections by Region,
1924–1940

Election year	Democrat Mean vote (pct.)	Std. dev.	Republican Mean vote (pct.)	Std. dev.	Democrat Mean vote (pct.)	Std. dev.	Republican Mean vote (pct.)	Std. dev.
	New England				Northeast			
1924	37.4%	12.7	61.3%	14.8	37.3%	18.0	57.5%	17.9
1926	39.6	18.7	59.4	19.1	38.4	22.2	58.8	22.1
1928	41.4	14.7	58.2	14.5	40.1	18.2	57.1	18.8
1930	44.2	15.4	54.8	13.4	41.8	21.2	54.8	23.1
1932	47.3	13.5	49.8	10.3	49.3	17.4	45.4	16.8
1934	48.6	18.4	49.9	18.3	53.0	14.3	42.4	16.8
1936	46.6	13.9	48.0	10.9	55.8	11.6	40.1	12.1
1938	45.3	14.9	51.3	15.2	47.8	12.7	48.9	13.4
1940	48.1	12.7	51.3	13.8	49.9	10.4	47.5	12.2
	East North Central				West North Central			
1924	34.7%	14.3	63.3%	13.9	34.0%	18.5	55.8%	10.3
1926	36.7	20.1	62.3	19.9	35.2	19.8	58.4	15.4
1928	37.6	11.9	60.4	13.6	35.3	16.4	59.6	14.1
1930	39.6	19.6	58.1	18.8	37.9	23.2	56.0	16.7
1932	46.1	9.5	49.0	10.7	52.4	8.3	45.2	8.1
1934	49.3	10.6	44.3	11.6	49.3	13.8	41.8	11.2
1936	50.5	11.9	43.4	10.9	46.2	16.7	44.2	9.2
1938	44.5	14.3	50.6	10.4	43.1	17.6	50.1	11.7
1940	44.9	14.5	50.9	10.5	41.0	13.8	53.5	8.4
	South				Border			
1924	86.7%	15.5	12.9%	15.5	60.5%	23.6	37.4%	23.3
1926	90.4	14.4	9.3	14.4	63.0	23.8	36.9	23.8
1928	86.5	18.4	13.2	18.5	52.1	15.6	47.2	16.7
1930	90.1	15.3	9.0	15.5	63.7	27.1	36.5	26.9
1932	92.8	10.4	6.1	10.8	67.3	15.9	30.1	14.7
1934	91.4	16.4	6.6	12.9	64.2	17.3	33.4	16.9
1936	89.7	13.9	9.8	14.9	66.1	13.8	33.2	14.2
1938	93.4	15.1	6.5	15.8	64.6	19.7	33.0	18.0
1940	91.2	16.5	6.5	11.5	65.7	16.7	32.7	18.2
	West							
1924	32.2%	34.9	58.9%	29.4				
1926	24.6	26.6	76.7	26.3				
1928	20.7	26.3	76.9	26.3				
1930	19.5	29.3	76.6	31.0				
1932	46.0	23.0	48.3	23.4				
1934	47.8	27.1	48.5	27.4				
1936	53.9	24.4	43.2	24.0				
1938	48.3	24.9	47.1	25.1				
1940	46.0	29.9	50.8	31.4				

NOTE: The region code is as follows: *New England* = Conn., Maine, Mass., N.H., R.I., Vt.; *Northeast* = Del., N.J., N.Y., Pa.; *East North Central* = Ill., Ind., Mich., Ohio, Wis.; *West North Central* = Iowa, Kans., Minn., Mo., Neb., N. Dak., S. Dak.; *South* = Ala., Ark., Fla., Ga., La., Miss., N.C., S.C., Tenn., Tex., Va.; *Border* = Ky., Md., Okla., W. Va.; *West* = Ariz., Calif., Colo., Idaho, Mont., Nev., N. Mex., Ore., Utah, Wash., Wyo.

might have expected given economic conditions: less than 3 percent across the Northern states. The dominant swing came in the 1932 election. In all but the New England states, the Democrats gained more than 7 percent, and in the West North Central states the gain was almost 15 percent. In New England the Democrats gained only about 3 percent. In the elections of 1934 and 1936 the Democrats gained consecutively in the Northeastern and East North Central states; in the West North Central states they lost consecutively. It is worthwhile to point out that the two regions where the Democrats gained continuously, the Northeast and East North Central, were the two most populous. A state-by-state analysis in these two regions shows that only Illinois and New York had swung decisively Democratic in 1932; Michigan, Pennsylvania, Ohio, and Massachusetts did not move into the Democratic column until 1934 or 1936. The 1938 election clearly brought a readjustment in the Republicans' favor, with Democrats losing votes and seats in every region except the Deep South. The last election in the series, 1940, shows a relatively competitive two-party system everywhere except in the solidly Democratic Southern and Border states. The broad dimensions of this system were maintained until at least the mid-1960's.

The standard deviations show the expected pattern (Table 4.4). In four of the seven regions the lowest standard deviation around the Democratic vote occurs in the 1932 election. The drop is particularly marked in the Midwestern states—from about 20 in 1930 to about nine in 1932. Although the drop is less dramatic in New England and the Northeast, the change is significant. Thus both the mean percentage of the vote and the variance around the vote are in the expected direction.

From Reconstruction on, the Democrats were the dominant party in the South. In the 1924 elections they captured 86.7 percent of the vote, and at no point in the period did they fall below 86.5 percent. In the 1932 election they gained 2.7 percent over their 1930 figure, and the variance around the vote drops to 10.4, indicating an across-the-board swing to the Democrats. At no time during the period were the Republicans a factor in congressional voting in the South.

The pattern in the Border states is interesting. In 1924 and 1926 the Democrats outpolled the Republicans by hefty margins. They outpolled them in 1928 as well, but the nomination of the Catholic Al Smith brought about a drop of over 10 percent in the Democratic vote. In the 1932 election they rebounded to increase their share to a two-to-one margin. Although in subsequent elections the Democrats did not hold their 1932 advantage, they never fell back to their pre-1928 level. Thus the Border states began the period strongly Democratic and picked up a few percentage points along the way. The variance in the vote drops sharply in both 1928 and 1932 as voters move first against Smith and the Democrats and then toward Roosevelt and the Democrats in an across-the-board fashion. The variance drops again in 1936 as Border voters reaffirmed their commitment to the Democrats. The Republican vote essentially mirrors the Democratic vote in both means and variances.

Even though the large gains in the Democratic vote after 1928 did not occur simultaneously across regions, the New Deal appears to have been much more of an across-the-board realignment than the Civil War and 1890's realignments, with fewer offsetting developments. Table 4.4 shows a dramatic increase in the Democratic vote in the 1928–36 period, followed by a readjustment toward the Republicans in 1938 and 1940. But the losses in these years only partially offset the 1932–36 gains, so that the overall lasting result was a sizable increase in the Democrats' share of the congressional vote.

Table 4.5 shows the swing in congressional election results in pairs of elections by region. In the New England states the Democrats gained votes in every pair from 1924 to 1932. The largest standard deviations of change occur between 1926 and 1928 and between 1930 and 1932. Interestingly, the swing to the Democrats was only gradual through 1932, and between that year and 1940 they lost a portion of the votes they had gained. The greatest shifts in voting occurred in the 1928 and 1932 elections. V. O. Key's finding that the 1928 election was realigning may have been unduly influenced by his New England sample. [15]

The swing to the Democrats in 1932 was more dramatic in the Northeast than in New England. The Democrats gained a mean of 8.6 percent of the vote across districts in the 1930–32 election pair, and the Republicans lost slightly more than 8 percent; the standard deviation figure is over 14 in each case, indicating an across-the-board change. However, in the Northeast as opposed to New England, the Democrats gained in both the 1932–34 and the 1934–36 election pairs (3.2 and 2.8 percent, respectively), with a high standard deviation of change for both Democrats and Republicans. The delay in the move to the Democrats occurred largely because Pennsylvania and New Jersey did not go Democratic at the congressional level until the 1934 and 1936 elections. In other words, the switch to the Democrats varies somewhat from state to state, accounting for the high standard deviation of change in the 1932–34 election pair.

The Republican comeback in the 1938 elections was also more dra-

TABLE 4.5
Mean Swing in Party Vote and Standard Deviation of Swing in Paired House Elections by Region, 1924–1940

Election years	Democrat Mean swing (pct.)	Std. dev.	Republican Mean swing (pct.)	Std. dev.	Democrat Mean swing (pct.)	Std. dev.	Republican Mean swing (pct.)	Std. dev.
	New England				Northeast			
1924–1926	2.1%	11.8	−1.8%	10.5	1.1%	10.8	1.3%	10.3
1926–1928	1.9	16.2	−1.3	16.6	2.6	15.0	−1.7	13.1
1928–1930	2.7	13.9	−3.4	12.6	0.9	13.0	−2.2	13.2
1930–1932	2.3	14.1	−3.5	14.3	8.6	14.1	−8.1	14.4
1932–1934	−0.4	10.7	0.1	10.6	3.2	18.1	−3.1	16.9
1934–1936	−2.0	9.8	1.9	12.6	2.8	11.4	−1.5	10.9
1936–1938	−1.3	10.3	3.4	7.3	−7.9	5.5	8.0	5.2
1938–1940	2.8	8.2	−0.1	6.1	2.1	6.5	−1.5	6.6
	East North Central				West North Central			
1924–1926	2.0%	14.6	−1.0%	13.0	1.1%	10.7	2.6%	8.9
1926–1928	0.9	14.2	−1.9	16.4	0.2	11.4	1.2	10.6
1928–1930	2.0	13.0	−2.4	12.6	2.6	17.9	−3.9	15.6
1930–1932	12.7	16.9	−11.7	15.6	10.4	15.1	−11.8	13.1
1932–1934	−3.3	8.9	−1.9	12.4	−0.5	8.3	1.8	7.8
1934–1936	1.4	6.5	−1.0	10.9	−3.1	6.3	2.4	6.6
1936–1938	−6.0	6.2	7.3	7.7	−3.1	5.5	5.9	5.3
1938–1940	0.4	6.1	0.3	5.9	−2.1	8.6	3.4	6.2
	South				Border			
1924–1926	3.7%	9.2	−3.6%	9.3	2.5%	19.9	−0.6%	20.0
1926–1928	−3.9	11.2	3.9	11.1	−10.8	17.7	10.4	17.7
1928–1930	4.4	11.6	−4.5	11.8	11.6	17.6	−10.6	16.7
1930–1932	0.9	8.8	−1.9	8.5	3.4	12.4	−4.7	15.2
1932–1934	2.1	7.3	−1.3	7.2	−0.9	11.9	1.2	11.0
1934–1936	−1.6	10.0	3.1	10.9	1.9	7.5	−0.2	6.8
1936–1938	3.7	11.7	−3.3	10.7	−1.4	9.5	−0.2	6.8
1938–1940	−2.2	0.6	0.1	14.0	1.0	13.6	−0.4	8.5
	West							
1924–1926	0.4%	17.9	17.7%	34.8				
1926–1928	−1.4	15.8	0.1	13.6				
1928–1930	−1.2	15.8	−0.3	22.7				
1930–1932	23.6	24.7	−25.7	26.4				
1932–1934	1.8	23.8	0.2	22.3				
1934–1936	6.1	20.4	−5.3	20.8				
1936–1938	−5.6	12.5	3.9	12.7				
1938–1940	−2.3	14.7	3.7	16.3				

matic in the Northeast than in New England. The Democrats lost almost 8 percent in the 1936–38 pair, and the Republicans gained about 8 percent. The standard deviation of change indicates stability from 1936 to 1940. The overall result of the New Deal realignment in the Northeastern states was to convert the region from a bastion of Republicanism to a competitive two-party electoral system.

The Midwest shows the same pattern: minor Democratic gains across all pairs of elections from 1924 to 1930, and an overwhelming swing to the Democrats in 1932. The Democrats' mean vote gain between 1930 and 1932 was 12.7 percent in the East North Central states and 10.4 in the West North Central. Moreover, the standard deviation of change is high in both regions: 16.9 in the East, 15.1 in the West. In the more populous region (East North Central) the highest standard deviation of change occurs between 1930 and 1932. In the more agricultural West North Central, the peak occurs between 1928 and 1930, although the figure for 1930–32 is also very high. The fact that the effects of the depression were felt earliest by farmers probably accounts for the lag between the West North Central region and the less agricultural East.[16]

In contrast to their performance in the Northeast, the Democrats lost votes in both Midwestern regions in 1934. They gained back a portion of the loss in industrial areas in 1936, but continued to lose votes in the agricultural ones, producing the results shown in the table: a much sharper loss in the 1936–38 election pair in the East North Central states (6.0 percent) than in the West North Central states (3.1).

The South was so overwhelmingly Democratic throughout the period that a marked swing was unlikely. The Democrats lost votes in the 1926–28 election pair largely because of Al Smith's religion and his advocacy of the repeal of Prohibition. Most of these votes were regained in the 1930 congressional elections; thus none of the other election pairs show as great a gain or loss as was found in the 1926 to 1930 elections. The pattern of the standard deviation of change shows little electoral change. In sum, the South began the period as a bastion of the Democrats, and by the end of the period, they had slightly increased their hold on the region.

The Border states followed a similar pattern, although the swing in the vote was more dramatic. The Democrats lost almost 11 percent in the 1926–28 election pair, again largely because of antipathy to Al Smith. However, the 1930 congressional elections saw a dramatic swing of more than 11 percent back toward the Democrats. In the next election they gained an average of more than 3 percent over their 1930 totals, while the Republicans lost almost 5 percent. The change in all subsequent pairs of elections is less than 3 percent and is insignificant. The greatest standard deviation of change occurs between 1924 and 1930, as one would expect given the shifts in voting associated with the 1928 presidential election. In sum, the region was heavily Democratic at the beginning of the period, and the New Deal transformation made it slightly more so.

The Western states show the greatest swings in vote from election to election. In part this is the result of the small number of representatives, in part the result of actual change. The 1930–36 period was characterized by a huge Democratic gain in 1932, and further gains in the next two elections. The standard deviation of the change is large in all three election pairs (1930–32, 1932–34, 1934–36), although the peak was reached in 1930–32. The net result is that a heavily Republican region became decidedly more Democratic in the New Deal realignment.

★ Electoral Summary

The overall results for the New Deal realignment clearly point to the nationalization of electoral factors in the 1932–36 period (73rd–75th Houses). Table 4.6 shows the aggregated results. The coefficient of variation is 3.04 for the Democrats in the critical period. The Democrats gained 9.1 percent over their prerealignment totals, whereas the Republicans lost 9.6 percent from theirs. The largest portion of the Democratic gain came with the shift from 1930 to 1932 (7.2 percent) and the concomitant Republican loss of 8.0 percent. The mean swings and the V coefficients in the pre- and postcritical periods support the nationalization hypothesis. In the precritical period both parties' mean swing was less than 2 percent, and the V's were at least twice as high as during the critical period. In the postcritical period the mean swing for both parties was approximately 4 percent, and the V's were between three and four times as high as during the critical period. These results clearly point to an across-the-board permanent movement to Roosevelt and the Democrats, whereas the Civil War and 1890's critical elections were compensatory in nature.

Let us again use the Flanigan-Zingale technique to demonstrate this. In contrast to the results shown for the 1860's and 1890's, the New Deal results show a clear-cut across-the-board shift toward the Democratic Party in the 1932 election. Nationally the Democrats gain 9.6 percent and the Republicans lose 6.2 percent, and these changes clearly outweigh the 2.1 percent and 2.3 percent (Democratic and Republican, respectively) compensating figures for the 1932 election. No

TABLE 4.6

Aggregate Party Vote Swings and Coefficients of Variation, 1924–1946

Period	Mean swing (percent)		Coefficient of variation	
	Democrat	Republican	Democrat	Republican
Precritical period, 1924–30	1.40%	−1.56%	8.32	−16.60
Critical period, 1932–36	9.12	−9.60	3.04	−4.15
Postcritical period, 1938–46	−3.79	4.01	−9.64	13.47
Controlling election, 1932	7.20%	—	2.14	—

other election in the 1924–40 series approaches the high level of change observed in 1932. Analysis of the regional results shows that the major portion of the Democrats' gain and the Republicans' loss came outside the South. Particularly important were the strong across-the-board shifts of 5.9 percent in the Northeastern states, 12.4 percent in the East North Central states, and 10.1 percent in the West North Central states.

The 1938 elections yielded an across-the-board 3.4 percent loss for the Democrats; and these losses were heaviest in precisely those regions where they gained the most in 1932—the Northeast and the Midwest. Thus the 1938 Republican victory is best seen as a slight adjustment away from the Democrats and toward the Republicans in an area that had been heavily Republican until 1932. No other figures in this period (1924–40), whether interactive or compensating, have values that approach even 3 percent. In fact, the across-the-board change figures for 1932 are significantly higher than any other figures in the three critical periods. Thus the New Deal is the one critical period that yields unequivocal results: the 1932 election was an across-the-board realignment toward Franklin Roosevelt and the Democratic Party.

★ Votes-to-Seats Ratios

Both the Civil War and the 1890's elections created one-party dominance in the House for fourteen years, in large part because the votes-to-seats ratio favored Republicans in Northern states. Roosevelt's election in 1932 also ushered in fourteen years of Democratic control of both the House and the Senate. However, because of the across-the-board nature of the election, the expectation is that the analysis will yield different results. The same procedure used in the two previous chapters was used to test for the votes-to-seats relationship.

Table 4.7 shows the Republicans with a national advantage through-

TABLE 4.7

Ratio of Republican House Seats to Democratic Seats Compared with Cube Law
Predictions Including and Excluding the South, 1924–1940

Election year	Entire nation			South excluded		
	Cube Law prediction	Actual ratio	Difference	Cube Law prediction	Actual ratio	Difference
1924	1.18	0.76	−0.42	0.33	0.38	0.05
1926	1.27	0.81	−0.46	0.34	0.42	0.08
1928	1.08	0.61	−0.47	0.31	0.28	−0.03
1930	1.68	0.99	−0.69	0.48	0.56	0.08
1932	4.78	2.38	−2.40	1.58	1.63	0.05
1934	5.41	2.88	−2.53	1.84	2.07	0.23
1936	5.60	3.38	−2.22	2.15	2.47	0.32
1938	3.52	1.49	−2.03	1.08	0.96	−0.12
1940	3.35	1.63	−1.72	1.08	1.05	−0.03

out the period. In every election from 1924 to 1940 the Democrats receive fewer seats than the Cube Law predicts. From 1924 to 1930, when the Democrats were in the minority except in the Southern and Border states, their actual number of seats was from −0.32 to −0.69 below the predicted number. Beginning with the 1932 realignment, when they became the majority party, they fell considerably below the Cube Law prediction, and they stayed well below it through the period, with a range of from −2.53 to −1.72. This seeming anomaly is explained by the party's status in the South: the Democrats so heavily controlled that area that the addition of Northern votes left them below the Cube Law prediction.

Excluding the South demonstrates these points clearly. Elsewhere the Cube Law is actually a good predictor of the votes-to-seats ratio. The 1932 elections show the Democrats +0.05 over the Cube Law prediction. However, the figures then rise to give the Democrats a 0.23 advantage over the Cube Law prediction in 1934 and a 0.32 advantage in 1936. In short, the across-the-board 1932 realignment to the Democrats was so massive that the Democrats dominated without a votes-to-seats distortion equal to the Cube prediction. Thus, in contrast to the two previous realignments, the Democrats' electoral dominance after 1932 was not largely the result of a votes-to-seats distortion caused by the single-member plurality electoral system.

★ Constituency Bases of the Congressional Parties

The realigning election of 1932 led to the Democratic dominance of congressional elections until 1946. The Democrats were dominant in both the industrial urban North and the agricultural rural South from 1932 to 1938. After 1938 they were competitive in the North and dominant in the South. If realigning elections change the composition of party preferences, then the constituency bases of the congressional parties should shift accordingly.

The farm depression of the 1920's had continued long after the industrial sector had recovered. The Republicans did little to remedy the situation, and the result was farm protests and policy proposals such as McNary-Haugenism for domestic price supports. James Sundquist, among others, argues that these farm protests were both a precursor and an integral part of the New Deal realignment.[17] Since the Republicans controlled government throughout the 1920's, we expect to find a rural electoral shift to the Democrats. A second, larger group of voters who switched to the Democratic Party was most readily identifiable by place of residence. The cities' blue-collar workers, ethnics, and blacks came into the Democratic column during the realignment.[18] In traditionally Democratic cities like New York the Democratic vote increased, and in predominantly Republican cities like Boston, the Democrats became dominant with the 1932 election. Working-class ethnics and blacks were hard-hit by the depression and voted Democratic. Thus we expect to see the congressional Democratic party reflect these changes. Specifically, the party should show gains across Northern industrial-urban districts as well as rural districts. This hypothesis, of course, fits the notion of an across-the-board surge to the Democrats. Testing this hypothesis entailed collecting the following data from the 1930 census—the number of blue-collar workers, the value-added by manufacture, and population density—and mapping them onto congressional districts. Since the size of constituencies varied, percentages were used and arrayed by median.

The ratio of Democratic to Republican seats by constituency type is shown in Table 4.8. As we see, during the New Deal era the Democrats made their greatest gains in industrial, urban, and blue-collar districts. In each case they increased the ratio of seats from around 0.5 in the 70th House (1927–29) to at least 1.8 in the 73rd House (1933–35). That is, in urban, labor, and industrial districts the Democrats went from about one-third of the seats to about two-thirds; in the 70th House, for example, they won only 34 percent of the seats in districts above the median in value-added by manufacture, against 65 percent in the 73rd House. The Democrats' domination of these districts continued unabated until the elections for the 76th House (1938), when the Republicans made significant inroads.

Rural, low-labor districts also show significant Democratic gains, but they are relatively small gains because the Democrats started with

TABLE 4.8

Shift in Constituency Bases, 1926–1938

(Ratio of Democratic to Republican seats in 70th–76th Houses)

District composition	1926	1928	1930	1932	1934	1936	1938
Labor							
Low	1.2	0.9	1.3	4.3	3.9	3.1	1.6
High	0.5	0.4	0.7	1.8	2.0	2.0	1.4
Industrial							
Low	1.1	0.9	1.3	4.3	3.9	3.0	1.6
High	0.5	0.4	0.7	1.8	2.0	2.1	1.5
Urban							
Low	1.1	0.9	1.3	3.7	3.4	2.7	1.4
High	0.4	0.4	0.8	1.9	2.0	2.0	1.3

SOURCE: 1930 Census data applied to current congressional districts.

NOTE: Labor districts are based on the percentage of blue-collar workers, industrial districts on the value-added of manufactures, and urban districts on population density. Low is defined as below the median, high as above the median.

a higher baseline of seats in those areas. Democratic party strength increased across all low-industry, low-labor, and rural districts, from a ratio of slightly over 1.1 to 1 in the 1926 elections to around 4 to 1 in 1932. In rural districts, for example, the Democrats won 54 percent of these seats in 1926 and 79 percent in 1932. Over the heyday of the realignment (1932–38) the Democratic percent of rural, low-labor, low-industry seats declined slightly but remained over 75 percent until the 76th House elections (1938). Thus, during the New Deal realignment Democrats gained across all types of districts.

After the Republican gains had stabilized the electoral alignment (1938 and after), the congressional Democratic party consisted of a combination of representatives from rural Southern and urban Northern districts. During the height of the realignment, Southern influence was limited because the South's proportion of the congressional party declined from about two-thirds of the seats in the 1924–30 elections to about 40 percent in 1932–36. After the Republican gains in 1938, Southerners held about 50 percent of the Democratic House seats. This regional pattern held until the mid-1960's.

To sum up, the major difference between the New Deal realignment and the two previous realignments is that the cross-cutting issues in the earlier realignments resulted in comparatively narrow electoral victories for the new majority party. In each case Northern industrial interests were pitted against Southern agrarian interests. The cross-cutting issue of the New Deal realignment—would the government attempt to alleviate the effects of the depression?—resulted in an overwhelming across-the-board realignment toward the Democrats. Both the Civil War and the 1890's realignments were characterized by vote swings to the Republicans in the North, which resulted in a strong pro-Republican seats-to-votes ratio. The New Deal realignment did not result in as strong a votes-to-seats bias because of the across-the-board nature of the election. The electoral results clearly indicate the presence of national electoral forces replacing local factors as the prime determinants of electoral results.

★ Congressional Turnover

As I argued earlier, critical elections should produce a high rate of turnover in the House, bringing with it a decrease in constituency-party cross-pressuring (or an increase in party cohesion) and changes in committee seats, thereby disrupting the old policy equilibrium. A higher level of party voting and a new policy equilibrium should result.

By 1932 the House of Representatives was a highly institutionalized body. The seniority system for determining committee positions was solidly in place, and the House had become a career for most of its members.[19] In the five Houses prior to the 73rd, less than 20 percent of the members were serving their first term, and the mean tenure was over four terms. Moreover, every Speaker of the House since 1911 had served over twenty years before rising to that office.[20] Less than 15 percent of the committee appointments, on average, were uncompensated violations of the seniority system, and this figure declined over the 1931–39 period.[21] Thus, the 1932 elections disrupted a much more highly institutionalized body than was the case in the two earlier critical elections.

The 1930 and 1932 congressional elections drastically changed the composition of the House. The 1930 freshman class constituted 19 percent of the House's membership. The election of Franklin Roosevelt in 1932 brought in 161 new members to the House (37.2 percent). Combined with the 1930 results, this meant that over half the House's membership had served less than two terms, and over 90 percent of the new members belonged to the new majority party. These turnover figures were the largest since the 1890's, and the new members were cohesive in their commitment to the President and to new policy initiatives to combat the effects of the depression.

The excitement and innovativeness of Roosevelt's first hundred days has been well documented elsewhere.[22] Nevertheless, one cannot read the *Congressional Record* of this period without taking away an impression of the Democrats' commitment to changing things. House precedents and rules were waived to get Roosevelt's programs passed. The debate on the National Banking Act is instructive. The bill was introduced on the opening day of the special session of the 73rd Congress (March 9, 1933) and passed without three readings or even a copy of the bill to peruse. Joseph W. Byrns (D–Tenn.) opened the debate with these comments:

It is of extreme importance that this bill, introduced a few moments ago by the gentleman from Alabama [Henry B. Steagall] carrying out the recommendations of the President preparatory to opening the banks of the country tomorrow, shall be adopted and become a law today. Mr. Speaker, the people of the U.S. have chosen the President as the leader not only of his party but as the leader of the Nation. To him they are looking for relief. He is their only hope. . . . We owe him our support.[23]

Bertrand H. Snell (R–N.Y.) responded: "The House is burning down, and the President says this is the way to put out the fire. . . . I do not know if I am in favor of this bill, but whether I am or not, I am going to give the President his way."[24] Congressman Steagall offered much the same argument for supporting the bill: "The people have summoned to their service a leader whose face is lifted toward the skies. We follow that leadership today."[25] Many Republican congressmen objected to the hasty treatment of so important a piece of legislation. As one noted, "It is, of course, out of the question, Mr. Speaker, that any man can grasp the full meaning of that bill by listening to its reading."[26] The final result was, of course, passage of the bill by a cohesive Democratic Party.

The congressional Democrats were equally receptive of other new policy proposals put forward by the White House or by their own colleagues. Throughout the New Deal era, innovative policies were passed because they were supported by a cohesive majority party. The new majority party's attitude was perhaps best summed up by William I. Sirovich of New York, who claimed: "The old order is passing. . . . New ideals, principles, and institutions are being called into immediate action."[27] Support for the New Deal had in fact been generated by the turnover of the 1932 election, and that support was maintained through at least the 75th Congress (1937–39).

The committee system had been an important component of congressional decision making for a considerable period.[28] And, as in the two previous critical elections, a dramatic turnover in committee members and chairmen paved the way for change by increasing the flexibility of the policy-making process. To test the committee-turnover hypothesis, the procedure outlined in Chapter Three was followed. Table 4.9 shows the results.

TABLE 4.9

Total and Partisan Turnover on Thirteen Selected Committees, 73rd House,
1933–1935

(Percent new members since 71st House)

Committee	Total turnover	Democrats	Republicans
Agriculture	85.2%	89.5%	75.0%
Appropriations	74.3	67.0	85.7
Banking and Currency	79.2	81.2	75.0
Commerce	64.0	85.7	62.5
Education	85.7	80.0	100.0
Foreign Affairs	80.0	88.2	62.5
Judiciary	88.0	88.2	87.5
Labor	85.0	85.7	83.3
Merchant Marine	73.9	82.4	50.0
Mines and Mining	95.5	100.0	83.3
Public Lands	95.7	100.0	83.3
Rules	67.0	62.5	75.0
Ways and Means	80.0	93.3	60.0

The results are striking. The lowest total turnover rate was 64 percent for the Commerce Committee, the highest 95.7 percent for Public Lands. Average total turnover was well over 80 percent, indicating the drastic nature of the change. Moreover, turnover was not limited to clientele committees; turnover on Appropriations and Ways and Means was 70 percent or greater, and over two-thirds of the members of the Rules Committee changed. The party turnover figures range from 50 percent for Republicans on Merchant Marine to 100 percent for Republicans on Education and for Democrats on Mines and Mining and Public Lands. In short, during the New Deal realignment all thirteen committees found themselves with a majority of new members. Since average turnover in the comparable period before the realignment was slightly over 20 percent, it is clear that the New Deal effected drastic changes in committee composition.

As noted earlier, in the modern era the norms of seniority and specialization have been important in facilitating committee continuity and stability. Committee leadership positions come available infrequently; leaders are brought along slowly. They must first put in long years on the committee, acquiring expertise and becoming keepers of committee norms and policy.

If in a very short time there should be drastic turnovers in membership, one would expect the norms of seniority and specialization to be affected—specifically, that during critical periods committee turnover would be so drastic that many of the leaders would not have acquired much seniority. Any committee chairman in the 73rd House

(1933–35) who was either not on the committee in the 70th House or below the median rank of seniority in that House can be considered a low-seniority chairman.

During the 1930's there were 44 House committees with more than five members. Within the short period of three elections, eighteen of them acquired chairmen who were not on the committee at all at the end of the 70th House or were below the median seniority rank. Robert Daughton of North Carolina, for example, was the tenth-ranking Democrat, the lowest-ranking minority member, on the Ways and Means Committee in January 1929; he was chairman of Ways and Means in January 1933. Heartsill Ragon of Arkansas was not a member of Ways and Means in the 70th House; he was the ranking majority member in the 73rd House. Adolph Sabath of Illinois was not on the Rules Committee in the 70th House; by the 73rd House he was the fourth-ranking majority member. The influx of new members plus the high turnover on committees facilitated such rapid advancement. Rather than continue the argument by enumeration, let me point to Table 4.10, which shows the 73rd House's eighteen low-seniority committee chairmen. It is plain that both important and relatively unimportant committees were led by men who did not have much seniority and were not the keepers of committee norms.

TABLE 4.10
Low-Seniority Committee Chairmen, 73rd House

Committee	Chairman
Accounts	Warren (N.C.)
District of Columbia	Norton (N.J.)
Election of President	Carley (N.Y.)
*Elections—1	Clark (N.C.)
*Elections—2	Gauagan (N.Y.)
*Enrolled Bills	Parsons (Ill.)
Expenditures in Executive	Cochran (Mo.)
Foreign Affairs	McReynolds (Tenn.)
*Insular Affairs	McDuffie (Ala.)
*Irrigation and Reclamation	Chavez (N.M.)
*Library	Keller (Ill.)
Military Affairs	McSwain (S.C.)
*Mines and Mining	Smith (W.Va.)
Patents	Sirovich (N.Y.)
*Public Lands	DeRoven (La.)
*Revision of Laws	Harlan (Ohio)
Territories	Kemp (La.)
Ways and Means	Daughton (N.C.)

NOTE: An asterisk indicates the Chairman was not on the committee in the 70th House. The other chairmen shown were below the median seniority on their committees in that house.

The most obvious effect of the discontinuity in committee leadership was that the committee system became more flexible or pliable in providing voting cues. In other words, there was less disjointedness between the new party's policy preferences and the committee leadership's preferences. In addition, the new committee leaders and members had not acquired the norms that made for recommendations of the status quo in their policy domains. The loss of norms and the confluence of leaders' and members' preferences increased the likelihood of cohesive partisan voting.*

★ Voting Patterns

The major stable issue dimensions of the New Deal realignment were government management, social welfare, and agricultural assistance. In addition, there were clusters of roll calls in some of the Houses involving what can loosely be grouped as civil rights issues. These categories fit Aage Clausen's and Barbara Sinclair's categories as closely as possible.[29] Unlike the issue dimensions of the two previous critical periods, those of the New Deal realignment have been quite intensively studied.[30] Therefore, the following discussion has more to do with specific reactions to them than with a description of the issues as such.

The government management dimension is present in all the New Deal Congresses. In the pre-realignment Houses there were partisan differences over Secretary of the Treasury Andrew Mellon's tax proposals, antitrust legislation, and tariff legislation. With the coming of the New Deal, the dimension reflects a shift in issue content. Sinclair correctly describes the shift as the movement from a relatively laissez-faire government role to the modern notion of government management[31]—namely, the belief that the federal government should directly intervene in the running of the economy. The culmination of this view is best expressed in the 1946 Full Employment Act, which makes the government responsible for employment.[32] During the New Deal period a strong support score indicates a favorable attitude toward activist government policies. In the 73rd House, for example, a high score means that a representative supported the Tennessee Valley Authority, Roosevelt's tax bill, the Reciprocal Trade Act, and so on.

---

*For an excellent example of the way turnover can affect the norms and operations of a committee, see Bruce Oppenheimer's work on the post-1974 Rules Committee— "Policy Implications of Rules Committee Reforms." Oppenheimer shows how turnover changed the committee from one that blocked the party leadership's desires to one that promoted them.

In later Houses it means support for the Wagner Act, the National Labor Relations Board, the Fair Labor Practices Act, and so forth.

The debate on the 1935 Public Utilities Act provides a good example of the partisan divisions over the question of government management. The most controversial feature of the bill was Section 11, which concerned holding companies. Representative Sam Rayburn (D–Tex.) took a dim view of such firms: "These creatures of our legal ingenuity are operated by a few clever men. They are used as the agencies for disenfranchising stockholders of thousands of necessary and prosperous operating companies." He went on to list seventeen separate reprehensible acts of holding companies, including creating special privilege, swindling the public, and functioning under Wall Street control. Rayburn concluded by stating, "What I want to do [and what this bill does] is to take from the backs of the clean, honestly operated companies of this country these *leeches* and *bloodsucking* holding companies."[33] His fellow Democrat, Representative Edward C. Eicher of Iowa, fully subscribed to this view, proclaiming: "The curse of a concentrated economic and financial power, exerted with other people's money, threatens the existence of our institutions. It must be banished from the land!"[34]

The opposition to the Public Utilities Act came overwhelmingly from Republicans. The House Committee voted 16-6 to report the bill; only one of the seven Republican members voted for it. Republicans argued that the bill was ersatz socialism. Representative John G. Cooper of Ohio stated their case:

Why destroy all holding companies because some of them have carried on abuse and unconscionable practices in the past? To dissolve and attempt to liquidate utility company control would mean direct loss to millions of citizens who have invested their money in utility securities. [In fact] the prime purpose of this legislation is public ownership of utilities. . . . Some foreign countries have passed through the miserable failure and experience of government ownership.[35]

William H. Wilson of Pennsylvania had deeper fears: "I made the contention that this bill was a plan for Government ownership of all industry."[36]

The social welfare dimension first appears in the 72nd House and is present in all subsequent Houses. In the 72nd House (1931–33) most votes dealt with the use of federal funds for relief and Speaker John N. Garner's $2 billion relief bill. After the coming of the New Deal, the question shifted from these matters to the whole gamut of Roosevelt's welfare programs. Thus, high social welfare scores indicate support for such programs as the Civil Conservation Corps, Works Projects Administration, Social Security, and aid to the blind. It should also be noted that before the New Deal the issue was whether or not to have welfare programs, and that during and after it, the issue was how *much* welfare and what kind. In short, the New Deal created the basic structure of the contemporary welfare state.

The Social Security program exemplifies partisan differences on the question of social welfare. The Democratic view was that the extraordinary circumstances of the depression called for new measures. As Representative Arthur H. Greenwood of Indiana stated: "From this depression we have learned that there must be new formulas for the security of humanity."[37] Democrats like Robert Daughton, chairman of the Ways and Means Committee, saw the program as essential to the financial security of deserving citizens:

Today we see frightful evidence of insecurity on every hand. The fact that 15,000,000 persons are receiving unemployment relief is perhaps our most striking evidence of insecurity. Nearly a million of these are over 65 years of age. . . . As long as their large number are unemployed, the great mass of American families, those in which there are employed wage earners, can feel no real security. We cannot afford to delay further the legislation necessary to protect our American workers against the many hazards of our industrial order which lead to huge relief rolls and threaten the foundations of our society.[38]

Republicans characterized the Social Security Act as reckless federal intervention and warned of dire consequences. "There will be a day of reckoning for those advocating [this] delusional plan" was the way one put it.[39] Moreover, opponents argued, the financial burden on employers would be monumental. Representative Allen T. Treadway of Massachusetts summarized this view nicely when he stated: "The burden which it [the Social Security tax] would impose on business and industry is heavy. This tax would increase unemployment and would be a burden on business." In any case, he added, "The federal government has no express or inherent power under the Constitution to set up such a scheme as is proposed."[40]

The agricultural assistance dimension is present in all Houses in the period. In the 69th and 70th Houses most of the roll calls centered on the question of a two-price system—the McNary-Haugen bill—which favored farmers who sold their products on the domestic market. With the drought of 1929 and the depression, the roll call votes began to reflect the modern forms of agricultural assistance, as provided in such legislation as the Agricultural Assistance Act, the

Soil Conservation Act, the Agricultural Relief Bill, and the Emergency Farm Mortgage Act. The debate on the Agricultural Relief Bill is instructive.

The Democrats were accused of bringing the bill out under what Republicans called a "gag rule." Democrats like Edward E. Cox of Georgia and William B. Bankhead of Alabama argued that in the current economic crisis farmers needed assistance to keep their farms. Even conservative Democrats like Richard M. Kleberg of Texas spoke in favor of the bill, arguing that if Roosevelt thought the bill necessary, the House had better vote for it. Republicans characterized the bill as financially unsound, unstatesmanlike, and even communistic. Here is a sample of their comments. Bertrand Snell (N.Y.): "The Republican Party never advises to chase rainbows as you propose today. This is not a statesman's bill. This is a pure Democratic patronage bill." Joseph W. Martin (Mass.): "I am opposed to this bill because I firmly believe it will result disastrously as have other ventures in the field of agricultural price fixing." Michael J. Hart (Mich.): "I am not going to follow communism."[41]

The roll calls that fall under the civil rights rubric vary substantially and cover areas as disparate as immigration and lynching. Though this dimension is less stable than the others, it is important to my argument because, unlike the other issue dimensions, it does not ostensibly deal with the cross-cutting national issues needed to unite the Northern and Southern wings of the Democratic Party. The scores, however, are instructive and worth including for illustrative purposes.*

The specific hypothesis is that the policy changes associated with the New Deal were passed by the huge Democratic majorities first elected in 1932; thus on social welfare, agricultural assistance, and government management, we expect high correlations between party identification and voting on these dimensions. Table 4.11 shows the results of the analysis.

The results clearly confirm the hypothesis. Social welfare becomes an issue dimension in the 72nd House and is strongly correlated with party throughout the period. Agricultural assistance is an issue dimension throughout the period but does not become heavily partisan until the 71st House (1929–31), supporting the argument of Sundquist and others that the farm movement of the late 1920's was a harbinger of the New Deal realignment. Farm prices were the first affected, and by late 1929 the Democrats were attempting to liberalize

---

*Readers are referred to Sinclair, "Party Realignment," Sinclair, *Congressional Realignment,* and Brady and Stewart, "Congressional Party Realignment," for details on the civil rights dimension in the New Deal era and afterward.

TABLE 4.11

Product-Moment Correlations Between Party Identification and Issue Voting,
69th–76th Houses, 1925–1941

House	Government management	Social welfare	Agricultural assistance	Civil rights
69	.84	—	.08	.17
70	.88	—	.24	—
71	.91	—	.94	.20
72	.94	.72	.77	.46
73	.97	.89	.90	—
74	.91	.94	.91	.22
75	.94	.86	.77	.18
76	.89	.69	.89	.22

the weak Agricultural Marketing Act passed earlier that year. In the 72nd House (1931–33) an agricultural policy stalemate developed between the Democratic majority and the Republican President. In the 73rd House the large Democratic majorities passed the first of the programs that meet Clausen's criteria for an agricultural assistance issue dimension. Thus, on both social welfare and agricultural assistance, the policy changes associated with the New Deal were passed by the newly elected majority party.[42]

As expected, the civil rights dimension severely divided the Democratic majority along regional lines. Regardless of the issue content— from Prohibition to anti-lynching—Southern and Northern Democrats broke ranks over civil rights issues.[43] This is consistent with our view of the New Deal realignment. That is, the cross-cutting issue of government involvement in alleviating the effects of the depression could legitimately cover agricultural assistance and social welfare policies, but it could not be extended to civil rights. The realigning issues were economic, not social; thus Southerners could and did oppose the liberal civil rights policies of Northern Democrats.

The government management issue dimension was present across all eight Houses and was strongly correlated with party identification throughout the period. However, as Sinclair has shown, the content of the roll calls on this dimension changes dramatically. In her words, "With the 73rd Congress the major government management dimension becomes a New Deal dimension."[44] Thus, even on a dimension dominated by strong partisanship, the policy changes associated with the New Deal on government management were passed by the new majority party. In sum, the dominant issue dimensions of the New Deal were associated with increased government economic activity, and from 1933 to 1938 "the new majority party had very large majori-

TABLE 4.12

Party Voting, 69th–76th Houses

	Percentage of party votes			Percentage of party votes	
House	90%–90%	50%–50%	House	90%–90%	50%–50%
69	5.3%	43.7%	73	18.9%	70.6%
70	5.6	48.6	74	14.2	59.9
71	13.6	58.2	75	11.8	63.9
72	13.8	57.7	76	17.6	71.4

ties in the Congress and it passed a large amount of significant and innovative legislation."[45]

Similar as the New Deal realignment is to the Civil War and 1890's realignments in the sense that policy changes were made by the new majority party, it differs in a number of ways. Most important, unlike them, it resulted in large Democratic majorities in the House and a unity of the North and South on policies favoring increased government activism. Moreover, since the majorities were so very large, the levels of party voting needed to pass policy changes were not as high as in the other realignment eras. An analysis of aggregate levels of party voting during the New Deal demonstrates this point (Table 4.12).

When party voting is measured by the 50 percent-50 percent criterion, the results show that only twice (the 73rd and 76th Houses) does the level of party voting reach 70 percent. In contrast, four of the six Houses in the 1897–1907 period have higher levels of party voting, and the *average* for the Civil War realignment was 74.7 percent. When the 90 percent-90 percent criterion is used, no House in the New Deal period reaches 20 percent; no House in the Civil War and 1890's realignments failed to do so. The aggregate party vote scores clearly show that party strength was not as high during the New Deal. But, then, with the huge Democratic majorities, it did not need to be. On economic issues the Democrats were relatively united, but less so than the majority parties in the earlier realignments were.

★ The Changing Shape of Voting on Issues, 1933–1939

The New Deal realignment resulted in significant shifts in public policy, which on the whole were attributable to the new majority party. This is of course similar to what happened in the two previous critical periods; the coalitions in the New Deal era, however, were less tied to region and economic interests. In the Civil War and 1890's realignments, the critical elections yielded two congressional parties with distinct regional and industrial-agricultural bases. In contrast, the electoral results of the 1930's brought together the Democrats' traditional Southern rural base and a new Northern urban, ethnic base. The second party was left with less than one-quarter of all House seats, and these representatives were, in V. O. Key's term, "stand patters," representatives by and large committed to the 1920's Republican laissez-faire policies.[46] Thus, polarization was a less important factor in the New Deal realignment than in the earlier ones.

When political parties have distinct centers of gravity on some regional, industrial, or ethnic continuum, one can readily explain why members behave as they do. Policy change becomes a function of the self-interest of the members aggregated as a political party. When political parties do not have distinct centers of gravity, one expects to find decreased levels of party strength and mixes of public policy. This argument, in fact, underlies a standard criticism of the American political system. From E. E. Schattschneider's *Party Government* (1942) to James M. Burns's *The Deadlock of Democracy* (1963) to Theodore Lowi's *The End of Liberalism* (1979), the underlying assumption is that the mix of interest groups and parties results in ad hoc or cyclic coalitions and policy confusion. Yet this did not occur in the first six years of the New Deal. Rather, the New Deal resulted in significant policy changes that, broadly speaking, moved American public policy toward welfare-statism. How can we account for this policy shift in view of the disparate groups in the Democratic coalition during the New Deal? As with previous realignments, the answer is to be found in the nature of the policies themselves.

Given the heterogeneity of the Democrats' electoral base, it would seem that policies that would be supported by Northern urban interests would not be favored by Southern rural interests. In fact, bills dealing with civil rights during the 1933–39 period are characterized by just such voting splits. On other legislation, however, such as the Agricultural Adjustment Act (AAA) or the Wagner Act, we find no such pattern. The coalition responsible for passing most of the New Deal legislation combined both Northern and Southern, rural and industrial interests. The Democrats were able to force this coalition by essentially logrolling these disparate elements around the issue of trying to alleviate the effects of the depression. Thus, the National Industrial Recovery Act (NIRA) allowed the affected industries to bargain among themselves to determine prices, while agricultural interests were accommodated by such legislation as the AAA and the Rural Electrification Act (REA). That is, each interest was dealt with separately, and representatives from rural Southern districts supported the NIRA, while their counterparts in Northern industrial districts supported the AAA and the REA.

In part these coalitions formed because of the severity of the economic shock they were called on to address and the fact that Roosevelt wanted the policies enacted. As we have seen, members frequently said they were voting for this or that piece of legislation not because they wanted or liked it, but because the President wanted it. It must be remembered that from 1932 to 1938, Roosevelt led the party to overwhelming victories. The 1932 landslide was followed by a *gain* in Democratic House seats in 1934, and then the overwhelming victory of 1936. No other President has ever had such striking electoral fortunes over a six-year, three-election period. As late as 1938, Lyndon Johnson overcame highly unfavorable odds and won a House seat by running on the slogan, "I will support the President in Washington."[47] This is in such stark contrast to contemporary results and campaigns as to be almost unbelievable. However, these impressive electoral results, and the unlikely nature of the coalition, could not last forever.

The emergence of a conservative coalition in 1938 effectively ended the President's ability to push further domestic policy changes through the Congress. The coalition became active on a bill that, like civil rights legislation, split the Northern and Southern wings of the party. The Fair Labor Standards Act was opposed by Southerners because it would have destroyed their sole advantage in attracting industry—cheap labor. In their efforts to defeat the bill, Southern representatives joined forces with Republicans. Their success in defeating the Fair Labor Standards Act and the increased Republican membership after the 1938 election put the conservative coalition in a position to block any further major policy proposals.

CHAPTER FIVE

Committees and Policy Making in Critical Eras

COMMITTEES ARE more than just a part of the policy process in the U.S. House of Representatives. Since World War II they have effectively *made* policy, according to such seminal works as those of Charles O. Jones (on the Agriculture Committee), Richard Fenno (Appropriations), John Manley (Ways and Means), and Nelson Polsby and Joseph Cooper (the seniority system). In general the historical picture these authors paint shows why committees' structure, norms, and rules encouraged policy incrementalism.[1] House committees were hierarchical; Ways and Means, Rules, and Appropriations were exclusive and powerful. Membership on these committees was earned: members first had to serve on less important committees, where their performance could be evaluated by the leadership, before being appointed to one of the major ones.[2] Turnover on the major committees was relatively slow, which served to inculcate new members with existing norms and rules.[3] Add to this portrait the selection of committee assignments by members seeking influence in areas relevant to their policy interests, and one recognizes that preferences and institutional structure combined to yield committees that were, in William Riker's term, sets of preferences.[4]

Although the 1974 congressional reforms changed some aspects of the committee system, the basic point still holds today—committee structure, norms, and rules promote policy incrementalism. To be sure, we may now speak more commonly of a "subcommittee government" that has brought more participants into the process; and there have been alterations in the referral process and other parts of the system. But despite these changes, Steven Smith and Christopher Deering conclude that the fragmentation of the pre-reform committee system is compatible with members' goals of reelection and personal power. "Jurisdictional fragmentation certainly helps. Members representing similar constituencies can join together to determine policy affecting those constituencies with minimal interference from disinterested members; . . . members with particular policy interests are given an opportunity to focus on and have a major influence over policy decisions in those areas."[5] Thus it is fair to say the post-reform House maintains the essence of the pre-reform arrangements, and though in the discussion that follows, I focus on committee studies in the pre-1974 period, I shall stick to the present tense.

This is not to say that different committees all use similar decision strategies except insofar as the strategy in every case favors incremental policy choices. Fenno's comparative study of congressional committees shows how the system works.[6] He classifies committees by the goals of their members and by their major constituencies—factors that together yield problems unique to each committee. The goal of the members of the Appropriations Committee, for example, is influence, and their primary constituency is the House itself, whose members desire funding for the various programs of interest to them. Since the Appropriations Committee's way to attain influence is to cut the President's budget requests, thus diminishing funding the House members desire, a strategic dilemma ensues. This dilemma has been resolved by the development of a committee bill strategy. The Appropriations Committee is made up of liberals and conservatives, Southerners and Northerners, Democrats and Republicans. Fiscal differences are expected to be compromised and ironed out first in subcommittee and then by the full committee. The final bill or bills are then supported by the entire committee on the floor. Fenno refers to this as an integrative strategy, and the mode is clearly consensual.[7] Reporting out a bill supported by all of the committee's disparate factions leaves the whole House with little alternative but to support it, especially since bills are normally reported with a special rule prohibiting amendments. On specific items the President's budget request is reduced, thus ensuring the committee's influence. As Fenno has shown, however, if one takes an over-time series of appropriation bills, the amount appropriated tends to rise, thus satisfying the House members' desire to fund programs. Moreover, the rate of increase is relatively stable. In sum, the over-time decisions are incremental, with funding roughly following the pattern

$$t_1 = \$x_{t_1}; \ t_2 = \$x_{t_1} + .05; \ t_3 = \$x_{t_2} + .05; \ etc.$$

The Interior Committee, by contrast, is characterized by members whose principal goal is reelection and a constituency composed of Western mining, timber, and ranching interests.[8] The committee's dilemma is how to support the differing, sometimes conflicting, inter-

ests of its members' constituencies. It has resolved the problem by
adopting a logrolling strategy and a policy of multiple use. That is, the
committee reports out a bill that satisfies the members' goal of reelection by allowing the different constituent interests to use federal lands
for different purposes. A representative from east Texas gets timber-
cutting rights for his constituents, a member from Colorado gets graz-
ing rights at reduced prices for *his* constituents, and a representative
from Montana gets mining rights. Each supports the others' policy
proposals, and the result is universal pork-barrel legislation.

Ways and Means Committee members also have influence as their
goal, but their constituency differs from the Appropriations Committee's; the constituency of Ways and Means is led by the President and
by business interests seeking tax breaks.[9] In addition, unlike Appropriations, Ways and Means is not required to report out a timely yearly
bill. The strategic result is that the committee is more partisan than
Appropriations; the usual policy result is the granting of special tax
breaks.[10] Neither the President nor the committee members want to
campaign for office on a record of increasing taxes, and business and
industrial interests usually present to the committee tightly reasoned
packages showing how tax breaks will help them without diminishing
overall revenues. Manley shows how, during a 1960's session, the committee heard testimony favoring a tax-cutting package proposed by
Lyndon Johnson and opposing a limited floor for deductions that
would have raised taxes.[11] Once again, the preferences of members
and the structure, norms, and rules of the committee combined to
provide stable policy results.

These are of course but a few examples of committee decision making, and a more exhaustive portrait would in any case be somewhat
dated. The rise of environmental interests, for example, must change
the policy equation for the Interior Committee to a certain extent.
And one could of course draw other, similar examples from other
House committees. Yet I would still argue that the overall policy
outputs of committees are incremental, owing in large part to the
combination of members' preferences and committee structure. In
the following pages we shall see how critical elections result in nonincremental policy changes by the Appropriations and Agriculture
committees.

In the modern House of Representatives the committee system has
reigned in no small part because of the continuity of membership.
Continuity ensures gradual changes in leadership and the transmis-
sion of committee norms and rules, which facilitate incrementalism,
to new members. In addition, committee jurisdictions amount to lim-

ited monopoly-right grants over certain policy areas.[12] Thus, for example, the Agriculture Committee has a monopoly on agriculture policy. Its membership is, within limits, self-selected and hence dominated by people representing agricultural interests. The more important a committee, the more restricted its membership. In part, restricting membership strengthens committees because their proprietary rights are distributed over fewer members, enabling individual members to wield more power within the committee. To be sure, a committee's monopoly rights can be contested or limited by claims of other committees, or by the actions of the House itself on a bill's final passage. The jurisdictional disputes over the 1977 Carter Energy Act are a case in point. And the House's attempts to amend tax bills on the floor testify to the desire, on occasion, to limit a committee's proprietary rights.[13] These limitations notwithstanding, it is still fair to assert that committees are, in general, awarded proprietary rights over policy areas, and that members seek committee assignments that help them attain their ends.

As we have seen, during critical election periods the turnover on House committees is very high. Fenno, noting how this affects committee decision making, observes: "The two occasions on which the greatest amount of open dissatisfaction, threatened rebellion, and actual rebellion occurred coincided with the two greatest personnel turnovers. . . . The tendency to rebellion increases as personnel turnover increases; the very stability of committee membership appears, once again, as a critical condition of [the style of decision making]."[14] Fenno is describing the Appropriations Committee in the 80th House (1947–49), when the newly elected Republican members, in the majority for the first time in fourteen years, were seeking to repeal much of the New Deal legislation. The fact that President Harry Truman was a Democrat who threatened and used the veto to thwart the proposed policy shifts, along with the Democrats' surprising electoral victory in 1948, ultimately prohibited any major shift. During critical election periods, however, the same party controls House, Senate, and Presidency for at least a decade.

Committee turnover during critical election periods should be interpreted as preference shifts brought about by electoral results. The shift in preferences and leadership results in changed norms, rules, and structure, which in combination yield nonincremental policy results. In this chapter the focus is on the House Appropriations Committee from 1895 to 1950, and the House Agriculture Committee during the New Deal era.[15] In regard to the Appropriations Committee the argument is that the exogenously driven electoral turnover, along with shifts in norms, leadership, and so forth, led to unified partisan activity on the committee and thus to nonincremental policy shifts, or a new equilibrium.

★ The Appropriations Committee

The Appropriations Committee is at the heart of the congressional policy process and is thus a natural choice. The committee has operated consensually since the end of World War II, compromising differences among its members. But the pressures to operate by consensus go back much further. Indeed, ever since the committee's formation in 1865, any major changes in the House's appropriations process have resulted from disputes over the committee's funding of programs and departments. When, in the 1880's, the House gave seven additional committees the right to appropriate funds, it was because the Appropriations Committee was not funding certain agencies (e.g. the one responsible for agriculture) at a high enough level. And when the House voted in 1919 and 1920 to change the budget process and recentralize power in the Appropriations Committee, it was essentially because the constituency-oriented committees were funding their agencies and programs at too high a level given the state of the economy. The committee's strategy to report consensual bills that balance the need to guard the Treasury and to fund programs incrementally can thus be seen as a long-standing strategy.[16]

During critical periods old policy patterns or equilibria are broken, and clusters of policy changes are enacted. If this is the case for policy in general, such results should be observable on the Appropriations Committee. The argument is that if preferences have shifted toward a new congressional majority party, then the committee's decision process will be partisan rather than consensual, and the chances for nonincremental appropriations are increased. High turnover and unified partisan behavior on the committee will yield nonincremental appropriations. In order to demonstrate this it is necessary to show that:

1. during the period from 1895 to 1950 the Appropriations Committee's behavior was usually consensual but at times partisan;

2. the absolute change in appropriations from year to year is associated with levels of partisan voting—specifically, partisan voting on the committee will be positively related to nonincremental appropriations;

3. during the critical periods 1897–99 and 1933–39, the levels of partisanship and nonincrementalism will be highest; and

4. committee turnover is high during the critical periods and thus associated with both partisanship and nonincrementalism.

In sum, the argument is that during a critical period electoral results cause high turnover, and the new majority on Appropriations behaves in a partisan fashion, which results in nonincremental appropriations.

In congressional history, 1890–1910 was the heyday of the Speaker's powers.[17] The committee and party systems were molded together by the practice of having party leaders chair the important committees. The result was a more hierarchical, centralized leadership structure in the House of Representatives than had previously obtained.[18] During this era party voting in the House peaked; thus one expects to find the Appropriations Committee voting in a more partisan fashion. To test this hypothesis, the committee's votes on the following kinds of roll calls were analyzed: amendments to appropriations bills, recommittal motions on appropriations bills, and final passage.[19] An average Index of Party Likeness score was computed for the entire committee, and the percentage of 90 percent-90 percent party-line votes was calculated. These scores were calculated for all Houses from the 54th through the 81st House (1895–1950). Since there were up to eight appropriating committees between 1895 and 1920, the scores were calculated for each committee during this period. The results are shown in Figure 5.1.

It is clear that within this span of years there were periods of partisan committee behavior. One is the period from the critical election of 1894 to 1915, a few years after the stripping of the Speaker's power in the 61st House (1909–11). The lowest percentage of almost straight party-line voting is 22 percent in the 54th House (1895–97); in the next two Houses the average rises to 50 percent. In the following period, 1916–33, the average is much lower; only two Houses attain levels falling in the range of the earlier period. The New Deal realignment results in an increased percentage of party votes from 1935 to 1939 (74th–75th Houses), when Roosevelt made a strong turn to the left. After these Houses the figures fall back toward the less-than-10-percent levels reported by Fenno for the post–World War II period. In addition, an analysis of average Index of Party Likeness scores for each House reveals an average of 27.2 for the 1895–1915 period, and of 51.6 for the post-1915 era. Since the lower the Index of Party Likeness score, the higher the levels of party voting, the earlier period was plainly characterized by party structuring of voting. Thus, by both measures it is clear that the members of appropriations committees have at times behaved in a partisan fashion, notably during the 1895–1915 period, when multiple committees appropriated, and during the

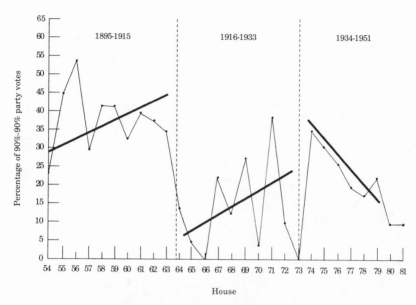

Fig. 5.1. Party voting on the House Appropriations Committee and other appropriating committees, 1895–1951. Source: compiled by author from the *Congressional Record* and *Public Acts.*

New Deal period, when Appropriations acted alone. The years 1895–1915 contain both a critical and a postcritical period when partisanship was high, which suggests two important points about partisanship and nonincremental appropriations decisions. I expect that during the critical period 1897–1901, changes in appropriations would be greater than they were in the post-1901 period, even though partisanship remained high. Essentially this means that partisan behavior was a norm in this era, and that it is the turnover in membership— change in preferences—that generates the shifts in appropriations. In addition, if partisanship is the norm during this era and in noncritical periods the committees pass incremental fiscal bills, then partisanship can yield both incremental and nonincremental results.* The nonincremental decisions will occur in critical periods when committee turnover is greatest. If I can show that the 1897–1901 and 1933–39 periods yielded the most partisan and least incremental appropriations, and that committee turnover in these periods was at a

---

*I am indebted to Joseph Cooper for this point. The argument is that a representative process ensures that all viewpoints will be heard internally; thus any policy output will be a compromise. A partisan process can vote in nonincremental changes as well as incremental outputs. In part this is true because in a partisan process you do not have to convince as many members—one over half of the majority party—if party voting is enforced after the decision is made.

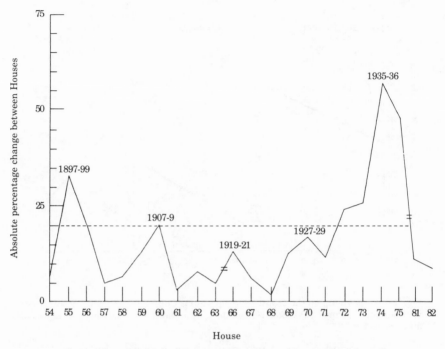

Fig. 5.2. Percentage changes in House appropriations, 1895–1953. The figure for each House is the average of the two annual bills.

high, the results for the committee study would be similar to those for the entire House.

Estimating the amounts of money appropriated during World Wars I and II, and to a lesser extent the Spanish-American War, is problematic. To reduce as much as possible the effects of war on appropriations decisions, I do not include defense appropriations in any of the 58 appropriations bills in the time series. In addition, I calculated changes in appropriations for agriculture, rivers and harbors, commerce, and labor as a check against changes in total appropriations. Because these checks did not show significant differences from the overall appropriations, only the overall figures, minus defense, are given. Figure 5.2 shows the absolute percentage changes from appropriations by previous Houses for the entire time series, excluding the two world wars. I include data from the 81st and 82nd Houses to show how increases dropped after realignment was over.

Two technical points are in order. First, I use absolute figures for appropriations because significant change can be either positive or negative. The Jacksonian era was characterized by the reductions in the scope of federal government. Ronald Reagan's "policy revolution" will ultimately be judged on the basis of how much he cut government. Second, the figures used are those for final House passage; they differ by less than 1 percent from those passed by the committees.[20] Essentially there is no difference between the two figures.

The results show that the highest absolute changes in appropriations occurred during the critical periods of the 1890's and 1930's. The only positive changes in excess of 20 percent obtain in the critical eras. The only other change of over 20 percent, in the 72nd House (1931–33), was a decrease, the result of President Hoover's attempt to balance the budget.

Thus far, I have shown that the Appropriations Committee behaved in a partisan fashion during both realignments and during the period from 1900 to 1915, and that absolute changes in appropriations are greatest during realignments. What remains is to tie together committee turnover, partisanship, and major changes in appropriations. Table 5.1 shows the average turnover on the Appropriations Committee, the average Index of Party Likeness for committee members on relevant votes, and the average positive increases in appropriations for 1897–1949. The hypothesis is that during the 1890's and New Deal realignment periods, committee turnover, party voting, and appropriations will be high, and that high partisanship during the 1901–15 period will not result in abnormally high change in appropriations. In addition it is expected that the 1916–32 and 1940–49 periods (excluding war expenditures) will follow the Fenno model of lower partisanship and incremental changes in appropriations.

The results support the argument. In the years 1897–1901 partisanship was high, with an average Index of Likeness of 20.5 (i.e. the average vote was about 80 percent-80 percent party line). The average increase in expenditures during these years was 27.0 percent, and the

TABLE 5.1

Appropriations Committee Turnover, Party Voting, and Increases in Appropriations, 1897–1949

Period	Number new committee members		Index of Likeness		Increase in appropriations	
	Mean (pct.)	Std. dev.	Mean	Std. dev.	Mean (pct.)	Std. dev.
1897–1901	46.6%	11.5	20.5	0.7	27.0%	8.5
1902–1915	35.9	18.1	34.3	4.2	7.6	7.1
1916–1932	26.0	13.6	57.6	12.4	4.5	18.9
1933–1939	34.3	10.9	29.7	1.2	34.1	19.4
1940–1949	24.4	8.0	54.0	9.3	9.6	14.3

turnover on the Appropriations Committee averaged 46.6 percent. The New Deal realignment was also characterized by high turnover—34.3 percent with an average Index of Likeness of 29.7 (about 70 percent-70 percent), and an average increase in expenditures of 34.1 percent. Thus the highest partisanship and highest change in appropriations occurred during realignment periods. The turnover on the Appropriations Committee was slightly higher during the 1902–15 period than during the New Deal realignment. However, since during more than two-thirds of this period the Speaker had the power to appoint committees, this difference in turnover can be readily accounted for by internal structural factors. Turnover on the committee brought about by electoral results appears to bring about the most dramatic changes in partisanship and in expenditures.

The 1902–15 period is characterized by relatively high partisan voting, but the average increase in appropriations is only 7.6 percent. The 1916–32 and 1940–49 periods have the lowest turnover, the lowest levels of partisan voting, and average increases in appropriations below 10 percent, a figure commonly used to define incrementalism.

These results show that nonincremental money decisions are related to electoral turnover and partisan voting. In terms of the theory offered here, the results are compatible with social-choice theory regarding policy equilibrium. Kenneth Shepsle argues that members seeking committee assignments are revealing preferences in the committees they select.[21] Thus he claims that "an election that 'shocks' the structure" of the previous House's committee has important consequences. The consequences result in part because "one of the benefits of committee membership is the monopoly control, shared with other committee members, over the agenda and deliberations in a particular policy jurisdiction. Monopoly 'rents' are earned by committee members; members capitalize these rents; that is, convert them into general institutional influence, by engaging in quid pro quo behavior that is common in congressional life."[22] Under normal conditions members of committees, especially the more important committees, guard the permeability of their "rents" by getting the new members' consent in regard to how things are done: "consent must be obtained before anything gets done." During critical periods the election results in a high turnover of members, shifts in preferences, and a drastic increase in committee permeability. When there is such a "large committee turnover . . . then the consent must be obtained before anything is done premise no longer applies."[23] In sum the combined effect of the "electoral shock" is to restructure the committee system in such a way that a new policy equilibrium can be obtained.

★ The Agriculture Committee

The results for appropriating committees corroborate the results for the House as a whole. However, these results do not portray in detail what one means by structural change, and the details of such change are important. In order to demonstrate the effect of structural change I turn to an analysis of the House Agriculture Committee during the 1890's and New Deal realignments. In the first period, I shall argue, the structure of the committee was changed in 1880, when the House granted Agriculture the right to appropriate independent of the Appropriations Committee. With this structural shift in place, the downturn in the farm economy and the turnover on the committee generated by the critical elections caused a rise in agricultural appropriations in the 1897–1901 period. In short, the argument is that the specific changes associated with the critical period were in part exogenously driven by the shift in farmers' economic fortunes.

In the New Deal era, I shall argue, the Agriculture Committee was presented with a serious structural problem with the passage of the Agricultural Adjustment Act. Specifically, the committee could not apportion the monies appropriated in the AAA until it had institutionalized a system of commodity subcommittees that could logroll price supports and other programs. This is, of course, in contrast to the 1890's example, where the structural shift preceded the appropriations increase.

First a word on the developments in the appropriating process from the inception of the Appropriations Committee after the Civil War. In 1867, with the government saddled with a high national debt and running huge deficits, the House created a committee with jurisdiction over all fiscal matters and an admonition to guard the Treasury. The new committee took its role seriously. From 1867 to 1879 the mean change in the budget was −0.21 percent. Meanwhile, in 1876 the House vested even more power in the committee by passing the Holman Rule, which allowed the committee to reduce departmental expenditures by cutting positions and salaries. Decreased expenditures over the 1867–79 period and the industrialization of the economy generated government surpluses and, by 1880, a greatly reduced national debt.

The committee's reward was a loss of power. In 1881 the 46th House, in a major revision of its rules, accorded the Agriculture Committee the right to appropriate monies on its own. The debate centered on two factors. First, members favoring the change felt that agriculture was underfunded. Second, they contended that the underfunding was due to the excessive power vested in the Appropriations Committee. As Representative William H. Calkins (R–Ind.) noted: "The fact is, this is simply a fight for power. . . . The ground of complaint is the immense power that the [Appropriations] committee now wields in this House. . . . Two hundred and seventy men are now under the guardianship of fifteen."[24]

The 46th House also granted the Commerce Committee the right to appropriate funds for rivers and harbors legislation; proposals from five other standing committees seeking the appropriations privilege were denied. But in 1885 the 49th House extended the privilege to five other committees, with the result that by 1887 Appropriations controlled only about half the budget. These decentralizing reforms generated increased expenditures by the seven committees directly appropriating funds for the departments and agencies under their jurisdiction. In sum, the exogenous demand for increased expenditures was accommodated by a structural change in the House's committee system.

After an initial jump, the year-to-year shifts in agricultural appropriations decreased. None of the 1892–96 budgets ever increased more than 3 percent; two actually decreased. The 1898–1900 budgets are the ones most likely to have been affected by the critical elections of 1894 and 1896. The story is as follows. The Panic of 1893 had caused a drastic drop in agricultural prices. In 1888 the December 1 price for a bushel of wheat was slightly over 90 cents; by 1894 the price had fallen to 30 cents. Oat prices fell from 42 cents a bushel in 1890 to 18 cents by 1896. The decline in agricultural prices led to increased political activity on the part of farmers, as the rise of the Populist and Anti-Monopoly political parties attests. The elections of 1894 and 1896 caused a complete turnover on the Agriculture Committee (Table 3.7), and the new members responded by increasing the agricultural appropriation. The response was delayed, however, until the full effects of the electoral change were evident—that is, until the Republican Party controlled the House, Senate, and Presidency. The full complement met on the budget for the first time in December 1897; thus the effect can only be seen in the 1898 budget figures. The budgets under the control of the 55th and 56th Houses (1897–1901) were the 1898, 1899, 1900, and 1901 budgets, and each provided for a minimum increase of over 7 percent in agricultural appropriations; two gave increases of 10 percent or more. Figure 5.3 shows the appropriations for agriculture over the 1891–1900 period.

The argument is that the upward shift in agricultural appropriations from 1898 to 1901 was the result of the committee turnover gen-

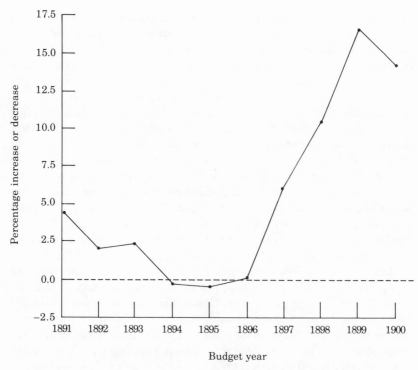

Fig. 5.3. Percentage changes in agricultural appropriations by budget year, 1891–1900

erated by the election results. The structure to increase appropriations had been in place since 1881; what was necessary was for the
preference shifts to be translated into electoral results. The increases
in that period are all the more impressive considering that the Republicans had won the elections. It was, after all, the Democrats
who adopted the pro-farmer Populist Party propositions in their 1896
platforms. Moreover, the Republicans overrepresented Northern industrial interests, the Democrats rural Southern and Western interests. In one sense the Republican coalition was capable of ignoring
farm interests. It did not do so at least in part because the new Republican members of the policy-making committee represented farm interests and favored increased appropriations. Interestingly, in two of
these four budgets the increase in agricultural funding was greater
than the overall budget increase. In short, if a committee has a jurisdictional monopoly and there is an influx of new members preferring
higher expenditures, they have the ability to increase expenditures
even under conditions where the dominant party could afford (electorally) to ignore or downplay the request for additional expenditures.

Some economic models assume that institutional structure is irrelevant; thus they would argue that the structural change that decentralized appropriations power was irrelevant or inconsequential. That is, a majority must have favored increased agricultural expenditures and, given this, expenditures would have risen regardless of the specific structural change actually made. The change could have come, for example, through new appointments to the Appropriations Committee or on the final floor vote. The specifics are irrelevant; what matters is that if a majority wishes to shift policy, it can do so regardless of structural arrangements.

It is, of course, difficult to counter such an argument without the capacity to replay history under different arrangements. Nevertheless, the structure-is-unimportant argument seems flawed in several ways. If the majority of the Appropriations Committee clearly favored funding at a lower rate, then finding a coalition to shift the decisions toward greater expenditures would have been extremely difficult, and replacing them *en bloc* impossible, since the committee members all had power bases that got them appointed to the committee in the first place. Given the Appropriations Committee's ability to delay and derail individual bills by parliamentary maneuvers, circumventing its decisions on the floor was not an option. The committee could and did keep bills off the floor, thus barring any appropriation at all in certain years. Given these difficulties, creating "new" appropriations committees was an extremely rational way to proceed. The Agriculture Committee had already revealed a preference for greater expenditures; empowering it to appropriate assured the desired policy result. If my claim is incorrect, then one might ask why, in the 46th House, the seven committees seeking the power to appropriate did not band together and seek an up-or-down vote for all their requests at the same time. Rather, the procedure was that each interest came separately to the floor for approval, and only Agriculture and Commerce won the right to appropriate. Obviously, in 1881 there was no majority for a complete stripping of Appropriations' power; rather, solutions were policy-specific.

Another reason to discount the structure-is-unimportant argument is that the flow of events was reversed in the New Deal period. As we have seen, in 1933–37 the House passed a large increase in the agricultural appropriation, and the committee had to create an after-the-fact structure that would allow it to divide the increased monies among the relevant commodity interests. Thus we turn to an explication of agricultural appropriations during the New Deal period.

Immediately after World War I the U.S. farm economy was plunged into recession. During the war the Allies' need for foodstuffs and American requirements for mobilization were such that production and services had expanded concomitantly, and the value of farmland and agricultural prices had risen sharply. The drop in farm prices after the war left farmers overextended in debt, taxation, and acreage. The weak export market, postwar deflation, and declining crop prices resulted in a depression. In 1919 annual farm income averaged $1,395.00; by 1921 it had fallen to $517.00. Aggregate farm debt was about $3.8 billion in 1918; by 1922 it exceeded $7 billion (in constant dollars).

All this generated pressure on Congress to shore up the farm economy. The main thrust of this pressure was toward three new policy preferences: to develop cooperative marketing programs, to raise the prices of agricultural products through government action, and to expand farm credit facilities. One important organizational development during this era was the formation, in 1920, of the American Farm Bureau Federation (AFBF), headquartered in Washington. Under its leadership, congressmen from rural districts established a caucus headed by the Republican L. J. Dickinson of Iowa. This caucus worked to organize a bipartisan pro-farm movement in both House and Senate, while the other half of the so-called Farm Bloc, the AFBF, conducted and tabulated local farm bureau referenda by congressional district and used the results to pressure congressmen into supporting pro-farm legislation. This organizational arrangement enjoyed the support of other farm groups as well as the Secretary of Agriculture. The Farm Bloc was given credit for passing the Packers and Stockyards Act of 1921, the Emergency Tariff of 1921, and the Capper-Volstead Act of 1922, among other bills. By 1924, however, prices in some commodities (e.g. cotton) had risen so much that bipartisan, cross-commodity action had become impossible.

Interest groups and congressmen representing commodities that were still depressed began to push programs that would increase prices, arguing that farmers were not fully sharing in America's prosperity. The core of these suggested policy shifts can be found by looking at a history of the McNary-Haugen agricultural subsidy bills considered by the House between 1924 and 1928.[25] For our purposes the dilemma was that the policy was driven by commodity differences, witness the fact that McNary-Haugen could not be passed until representatives of disparate agriculture interests came together to support it. The first bill died when cotton and dairy interests opposed it because it favored the wheat producers of the North Central states. Subsequent reintroductions of the bill featured the active participation of groups such as the American Council of Agriculture, the Corn Belt Committee, and the Committee of Twenty-Two. A form of the bill was passed twice in the 69th House (1925–27), when cotton and tobacco interests were added to the coalition. President Coolidge vetoed the bill both times. Hoover, too, adamantly opposed McNary-Haugen, preferring instead tariffs and cooperative marketing solutions.

The shift from subsistence and small cash-crop agriculture to agriculture as a commodity-based business generated shifts in preferences. The major indicators of shifting preferences were increases in commodity-based farm interest groups and Agriculture Committee hearings focusing on commodity problems. Nancy Kursman shows at least a fourfold increase in commodity-based farm groups between 1915 and 1930 and a similar fourfold rise in committee hearings on commodity-based problems from 1920 to 1930.

The Great Depression exacerbated the farm problem. Prices for farm products fell dramatically, and farm foreclosures rose from 17 per 1,000 in 1927–30 to 30 per 1,000 in 1932–33. The immediate response of the Roosevelt administration was to pass the Agricultural Adjustment Act of 1933. This legislation was an emergency relief program. The thrust of the original AAA was based on the McNary-Haugen principle of price supports and parity that would give farmers purchasing power equivalent to their purchasing power in the 1909–14 base period. The act featured production controls for basic commodities in exchange for cash benefit payments. Unlike the 1920's legislation, the 1933 AAA was originated not by farm pressure groups working through the House, but by the executive branch. The same was true of other early New Deal agricultural legislation, such as the Emergency Farm Mortgage Act and the Farm Credit Act. In fact, the AAA appropriation appeared in the executive budget, not the congressional budget.

But whatever the initial intentions of the executive branch in passing the 1933 AAA, events soon changed them. In 1936 the Supreme Court declared the processing-tax section of the bill unconstitutional. Congress, meanwhile, in an attempt to maintain continuity of aid, had passed stopgap legislation such as the Soil Conservation and Domestic Allotment acts. In the course of this effort, policy shifted from farm prices to the maintenance of farm income. Rather than accept a tax on processors, the Congress was to fund commodity subsidies. In short, from 1933 to 1938, policy shifted from emergency legislation to long-term policies featuring price subsidies, crop insurance, farm loans, and marketing quotas.

The President had given agricultural appropriations a large early boost with the AAA. The depression had resulted in a shift of preferences, and the massive turnover in the House yielded an agricultural policy designed to ameliorate the effects of the depression. However, this shift had been achieved without any restructuring of the Agriculture Committee. Turnover on the committee was great—85.7 percent from 1930 to 1933—but the legislation was executive and emergency-oriented, not congressional and maintaining. Given the commodity-based nature of the funding, the Agriculture Committee's problem was how to divide the increased appropriations in a way that would generate continuing support for agricultural income supports. The greatest challenge was to structure the committee to present a united front. The committee responded by establishing commodity-based subcommittees, thus institutionalizing the pork-barrel nature of agricultural politics that Charles O. Jones has detailed.[26] Kursman tells us how great were the exogenous pressures put on the committee, documenting a full 60 percent increase in commodity-based lobbies from 1932 to 1940.[27]

Before 1933 only the full committee held hearings; there were no permanent subcommittees. In the 73rd and subsequent Houses the committee was divided into formal subcommittees. From 1902 to the mid-1920's the Agriculture Committee's chairman had run commodity hearings; the new arrangement featured relatively permanent subcommittee chairs. In 1937 subcommittees were numbered and made permanent (some 20 years later, the 84th House established standing, named subcommittees). Some of the commodity-based subcommittees with their committee numbering scheme in the 74th House were (2) Potatoes under AAA, (3) Oleomargarine, (4) Wheat, (6) Cotton, (7) Tobacco, and (8) Rice. Standing subcommittees of the 75th House included (1) Commodities under AAA, (2) Sugar, (3) Dairy and Insurance, and (5) Surplus Commodities.

The subcommittees early recognized that in order to perpetuate and maintain the farm program, they would have to hold regular meetings on price supports. By 1936 such meetings were routine, with members of each subcommittee prepared to protect their interests. The debate over the 1938 AAA shows how the process worked. Representative Gerald J. Boileau (R–Wis.) stated: "The gentleman knows that the Committee on Agriculture was broken up into subcommittees to consider various phases of this bill. I happen to be on the subcom-

mittee considering milk and dairying, and that is what I am protecting."[28] Thus, the House Agriculture Committee restructured itself
over the 1933–38 period in response to the emergency passage of the
1933 AAA. The passage of the 1938 AAA meant that the committee,
through its subcommittees, controlled commodity subsidies; and the
budget line was transferred from the executive to the congressional
budget.

In order to test whether or not the shift to this new structural arrangement resulted in a new policy equilibrium, a piecewise dummy
regression with known joint points was run on agricultural appropriations.[29] This technique was used because it tells us whether or not a
new policy system resulted from the structural changes set in motion
by the 1938 AAA. Richard Quandt devised this technique to determine systemic changes in the economy when the only data one had
were known points measured as 0 or 1.[30] Thus the model identifies
period-specific slopes and intercepts. To correct for years of inflation
and deflation, the total amount appropriated for agriculture was adjusted for the price deflator for each year from 1916 to 1950. Using
these figures the absolute levels of change in agricultural appropriations from one budget year to the next were calculated and run as the
dependent variable. The equation is:

$$yt = b_1 x_1 t + b_2 x_2 t + b_3 x_3 t + b_4 x_4 t + e$$

where

yt = absolute change in yearly appropriations
x_1 = a dichotomous variable with 1 for every year from 1916 to
       1937 and 0 for every year from 1938 to 1950
x_2 = a counter for the years 1916 to 1950
x_3 = a dichotomous variable with 1 for every year from 1938 to
       1950 and 0 for every year from 1916 to 1937
x_4 = a counter for the years 1938 to 1950
e = error term

The model was estimated by a first-order autoregressive model in
which $y = xb + e$ and $e = pe(t-1) + u$, where p is the autoregressive pa-
rameter rho and u is an independent disturbance. Rho was estimated
with a least-squares procedure, and to correct for autocorrelation a
Cochrane-Orcutt iterative procedure was used.[31] The expectation is
that the intercept for the 1938–50 period will be significant. In addition the slope for the 1916–37 period may be significant, given the
success of the Farm Bloc. Table 5.2 shows the results.

The results confirm the hypothesis. The intercept for the subcom-

TABLE 5.2

*Piecewise Regression for the Structural Shift in the
Agriculture Committee*

Variable	Coefficient	Significance
x_1: intercept 1916	.041	insignificant
x_2: slope 1916–37	.406	significant .05
x_3: intercept 1937	.472	significant .05
x_4: slope 1938–50	−.023	insignificant

NOTE: r square = .45. Durbin Watson 1.97.

mittee system inaugurated in the 1933–37 period and the passage of the 1938 AAA shows a significant upward and permanent shift in the appropriations for agriculture. The slope for the 1916–37 period is also significant. This result is not surprising given the early success of the Farm Bloc. In fact, changing the starting date to 1921 and rerunning the analysis yields an increase in the value of the slope coefficient. Figure 5.4 shows the agricultural appropriations by year for 1921–50. (Observe that the scale for 1921–34 rises to only $250 million, which is close to the bottom of the scale for 1935–50.) The figure clearly shows a steady increase in appropriations from 1922 to 1933, and further increases from 1935 to 1939. The jump from slightly less than $200 million in 1936 to over $1 billion by 1939 shows the systemic difference.

The period from 1942 to 1950 shows a steady state at around $600 million. Thus the results from the piecewise regression make sense: a significant slope change in the 1916–37 period and a significant intercept change for the 1938 AAA. The passage of the 1933 AAA failed to resolve the farm issue for the House in the following ways: (1) the decision was essentially made not there, but in the executive branch; (2) the bill was viewed as an emergency act; (3) the policy was based on processing taxes, not on permanent subsidies; and (4) the commodity subsidies were not finalized. Between 1933 and 1937 the House resolved these difficulties by forming commodity-based subcommittees to divide the benefits. Through these subcommittees the Agriculture Committee built itself a unified coalition, and it used the coalition to convert the policy from a temporary solution to a permanent one, transferring the line from the executive to the congressional budget. The result was, of course, higher expenditures for agriculture and a new policy equilibrium. Surely the committee's choice to restructure itself into commodity subcommittees influenced both the policy process and the policy outputs.

In general these results show that both the endogenous structure

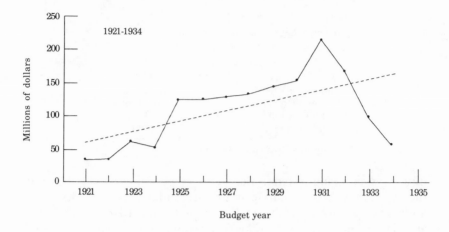

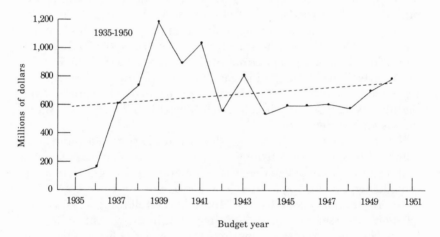

Fig. 5.4. Agricultural appropriations by budget year, 1921–1950

of the House and exogenous economic and electoral forces affected the shape of the agricultural budget. The upward shift in agricultural appropriations in 1897–1901 was largely the result of the electoral consequences of the Panic of 1893 and the decentralized structure of the Appropriations Committee. The upward shift in agricultural appropriations in 1938 was largely the result of the Agriculture Committee's restructuring into subcommittees, which balanced commodity interests and facilitated coalition building, and, of course, the electoral results associated with the Great Depression.

The party voting scores for the passage of the AAA of 1938 were heavily partisan. Although I cannot report the votes in the Agriculture Committee, since they were not recorded, congressional voting on agricultural assistance legislation was clearly structured by party throughout the New Deal era. The correlations between party identification and favorable votes in this domain are as follows: 1933–35 (73rd House), 0.90; 1935–37 (74th House), 0.91, and 1937–39 (75th House), 0.77. The lower correlation between party and voting in the 75th House came about when some Republicans from rural areas began supporting some agricultural assistance programs. Members of the House Agriculture Committee were separated out, and the same correlations were run; this analysis showed no significant differences save the slightly higher pro-support scores for Republicans on the committee. Nevertheless, agricultural assistance programs, including the AAA, were voted in by Democrats over solid Republican opposition. Thus, as was the case for the earlier appropriating committees, partisanship rose during periods of policy shifts.

Studies of other committees' activities during critical periods would surely reveal different structural arrangements, depending on members' motivations and committee constituencies. Such analyses will have to be done by other researchers. For my part, I will simply conclude that at least for appropriations and agricultural policy, both electoral and structural factors contributed to changes in policy equilibrium.

CHAPTER SIX

Competitive Party Systems and the Votes-to-Seats Ratio

★ WITH THE PUBLICATION of the important 1980 Clubb-Flanigan-Zingale work, *Partisan Realignment: Voters, Parties, and Government in American History*, students of American realignments began to focus on endogenous variables to account for policy shifts. This was in part because neither the Civil War nor the 1890's realignment represented an impressive shift of voters. As the authors said, with respect to the Civil War: "Electoral change during these years seems to be largely interpretable in terms of Southern secession, occupation and Reconstruction." And with respect to the 1890's: "Here again . . . while indications of lasting electoral change are clear, the realignment of 1896 appears substantially less impressive than might have been expected."[1] Thus far we have seen how electoral results in each of these eras produced turnover in the House and consequently disrupted the continuity and structure of House committees, thus enabling the dominant congressional party to shift the policy equilibrium. Yet it is important to recognize that this model of policy change is electorally driven.

In each of the three critical periods under study, the election resulted in a new and dominant House majority party, which also controlled the Senate and the Presidency for at least a decade. This extended electoral control has been shown in the Civil War and 1890's periods to be tied to the votes-to-seats relationship. Neither of these critical periods generated an electoral shift as impressive as that of the New Deal era. Both the Civil War and 1890's critical eras were compensating in nature, with electoral gains for the Republicans in the North offset by gains for Democrats in the Southern and Border states. In both periods relatively minor shifts in votes resulted in extensive and lasting gains in House seats for the Republicans. A partial explanation for these gains in seats is that the votes-to-seats ratio favored Republicans, particularly in the North. It has been shown that the Republicans benefited more than the Cube Law predicts.

In this chapter the nature of the votes-to-seats ratio during critical periods is examined. We begin with a discussion of seats, votes, and the spatial organization of elections. After discussing the effect of single-seat, plurality-winner electoral arrangements on votes-to-seats ratios, we will examine the constituency party distribution (CPD) for each critical period. In addition, the analysis isolates those congressional districts that accounted for the Republican majorities in the Civil War and 1890's eras. We conclude with an explanation of how relatively minor vote swings can result in significant and lasting seat swings.

The Cube Law relationship between votes and seats is based on the assumption that the CPD is normally distributed, with a mean of 50 percent and a narrow range of observed values. G. Gudgin and R. J. Taylor describe the phenomenon as follows: "It is the existence of the normal CPD, and in particular the narrow range of observed values for the standard deviation which are important [for understanding the Cube Law]."[2] When the two-party vote is normally distributed, in the familiar bell curve, and the standard deviation is limited, the relationship between votes and seats is expressed by the power curve shown in Figure 6.1. When the CPD is normal and the Cube Law applies, then for every increase of 1 percent in the vote over 50 percent, there is a 3 percent rise in the number of seats won; thus the name Cube Law. It is obvious that to the extent that the conditions of a normal distribution and limited variance are violated, the power curve will vary from the Cube Law curve.

The two dominant statistical properties of a CPD that affect the votes-to-seats ratio are skewness and kurtosis. The asymmetry of a frequency distribution is measured by its *skewness*. The skewness measure (B_1) is based on the third moment about the mean on the formula

$$B_1 = \sum \frac{(V_1 - \bar{V})^3}{\sigma}.$$

$B_1 = 0$ when the distribution is symmetric (including the normal curve). If $B_1 > 0$ (positive), then the mode is to the left of the mean; if $B_1 < 0$ and negative, the mode is to the right of the mean. If the mean vote is around 50 percent, a slight positive skewness means a large number of votes are wasted in marginal constituencies, and a negative skewness indicates efficient voting—or few votes wasted. Figure 6.2 shows the effects of positive and negative skewness. In the case of positive skewness, large numbers of wasted votes are found in the high tail.

Kurtosis is a general measure of the shape of a distribution in terms

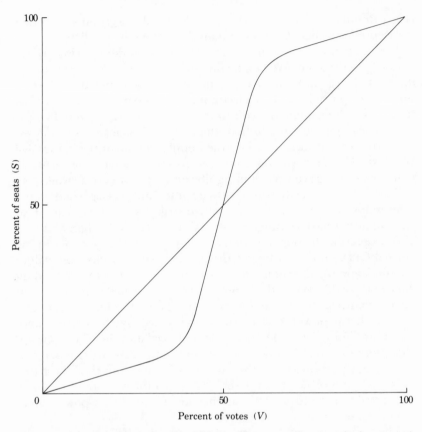

Fig. 6.1. Cube Law power curve. The Cube Law is expressed as $S = V^3/V^3 + (1 - V)^3$.

of peakedness through flatness to a U-shaped distribution. Kurtosis (B_2) is defined as:

$$B_2 = \left[\sum \frac{(V_i - \bar{V})^4}{\sigma^2} \right] - 3.$$

A normal distribution has a value of 0, $B_2 = 0$. When the distribution is more peaked than normal and has compensating thick tails, $B_2 > 0$, and the distribution is *leptokurtic*. When the distribution is flatter than normal and has deficiencies in the tails, it is *platykurtic* and $0 > B_2$. Thus, kurtosis is a measure of the pattern of a distribution about its mean that is independent of variance.*

---

*Technically, kurtosis measures the thickness of the tails of a distribution. In the case of a well-behaved curve, kurtosis gives a good estimate of the peakedness of a distribution. The results shown in this chapter measure the shape of the curves around 50 percent. The number of competitive seats is included to demonstrate this point.

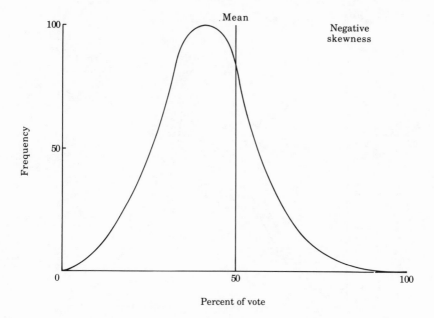

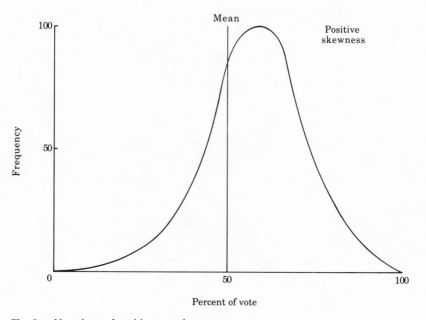

Fig. 6.2. Negative and positive vote skewness

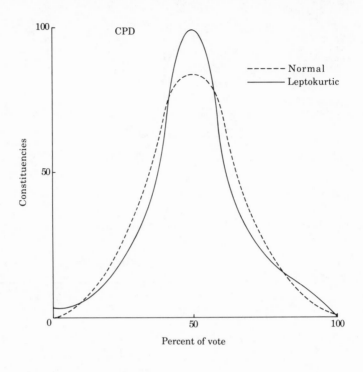

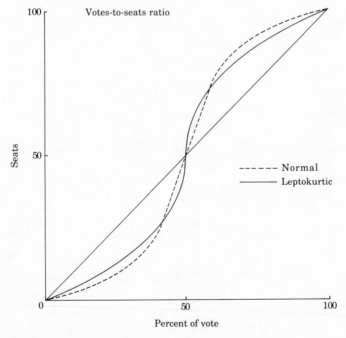

Fig. 6.3. Effect of leptokurtic CPD on votes-to-seats ratio

The level of kurtosis in a CPD measures the level of party competition because it concerns the central portion of the CPD where seats change hands. The higher the value of kurtosis (positive $B_2 > 0$), the greater the number of competitive seats. Since the number of competitive seats directly affects the votes-to-seats ratio, the kurtosis of a CPD is related to the votes-seats curve. Gudgin and Taylor show that kurtosis is much like variance in its effects on electoral stability.[3] Consider, for example, two CPDs with the same variance, where one curve is leptokurtic and the other normal. In this case the leptokurtic distribution will have more competitive seats and will produce a votes-to-seats relationship equivalent to a normal distribution with compact variance. Platykurtosis will have the opposite effect. As indicated in Figure 6.3, the leptokurtic curve translates into a steeper votes-to-seats power curve at the 50 percent point.

In the platykurtic case, the most obvious application for our purposes occurs when each party has a large number of safe seats; thus the distribution has two modes toward each end of the distribution and a relatively flat center where seats might change hands. Gudgin and Taylor correctly point out that for such platykurtic curves, "All such distributions (including that of the U.S.A.) cannot be modeled adequately by power laws."[4] In this case the votes-to-seats relationship must be taken directly from the CPDs themselves. Since the purpose here is to show how the CPD changes over time, and what the specific relationship is between CPDs and seats, it is not necessary to pursue the specifics of modeling a power curve for platykurtic distributions. In sum, the skewness and kurtosis of CPDs in first-past-the-post systems can be used to describe how during the Civil War and 1890's critical periods, minor vote shifts produced relatively permanent seat shifts to the Republican Party.

The argument is that before the Civil War and 1890's critical elections, the party system should be characterized by a large number of competitive seats. The CPDs should have positive kurtoses ($B_2 > 0 =$ leptokurtic) before the elections, and during the critical period the kurtosis figures should decrease, since many of the competitive seats will have been shifted into safer seats. The Republican Party CPDs should be skewed negatively ($B_1 < 0$), giving the party an advantage over the Democrats in seats won: a negative skewness, as noted, implies more efficient voting. The period following the critical election should be characterized by relatively lower Republican kurtosis figures and continued efficiency in Republican voting (negative skews). Once we have demonstrated the above, we turn to an analysis of where the Republicans attained their fourteen-year majorities in the House.

★ Constituency Party Distributions in the Three Periods

The first characteristic of the distribution of seats worth exploring is the actual percentage of House seats where a switch of 5 percent of the vote would have changed the party representing the district. Tables 6.1 and 6.2 show the percentage of competitive House seats and the corresponding kurtosis figures; Figures 6.4 and 6.5 show the same results graphically.

The results for the Civil War era (Table 6.1) show a drop in the number of competitive seats, beginning in 1854. The figure falls below 40 percent and stays there until the very competitive election of 1862. The 1864 and 1866 elections have fewer competitive districts, but then, in 1868, as Southern states begin to be readmitted to the Union, the figure rises once more, to remain above 40 percent through the 1874 elections. The kurtosis figure drops to 0.6 in 1854 and then is 2.0 or more for the next two elections. In the controlling election for the Republicans, 1860, the kurtosis drops to 1.6. As expected, the competitive election of 1862 drives the kurtosis figure up, but in the next three elections the figure remains below 2.0. The readmission of the Southern states restores a competitive two-party system, as indicated by the high kurtosis figures. Figure 6.4 graphically tells much the same story. Clearly, the election of 1854 shows a shift away from the Democrats, as evidenced by the leftward shift in the curve. Elections from 1856 to 1862 show a slightly more competitive system, but the left tails of these curves remain higher than the Democratic gains on the far right. After a considerable increase in Republican safe seats (a leftward shift) in 1864 and 1866, the Democrats made

TABLE 6.1

Competitive Districts and Kurtosis for Democratic CPDs, 1850–1874

Election year	Competitive districts (percent of total)	Kurtosis (B_2)	Election year	Competitive districts (percent of total)	Kurtosis (B_2)
1850	59.4%	2.5	1864	32.0%	1.2
1852	48.1	1.4	1866	35.3	1.4
1854	30.4	0.6	1868	41.0	1.6
1856	37.4	2.6	1870	42.1	2.8
1858	37.8	2.0	1872	40.6	2.5
1860	39.2	1.6	1874	40.1	2.9
1862	40.7	2.8			

NOTE: In this and the following tables, a competitive district is one where a switch of 5% of the vote would have swung the district from one party to the other. The higher the B_2 figure, the greater the number of competitive seats.

TABLE 6.2

Competitive Districts and Kurtosis for Democratic CPDs, 1884–1910

Election year	Competitive districts (percent of total)	Kurtosis (B_2)	Election year	Competitive districts (percent of total)	Kurtosis (B_2)
1884	40.5%	2.2	1898	33.0%	1.0
1886	37.8	0.6	1900	29.7	1.0
1888	43.1	2.7	1902	24.3	0.1
1890	41.9	1.0	1904	18.0	0.1
1892	34.0	3.2	1906	23.6	0.0
1894	23.2	1.6	1908	27.0	0.5
1896	34.5	1.6	1910	36.3	0.3

good some of their losses in subsequent years, and by 1874, as indicated by the rightward shift, they have more safe seats than the Republicans. And, of course, it is in 1874 that the Democrats had their first House majority since 1858. While the end points of the graph show seats won or lost by 25 percent or more (aggregated), the kurtosis figures in the tables are for actual values (not aggregated). Thus the graphs help illuminate how the thicker tails of a leptokurtic curve indicate increases in safe seats.

Table 6.2 shows that, in the 1890's era, the number of competitive seats falls sharply in 1892 and again in 1894. The number of competitive seats declines from 1896 until 1902 and then begins to rise in 1906 until it reaches 36.3 in 1910. The kurtosis figures are, in general, higher in the precritical period (1884–92) than they are in the critical period. The period following the 1896 election is clearly less leptokurtic than the two preceding periods. Figure 6.4 shows these results in graphic form. The 1894 election dramatically shifts the curve leftward, and this Republican bias continues until 1910, when the Democrats regained the House for the first time since 1892.

Thus, in both the Civil War and the 1890's, a pattern of decreases in the number of competitive seats and corresponding decreases in kurtosis is observed. Still, it has not been shown how this favored the Republicans. To do so, it is necessary to show that the Republican CPDs are more negatively skewed—more efficient voting—than the Democratic CPDs in the Civil War and 1890's periods, and that this voting efficiency manifested itself in seats won in marginal districts. Tables 6.3 and 6.4 show the percentage of marginal seats won by Republicans in the respective periods and the skewness of both parties' CPDs.

As can be seen, in the Civil War era, the Republicans began to win more than 50 percent of the marginal seats in 1856 and continued to win heavily until 1874. The Republicans enjoyed more efficient voting

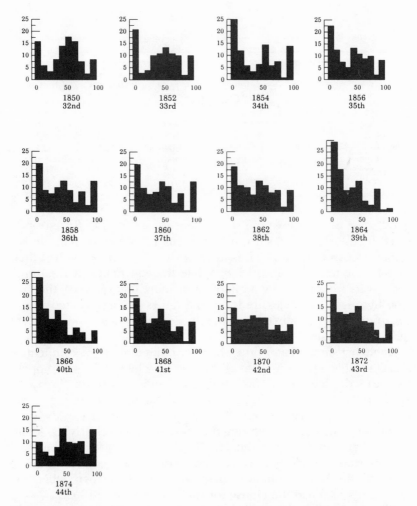

Fig. 6.4. Democratic CPDs, 1850–1876. In this and the analogous figures that follow, the years shown are election years. The y axis is percent of seats.

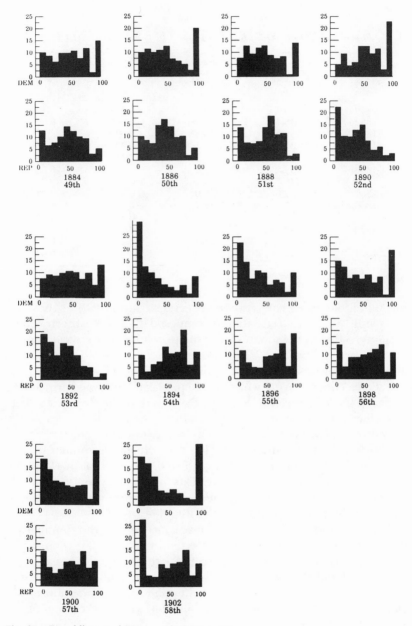

Fig. 6.5. Republican and Democratic CPDs, 1884–1902

TABLE 6.3

Percentage of Republican Wins and Skewness in Competitive Districts, 1850–1874

| Election year | Competitive districts | | Skewness | |
	Percent of total	Percent Republican wins	Republican	Democrat
1850	59.4%	40.1%[a]	−0.49[a]	0.13
1852	48.1	46.4[a]	−0.68[a]	0.04
1854	30.4	34.3[a]	−0.90[a]	0.37
1856	37.4	51.1	−0.99	0.73
1858	37.8	52.2	−1.31	1.26
1860	39.2	59.4	−1.02	0.56
1862	40.7	53.1	0.43	−0.81
1864	32.0	75.0	0.46	−1.01
1866	35.3	72.7	−0.46	0.27
1868	41.0	63.9	−0.34	0.07
1870	42.1	57.8	−0.79	0.69
1872	40.6	58.1	−0.85	0.13
1874	40.1	47.4	−1.19	0.44

[a] Figures are for non-Democrats.

during all but three congressional elections, and in two of those (in 1862 and 1864) the electorate was composed of only Northern voters. It is interesting to note that during the precritical and critical periods Republicans always had CPDs characterized by negative skewness, and the Democrats always had positive skewness. That is, in the 1850 to 1860 elections, during which the Republican Party was formed and replaced the Whigs as the Democrats' opposition, the Republican vote was efficiently distributed while the Democrats wasted votes in the right-hand tail of the distribution. Figure 6.2 shows how the mid-1850's elections shifted the curve to the left (i.e., created a number of safe seats for the Republicans). In sum, Table 6.3 shows that the Republicans won a majority of competitive seats in 1856 and continued to do so until the 1874 elections, and the skewness figures show a more efficient distribution of the vote for the Republicans.

Table 6.4 shows that in every House controlled by the Republicans (and they controlled all but those elected in 1884, 1886, 1890, 1892, and 1910), they won over 52 percent of the competitive seats, and in three of the five Houses they lost they were under 50 percent. Throughout the entire period the Republican vote was more efficiently distributed than the Democratic vote. Every skewness figure for the Republicans is negative, every skewness figure for the Democrats positive. Thus, as in the Civil War era, during the competitive precritical period when the Republicans won control of the House in 1888, they also won a majority of the competitive seats. Then, during

TABLE 6.4

Percentage of Republican Wins and Skewness in Competitive Districts, 1884–1910

Election year	Competitive districts		Skewness	
	Percent of total	Percent Republican wins	Republican	Democrat
1884	40.5%	50.7%	−0.53	1.28
1886	37.8	36.2	−0.64	1.24
1888	43.1	61.9	−1.00	1.43
1890	41.9	47.5	−0.40	1.20
1892	34.0	43.9	−1.07	1.28
1894	23.2	64.9	−0.80	0.70
1896	34.5	64.1	−0.40	0.97
1898	33.0	54.5	−0.55	1.03
1900	29.7	52.8	−0.87	1.05
1902	24.3	52.9	−0.59	0.42
1904	18.0	56.7	−0.77	0.63
1906	23.6	53.8	−0.59	0.54
1908	27.0	61.1	−1.01	0.89
1910	36.3	51.8	−0.59	0.56

the critical period, the number of competitive seats dropped, and in both 1894 and 1896 the Republicans won over 64 percent of the remaining marginal seats. The period of dominance was characterized by consistent Republican majorities in competitive seats.

In sum, in both the Civil War period and the 1890's, Republican majorities were created in part by their efficient voting distributions and their ability to win a majority of the competitive seats.

Although these data are suggestive, they are not definitive. To be totally persuasive, I need to show that the drop in the number of competitive seats during the critical election periods resulted from a long-lived shift to the Republican Party. Demonstrating that the shift of a relatively few voters could account for a major shift in seats entails an analysis of both competitive districts and the spatial configuration of voters.

The major factor accounting for particular distributions of CPDs is of course the spatial organization of voters. If voters are distributed equally across all districts, then the party with a mean above 50 percent will win all districts. Consider, for example, a three-district two-party system in which votes are distributed equally and one party has a mean of 52 percent (thus 52–48; 52–48; 52–48). In this case, clearly, one party wins all three seats. This, however, assumes zero variance, and as we know, that is not true of the distribution of the vote in American elections. Consider, then, these two variants of a three-district system: (1) 5–95; 75–25; 76–24; and (2) 48–52; 45–

TABLE 6.5

Mean Vote, Kurtosis, Skewness, and Competitive District Wins for Republican Party in Northern States, 1850–1874

Election year	Mean vote (percent)	Kurtosis (B_2)	Skewness (B_1)	Competitive districts	
				Percent of total	Percent Republican wins[a]
1850	46.9%	3.8	−0.41	58.2%	37.9%
1852	45.4	5.8	−0.13	51.1	35.2
1854	54.5	3.8	−0.83	32.9	58.9
1856	51.4	0.6	−0.20	37.3	55.0
1858	51.3	5.5	−1.86	48.4	64.3
1860	51.9	4.1	−1.58	45.6	58.8
1862	52.6	3.4	0.43	41.5	50.9
1864	58.8	1.8	0.46	34.5	71.0
1866	56.1	2.3	−0.47	37.7	69.5
1868	53.8	1.9	−0.34	40.3	64.0
1870	50.3	2.1	−0.57	47.1	62.8
1872	53.4	4.1	−1.14	40.8	60.8
1874	45.2	2.2	−1.38	45.1	47.3

[a] Non-Democratic parties.

55; 63–37. In both cases the first party's mean vote is 52 percent, but in example (1) it wins two seats, in (2) only one. The American electoral system, since at least the Civil War era, has been characterized by a regional-spatial configuration of party voters. That is, Democrats have been more concentrated in Southern and Border states, Republicans in Northern states. The analysis of the votes-to-seats ratio in both periods showed Republicans with a large advantage in Northern states. Thus it follows that the advantages to Republicans shown above, a negative skewness and leptokurtic distributions, should be even more pronounced if we control for region. If in fact the CPDs show the appropriate shapes, it will be clear that slight voter shifts can result in major seat shifts. In short, if it can be shown that Northern districts were extremely competitive prior to the critical elections, then it is clear that a slight shift toward the Republicans in the North could result in a pro-Republican (rightward) shift in the CPDs. This rightward shift to the Republicans can be the result of three factors: (1) the mean shift in the vote toward the Republicans reduces the number of competitive districts by increasing the number of safe Republican seats; (2) the mean shift does not significantly reduce the number of competitive seats but ensures that Republicans will win a majority of competitive seats; and (3) a combination of (1) and (2) such that Republicans increase their number of safe seats and win a majority of the competitive seats. Since Tables 6.1 and 6.2 showed that

TABLE 6.6

Mean Vote, Kurtosis, Skewness, and Competitive District Wins for Republican Party
in Northern States, 1884–1910

Election year	Mean vote (percent)	Kurtosis (B_2)	Skewness (B_1)	Competitive districts	
				Percent of total	Percent Republican wins
1884	50.8%	6.8	0.19	58.7%	51.5%
1886	49.2	6.4	−0.17	60.9	43.5
1888	50.5	6.0	0.31	58.9	60.9
1890	46.4	3.7	0.18	47.1	32.9
1892	46.8	2.5	0.38	51.2	32.6
1894	53.7	3.6	−0.26	45.2	52.4
1896	55.9	2.5	0.32	38.6	63.7
1898	52.2	3.5	0.48	46.2	59.1
1900	53.9	2.1	0.45	43.8	53.3
1902	51.6	4.4	−0.31	43.0	55.6
1904	57.1	2.0	0.51	33.2	55.6
1906	53.4	2.8	0.19	41.9	56.6
1908	52.9	4.0	−0.48	42.8	52.8
1910	47.9	5.2	−0.11	47.7	41.5

the decrease in competitive seats and the drop in the leptokurtosis of Republican CPDs was less pronounced in the Civil War era than in the 1890's, the expectation is that the Civil War period will be like (3) above, and the 1890's like (1).

To determine whether or not this is the case requires an analysis of the following data: (1) the levels of kurtosis found in the pre- and postcritical election period; (2) the shift in the mean vote toward the Republicans in the periods under consideration; (3) the percentage of Republican victories in competitive districts over the relevant time periods; and (4) the confluence of these trends (i.e., whether all of these relationships are more pronounced in the Northern states since this is where the Republicans' seat advantages were won). Tables 6.5 and 6.6 show the results. The figures for 1850–58 in Table 6.5 are for all non-Democratic candidates, and those for 1860–74 are for Republicans.

The 1854 election is the turning point in the anti-Democratic vote. In this election the mean non-Democratic vote goes over 50 percent and stays there until 1874. Until the 1862 election, with the exception of 1856, the kurtosis of the CPDs is quite high, almost twice as high as the figures for the whole country (Table 6.1). From 1864 until 1872 the peakness of the CPDs is reduced, largely as a result of the Republicans' electoral success during the Civil War. The number of competitive districts falls somewhat from 1860 through 1868, but less dramatically than in the 1890's. Thus there is reason to believe that the

Republicans' seat advantage resulted from the combination of an increase in safe seats and victories in competitive seats.

Throughout this period, but especially in the critical 1858 and 1860 elections, the Republican vote was more efficiently distributed—that is, negatively skewed. In regard to competitive seats, non-Democratic candidates won less than 40 percent until the 1854 election, at which point and continuing until 1874, the non-Democrats and then the Republicans won a majority of competitive seats. Interestingly, in the critical 1858 and 1860 elections, respectively, the Republicans won 64.3 and 58.8 percent of competitive seats. From 1864 until 1874 they never fell below the 60 percent level in competitive seats. It seems clear that the Republican control of the House from 1858 to 1874 rested on their control of competitive seats plus a shift of some seats from competitive to safe. In fact, from 1862 until 1874, Republicans controlled an average of 74.9 percent of the seats won by 25 percent of the vote or more. In the critical elections of 1858 and 1860 the Republicans won 58.8 and 58.6 percent of safe seats.

Figure 6.6 shows the Republican CPDs in a precritical, critical, and postcritical election, controlling for North-South differences. The 1850 graphs show a competitive system in both the North and the South, but especially the North. Those for 1860 show the rightward shift to the Republicans in the North, and the Democrats' position as *the* party in the South. And the 1870 graphs show that with the readmission of some Southern states, the Republicans, under Reconstruction, won some Southern seats, and maintained an advantage in the North.

Table 6.6 shows that from 1884 until 1894 there was a two-party competitive system in the North. The vote hovers around 50 percent, with the Republicans winning slim majorities twice and the Democrats winning three times. The 1894 election shifts the Republican mean vote to 53.7 percent, and until 1902 the Republicans retain their advantage. The kurtosis figures show a very peaked curve until the Democratic landslide of 1890; from 1892 until 1910, with the exception of 1902, the peakness of the curve is reduced. The 1890 Democratic landslide also marks a decline in the number of competitive seats, and from 1894 on, the number of competitive seats remains below 50 percent. The party wins in competitive seats flip-flop until 1894, with Democrats winning a majority of competitive seats three times in the five elections. Thereafter, the Republicans win the majority of competitive districts until the 1910 election. The skewness figures do not indicate any Republican advantage arising from efficient voting, although the figures are low enough to have little effect (i.e.,

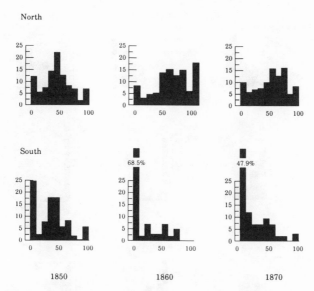

Fig. 6.6. Republican CPDs in three Civil War–era elections by region, 1850–1870. The 1850 distributions are for the Whig Party.

very little skew). Thus, as in the Civil War period, the Republicans' control of House seats was based on their ability to win majorities of competitive seats and increase the number of their safe seats. In fact, from 1894 to 1910 the Republicans controlled over 75 percent of safe Northern seats.

Figure 6.7 shows the Democratic and Republican CPDs in a precritical, critical, and postcritical election, controlling for North-South differences. The 1888 graphs show a two-party, competitive system in the North and Democratic dominance in the South. The 1896 graphs show the rightward shift to the Republicans in the North and the leftward shift to the Democrats in the South. And the 1900 graphs show the Republicans maintaining their advantage in the North, while the Democrats dominate a noncompetitive South.

The precritical periods in both the Civil War era and the 1890's were periods of intense two-party competition in the North, where control of the House shifted from party to party depending mostly on which party captured a majority of the competitive seats. The critical election or elections shifted the mean percentage of the vote to the Republicans, or against the Democrats. This shift gave the Republicans an increase in safe seats and a majority of the competitive seats until the 1874 and 1910 elections. In both cases the critical election results were obtainable given the competitive nature of the CPDs. In

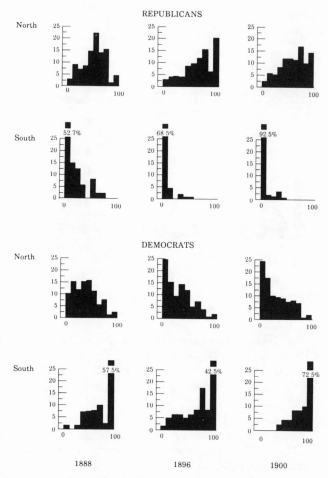

Fig. 6.7. Republican and Democratic CPDs in three 1890's-era elections by region, 1888–1900

short, the relatively minor vote shifts resulted in permanent seat shifts owing to the nature of the spatial distribution of the party vote. This is in contradistinction to the New Deal era, when the critical election was an across-the-board phenomenon. It is worthwhile to examine the difference, and I turn next to an analysis of the New Deal realignment.

From 1874, when the Democrats regained the House for the first time since 1858, until 1892 there was a substantial number of competitive districts. The ten House elections from 1874 to 1892 had an average of 39.4 percent competitive districts, and the average kurtosis was +2.3, which indicates the peakness of the distributions. In contrast, the elections from 1910 to 1930 had an average of only 21.6 percent competitive seats, and an average kurtosis of −.03. In fact, only the 1910, 1916, and 1920 elections had a positive kurtosis, the highest of which was 0.5. Thus the 1932 election took place in an electoral context characterized by relatively few competitive seats and many safe seats. The 1874–94 period had an average of just 27.8 percent safe seats per election, compared with 52.9 percent in 1910–30. Put another way, the shape of the CPDs had shifted from peaked to U-shaped. Figure 6.8 shows the distribution of the Democratic vote for 1924–40 and 1946, and clearly shows the U shape of the curve prior to the critical election of 1932.

The 1932 election was clearly an across-the-board realignment to the Democrats. That is, the Democrats gained in almost all districts. Since they had already dominated elections in the Southern states, we ought to see the greatest shift occurring in the North. Table 6.7 shows the mean Democratic vote, the skewness and kurtosis of the Demo-

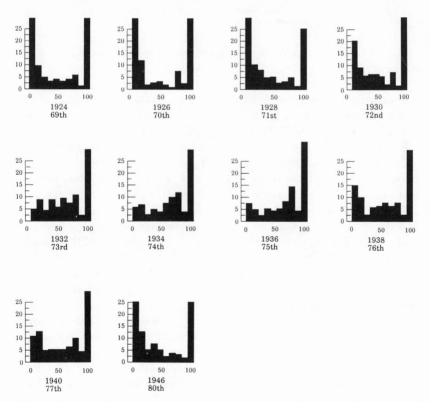

Fig. 6.8. Democratic CPDs, 1924–1946

TABLE 6.7

Mean Vote, Kurtosis, Skewness, and Competitive and Safe District Wins for Democratic Party in Northern States, 1924–1946

				Competitive seats		Safe seats[a]	
Election year	Mean vote (percent)	Kurtosis (B_2)	Skewness (B_1)	Percent of total	Percent Democrat wins	Percent of total	Percent Democrat wins
1924	41.6%	1.7	0.99	19.4%	48.4%	52.3%	18.7%
1926	44.8	1.2	0.92	14.7	38.1	53.8	25.1
1928	42.7	1.3	0.89	22.2	33.7	45.3	37.8
1930	48.4	0.7	0.63	25.8	37.6	44.9	43.0
1932	53.7	1.3	0.93	38.0	51.1	27.8	73.7
1934	54.3	1.3	0.68	36.0	64.7	28.6	73.4
1936	54.6	1.0	0.09	30.9	60.8	33.9	72.0
1938	49.7	1.1	0.34	30.9	54.7	37.7	47.8
1940	50.3	1.6	0.37	29.6	52.6	28.8	52.8
1942	46.7	1.5	0.40	24.0	45.0	42.1	37.6
1944	49.5	2.2	0.36	27.6	47.8	39.4	39.6
1946	44.3	2.9	0.97	24.0	32.5	45.6	24.3

[a] Won by a margin of 25 percent or more.

cratic CPD, and the percentages of competitive and safe seats in each election from 1924 to 1946 in the Northern states.

The results clearly show how the Democrats became the majority party during the New Deal era. Over 1924–30 their proportion of the House vote in Northern states rose from 41.6 percent to 48.4 percent, and from 1932 to 1938 they averaged 54 percent. The number of competitive seats rose by a factor of 2 between 1924 and 1932, from 19.4 percent to 38.0 percent. Before 1932 the Democrats never won a majority of competitive seats; in fact, with one exception they did not win even 40 percent of these seats. Thereafter they won the majority of competitive seats until the 1942 election. The number of safe seats was quite high over the 1924–30 elections, averaging 49.1 percent, and the Democrats won an average of only 31.2 percent of these seats. The number of safe seats dropped dramatically in the 1932 election, and in the 1932, 1934, and 1936 elections the Democrats won over 70 percent of them. Over the 1938 to 1946 period the number of safe seats increased, and until 1946 the Democrats held slightly less than 50 percent of these seats. In short, the 1932 election shifted the entire CPD curve to the right, increasing the number of competitive seats and the number of Democratic wins in these seats. The number of safe seats decreased, but it was Republican safe seats that were lost, while in contrast the Democrats held their existing safe seats and gained a few new ones.

Figure 6.9 shows the Democratic CPDs in a precritical, a critical, and a postcritical election, controlling for North-South differences. The picture clearly makes the point. In 1926 there are few competitive seats in the North, and the Republicans have a big advantage in safe seats. The 1932 election shifts the curve rightward in the Northern states and increases the number of safe Democratic seats. The 1938 election readjusts the curve leftward, increasing the number of safe Republican seats while leaving the Democrats with a sizable number of safe seats and a slight advantage in competitive seats. The House seats in the South curve shows no significant change during the period. In 1926 91.5 percent of all Southern seats were safely Democratic. This figure increases to over 95 percent in both 1932 and 1938, but does not affect the net number of Democratic seats in the House. The CPDs in Table 6.7 reflect first the decline of competitive seats prior to 1932, then from 1932 through 1938 the increase in the size of the tails (i.e., the increase in safe Democratic seats) and from 1940 through 1946 the increase in the number of competitive seats.

The New Deal critical elections were unlike those of the Civil War and 1890's because the election results were a noncompensating, across-the-board shift to the new majority party in the North. The South was heavily Democratic before 1932, and remained so during

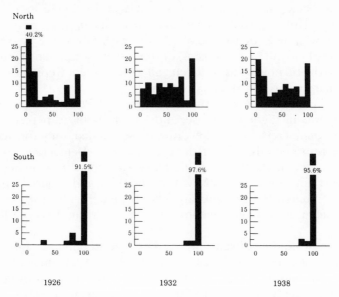

Fig. 6.9. Democratic CPDs in three New Deal–era elections by region, 1926–1938

and after the critical election. In contrast, the Civil War and 1890's periods did not shift the curve as dramatically rightward to the Republicans, and gains in Northern states were accompanied by losses in Southern states. Thus, there was nothing marginal about the Democratic win in the New Deal period. The across-the-board shift to the Democrats can easily be translated into their huge seat advantage in the House.

★ Spatial Changes in the Civil War and 1890's Eras

The analysis thus far has dealt only with election-by-election results. Let us now turn to an analysis of which regions and districts switched in the direction of the Republicans in the two non-across-the-board realignments, those of the Civil War and 1890's eras. The strategy is to present the results in three stages: the precritical period, the critical period, and the period of party control.

Chapter Two showed that during the Civil War period, the first major shift away from the Democrats occurred in the 1854 election in the Midwestern and Eastern states. The Republican Party was not the only beneficiary of the anti-Democratic vote in this election. The American, Free Soil, and Whig parties, in various degrees, benefited. The most dramatic shift to the Republican Party occurred in Illinois, Indiana, Maine, Michigan, Ohio, and Wisconsin. These states had a total of 54 House seats in the 33rd House (1853–55); 37, or about 69 percent, were held by Democrats. In the 34th House (1855–57) Republicans held 46, or 85 percent, of these seats, a dramatic turnover. In Ohio the turnover was complete: all 21 seats went Republican, and all by margins greater than 55 percent.

New York, New Jersey, Massachusetts, and Pennsylvania had 74 House seats in the 33rd House, and 44, or about 59 percent, were held by Democrats. When the 34th House opened, only fourteen of the 74 representatives from these states were Democrats. In New Jersey and Pennsylvania the Whig Party was the major beneficiary of the anti-Democratic vote; in New York the Whig and American parties and a combined Whig-American ticket benefited. The 1854 election in Massachusetts brought an entire slate of American Party candidates to office.

These two blocks of states were where the Republicans built their new majority. The first block remained Republican through 1860. The second moved toward the Republicans over the next three elections at a differential rate. In 1856 Massachusetts moved into the Republican column, electing Republicans for ten of its eleven seats. New

TABLE 6.8

Spatial Configurations of Republican Wins in the Civil War Realignment

(Percent)

Category	1846–52 elections	1854–58 elections	1860–74 elections	Difference over period
Midwest				
Competitive seats	80.0%	47.5%	53.6%	−26.4%
Republican share of all seats	35.2[a]	73.3	74.7	39.5
Republican safe seats[b]	3.8	44.7	34.9	31.1
Northeast				
Competitive seats	77.0%	50.9%	42.5%	34.5%
Republican share of all seats	45.3[a]	47.7	72.2	26.9
Republican safe seats[b]	10.8	22.5	42.5	31.7
All other non-Southern				
Competitive seats	54.7%	52.2%	31.5%	−23.2%
Republican share of all seats	50.5[a]	10.9	45.6	−4.9
Republican safe seats[b]	22.1	6.5	32.9	10.8

[a] Non-Democratic parties.
[b] "Safe seats" here and in Table 6.9 means wins by more than 55 percent of the vote.

York, with 33 seats, moved Republican in 1856, electing 21 Republicans, and then 29 in 1858. Pennsylvania did not move toward the Republicans until 1858, when it elected 21 Union (later Republican) Party members out of a 25-member delegation; and in 1860 Republicans captured 20 seats. Table 6.8 shows election patterns from 1846 to 1874 for these two blocks of states and all other non-Southern states. The percentages are based on the total number of contests within the block over the period. Safe seats here are defined as those won by more than 55 percent of the vote.

The results show a drop in the number of competitive seats from the precritical to the critical period and increases in both Republican victories and Republican safe seats. The Republicans control over 70 percent of Midwestern seats in the 1854–58 period and maintain that margin in the era of Republican control. In the Northeast the pattern develops more slowly. Republicans win only 47.7 percent of all seats in the 1854–58 period and then increase their share to over 70 percent in the era of Republican control. Although the other Northern states also show a decrease in competitive seats, the Democrats maintained majorities there through the 1858 election. In fact, the Republican vote decreases about 5 percent over the years 1846–74, and the increase in Republican safe seats is about one-third of that found for the Midwest and Northeast.

In regard to seats won by 10 percent or more during the all-important 1860–66 period, there were 66 seats that were Republican in all four elections; 20 were Midwestern, 42 Northeastern. Massachusetts and Maine were the most strongly Republican; all their House seats were filled by Republicans through the period, and over 90 percent of these victories were by 55 percent or more. Upstate New York had twelve relatively safe Republican seats; in these 48 elections (12 seats × 4 elections) only six were decided by a margin of less than 55 percent. Thus it is fair to conclude that the regions that brought the Republicans their majority sustained them during the Civil War elections.

This holds true throughout the period of Republican dominance. For example, of the 55 House seats that were filled by Republicans in every election from 1860 to 1874, sixteen were Midwestern, 37 Northeastern. Massachusetts, Maine, and upstate New York were the strongest Republican areas, contributing 26 of the 55 seats. In fact, from 1860 to 1874 the Massachusetts and Maine state delegations were entirely Republican.

If we shift the focus from districts to states, we find sixteen states electing Republicans at a two-to-one ratio over Democrats in 1860–74: California, Connecticut, Illinois, Indiana, Iowa, Kansas, Maine, Massachusetts, Michigan, Minnesota, New Hampshire, Ohio, Rhode Island, Vermont, West Virginia, and Wisconsin. It is worth noting that states entering the Union after 1854 overwhelmingly favored Republican candidates. In addition, those states gaining the most seats in the 1862 and 1872 census-driven reapportionments were also strongly Republican. From 1862 to 1874 the Northern states had a net gain of 50 seats, with Illinois, Iowa, Michigan, and Minnesota accounting for one-half of them, and these states were very Republican states. In contrast, the Deep South lost nine seats during the period, with Virginia alone losing six from 1850 to 1874. In short, Republican dominance was not only built on existing House districts, but was also aided by the addition of new states and new districts.

The 1890's period is easier to deal with since House elections were contested essentially between Democrats and Republicans, and the switch to the Republicans occurred in the 1894 and 1896 elections. The Midwestern states were the major block moving toward the Republicans: Illinois, Indiana, Iowa, Kansas, Michigan, Minnesota, Ohio, and Wisconsin. Illinois moved from eleven Democrats and eleven Republicans in 1892 to two Democrats and 20 Republicans in 1894 and held a seventeen-to-six Republican advantage in 1896. In a similar pattern, from 1892 to 1894 Republicans gained eleven seats in Indiana, four seats in Michigan (nine if 1890 is the base), eight in Ohio, seven in Wisconsin, and three in Kansas. The Republicans gained seats in other Midwestern states, but the major gains that were sustained over the period of Republican control, 1896–1908, came from these states.

In the Northeast the states that moved most strongly Republican between 1890 and 1894 were Connecticut, Massachusetts, New Jersey, New York, and Pennsylvania. Massachusetts went from five Republicans in 1890 to twelve in 1894. And between 1892 and 1894 Connecticut went from one Republican to four; New York and Pennsylvania from fourteen and 20 to 29 and 28, respectively; and New Jersey from two to eight. Again, as in the Midwest, other Northeastern states voted in more Republicans in 1894, but the states listed above provided the most sustained support over the 1896–1908 period. Table 6.9 shows the percent of competitive seats, Republican victories, and safe Republican seats for both the pre-1894 period and the 1894–1908 period. The expectation is that the percentage of competitive seats should decrease, and that the percentage of Republican and safe Republican seats should increase. Moreover, the percentage shifts should be greater in the Midwest than in the East, which had a higher Republican base.

The results corroborate the hypothesis. In the Midwest 55 percent of the seats were competitive in the pre-1894 period, compared with only about 53 percent in the 1894–1908 period. The Republicans'

TABLE 6.9

Spatial Configurations of Republican Wins in the 1890's Realignment

(Percent)

Category	1890–1892 elections	1894–1910 elections	Difference over period
Midwest			
Competitive seats	85.0%	52.7%	−32.3%
Republican share of all seats	40.0	84.2	44.2
Republican safe seats	4.0	43.2	39.2
Northeast			
Competitive seats	56.9%	45.8%	−11.1%
Republican share of all seats	48.2	71.0	22.8
Republican safe seats	17.8	42.5	24.7
All other non-Southern			
Competitive seats	60.3%	58.1%	−2.2%
Republican share of all seats	31.2	49.8	18.6
Republican safe seats	8.5	19.7	−11.2

share rose from 40 percent of all Midwestern seats to more than 84 percent. And their safe seats jumped dramatically, from 4 percent to over 40 percent. The Northeastern states show the same pattern, but as expected, the percentage changes are smaller: an 11 percent decrease in competitive seats, a 23 percent increase in safe seats. The "other non-Southern states" (see Table 6.8) were run as a control, and the results show how the Midwestern and Northeastern states stand apart. In the rest of the North, competitive seats decrease only 2.2 percent, and Republican wins and safe seats increase only some 19 percent and 8 percent, respectively. And it should be noted that in these states the Republicans do not capture a majority of the contested seats in either period. Thus, it can be concluded that a swing of a relatively few voters in these two blocks of Northern states transformed a competitive two-party system into a one-party-dominant system for a period of sixteen years.

Only one small question remains. Did the Republican Party's seat margin come from competitive districts or from noncompetitive districts? That is, how many of the seats won by the Republicans in both periods came from districts where a swing of 5 percent or less would have changed the district's representation? The thesis in this chapter is that in both the Civil War and the 1890's critical period, the Republican votes-to-seats advantage occurred because there were so many competitive (45 to 55 percent) districts. That is, the Republicans could attain a House majority with a relatively minor swing in votes because they were winning competitive districts.

The 1854 election is the most important during the Civil War era because, as has been shown, that election saw a massive movement away from the Democrats. The anti–Democratic Party vote in 1854 benefited different parties in different regions; thus I shall use the term non-Democratic and in the next chapter deal with the question of how the Republicans put together a majority between 1854 and 1860. There were 105 districts represented by Democrats in 1852 that switched to other parties in 1854. There were, of course, many Southern districts that went Democratic in 1854; thus the 105 seats do not represent the net loss to the Democrats. It is, however, in those seats that we find the origins of the Republican majority. Eighty-one of the 105, or 77.1 percent, had been competitive in the 1852 election. It is clear that over three-quarters of the original anti-Democratic surge came from districts where minor vote swings resulted in a major seat change. Moreover, 72 (68.6 percent) of the 105 anti-Democratic seats in 1854 were Republican in 1860, and over one-half (54.2) were safe seats (won by margins greater than 55 percent). In sum about three-quarters of the seats that gave the Republicans their realignment margin came from the competitive sector of the constituency party distribution.

The 1890's critical period follows much the same pattern. The 1894 election, as shown above, was the most important in the era. There were 110 seats that shifted from Democratic in 1892 to Republican in 1894. Of the 110 new Republican seats, 91 or 82.7 percent had been competitive in 1892. Thus slightly over four-fifths of the Republican swing seats came from districts where a vote change of 5 percent or less could result in a seat change. Sixty-eight (61.8 percent) of these seats remained Republican in both the 1896 and 1898 elections. In contrast to the Civil War period, however, only a third (35.3 percent) of these were safe seats. In sum, as in the Civil War period, the vast majority of the seats that gave the Republicans majority status came from the competitive sector of the constituency party distribution. This result is not surprising given the competitive nature of the electoral system prior to both realignments.

★ Summary

Neither the Civil War critical period nor the 1890's critical period was characterized by significant shifts in voting, yet both produced stable Republican majorities in the House and Senate. Earlier in this chapter this anomaly was seen to be the result of a votes-to-seats ratio in excess of the Cube Law. The Cube Law was shown to be dependent on a normally distributed cumulative party distribution with limited variance. Since the American party system is not typically "normal," the votes-to-seats distortion found in the Civil War and 1890's eras is seen as a result of the shape of the CPDs. In both critical periods the party distribution prior to the shift was leptokurtic—that is, highly peaked with many competitive seats. Given such a peaked distribution, a permanent shift of a small percentage of voters would result in a new stable majority party. The results showed that the precritical periods in both eras were characterized by peaked distributions, efficient Republican voting, and a slight shift toward the Republicans in the mean vote.

Our attention then turned to ascertaining the spatial configuration of party voting. The initial assumption was that in both the Civil War and 1890's eras, the shift to the Republicans would be concentrated in the Northeastern and Midwestern states. The data revealed that in the Civil War era the 1854 election shifted support away from the Democrats. In the Midwest the shift was to Republican candidates; in the

Northeast the Whigs and the American Party were the primary beneficiaries of anti-Democratic voting. By 1858, however, the Republicans had replaced both these parties as the second major party, and in both regions Republicans dominated elections until the mid-1870's. In the 1890's era the Midwestern and Northeastern states shifted to the Republicans in 1894 and remained predominantly Republican until 1910. Thus in both periods a small Republican shift in the Midwest and the Northeast converted a highly competitive two-party system into regional one-partyism.

CHAPTER SEVEN

Conclusion

★ THIS BOOK began with an argument that linked changes in mass electoral behavior and the House of Representatives with dramatic changes in public policy. In the process of examining these linkages, I found that many of my preconceptions changed and new questions arose. No question has been more important than the role of political parties in linking elections, institutions, and policy shifts. Political parties in the electorate, as organizations, and as government, were central to explaining how policy shifts occurred in each of our three eras, and in this final chapter I deal with three questions related to this theme. (1) Would the two nineteenth-century realignments have occurred without the particular constituent party distributions that generated favorable Republican votes-to-seats ratios? (2) Are the electoral results reported in this book compatible with the theory of retrospective voting? And (3) What are some of the implications of my findings for contemporary American politics?

★ A Revised View of Realignments

The finding that both nineteenth-century realignments were dependent on a highly competitive party system leads one to ask the first question. To restate it in more concrete terms, did the Kansas-Nebraska, slavery, and money issues produce these realignments, or should they be ascribed instead to advantages in the votes-to-seats ratios? In order to answer this question, it is necessary, first, to outline the standard view of what drives realignments and then to offer my own.

The standard view of realignments holds that as we move (in time) away from a realignment party identification weakness (dealignment), at some point a new, cross-cutting issue arises to generate a new critical election. That election realigns party preferences around the cross-cutting issue (or issues), and public policy shifts to reflect the new alignment. Thus what drives realignments is the interaction of the fading of old issues with the decline of party identification based on them.

The argument in this book differs by holding that the effect of cross-cutting issues on the composition of Congress and on policy depends on both the issues *and* the shape of the constituent party distribution. The argument does not hold that weakened party identification is a necessary condition. Rather, the point is that a change in the spatial distribution of partisanship can result in the congressional turnover necessary to generate the policy changes associated with realignments. If, for example, 5 percent of the voters shift for or against a party, and the constituent party distribution is U-shaped (lots of safe seats), turnover in the House will be minimal and the conditions for policy shifts absent. If the same 5 percent shift occurs where the party distribution is competitive, there will be high turnover in House seats (a high swing ratio), which can generate the policy shifts associated with realignments. In each of the nineteenth-century realignments, the cross-cutting issues generated vote shifts of about 5 percent, and because they occurred within the context of highly competitive party distributions, they generated the congressional turnover necessary to change public policy. Thus voters in subsequent elections could vote to affirm the policy changes legislated by the Congress.

This analysis helps to explain why students of contemporary politics have difficulty in discerning realignments. With the single exception of the New Deal (in which a massive voter shift occurred), the twentieth century has not produced a clear realignment. In part this is because the CPDs (see Fig. 7.1) have been U-shaped or noncompetitive; thus voter shifts of around 5 percent in congressional elections *cannot* produce the turnover necessary to change policy. Ronald Reagan's electoral victories in 1980 and 1984 shifted the congressional vote toward the Republicans, but given the party distribution there was not enough turnover to create the conditions (committee changes and other shifts discussed in Chaps. 2–4) to change policy in a significant or permanent manner.

While there is no direct test that can discriminate between these two views of realignment, a brief discussion of why there was no clear realignment in the 1960's and 1970's might be useful. If the decline-in-partisanship view of realignments is correct, those decades should have been a prime period for a realignment. Study after study revealed a definite decline in the levels of party identification. Indeed

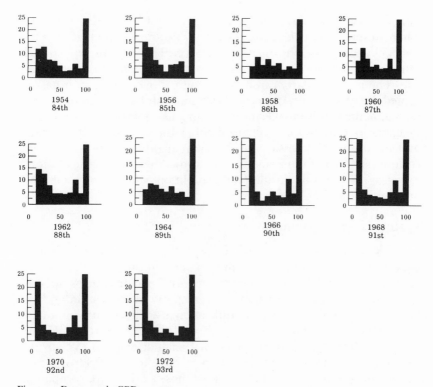

Fig. 7.1. Democratic CPDs, 1954–1972

many analysts expected, predicted, and even claimed realignments. The decline in party loyalty plus the turbulence associated with the great issues of the times—civil rights, Vietnam, and the Great Society, among others—led scholars to believe that a realignment was imminent. The fact that one did not occur was in my view not for lack of a cross-cutting issue (or issues), but because the CPD was noncompetitive. Thus even though the issues of the 1960's and 1970's shifted votes, the shifts were not great enough (across the board) to generate the turnover necessary for policy changes, and voters in subsequent elections did not have a set of policy changes to affirm. Given the present shape of the party distribution curve, only an across-the-board realignment (like the New Deal), where there is a major shift in the mean vote toward one party, could generate the turnover necessary for realignment replete with policy shifts.

In sum, for a full-blown realignment to occur the electoral shift must generate undivided electoral control of the House, the Senate, and the Presidency for the new majority party. Once in power, the new majority must legislate policy changes of a significant nature. Then, in subsequent elections, the electorate affirms and reaffirms the policy changes passed by the majority party. This explains why in each of the realignments studied the span of control lasted for over a decade. The minority party can become competitive only after it has accepted the fundamental aspects of the policy shifts associated with the realignment. Landslide electoral margins like Johnson's in 1964 and Reagan's in 1980 did not generate either the span of control or the undivided control necessary for the full realignment process to occur. In contrast, each of the realignments studied here meets the electoral as well as the institutional and policy conditions sufficient to establish a new equilibrium in American politics.

★ Retrospective Voting

In the clearest statement of retrospective voting, Morris Fiorina conceptually incorporates the time dimension, arguing that voters' retrospective judgments about presidential performance and economic performance affect both current party identification and future expectations. Past party identification also affects current identification, and current identification affects future expectations. Figure 7.2 shows his schema. In this section I shall attempt to explain the electoral results in our three critical periods in terms of retrospective voting. In the process of showing how those periods are compatible with retrospective voting, I will compare realignments. For present purposes I will be content to show that my explanation of electoral results is compatible with the theory of retrospective voting. I do not have access to the survey data necessary to test the theory itself.

All the factors Fiorina discusses can affect the voter's decision. His model is useful because it is general and can accommodate the fact that any one election may be the result of a different weighting of the factors. In the case of critical elections it is clear that there are more national electoral forces at work than usual. Major breakdowns of the U.S. economy—the Panic of 1893 and the Great Depression—were clearly the driving forces behind the electoral shifts of the 1890's and the New Deal eras. Thus we should expect to find that an explanation featuring retrospective economic voting is compatible with the electoral results observed in these two eras.

I agree with V. O. Key, Jr., that "the vocabulary of the voice of the people consists mainly of the words yes and no; and at times one cannot be certain which word is being uttered."[1] In critical periods the yes or no of the people is clearly understood. It is to be understood first as

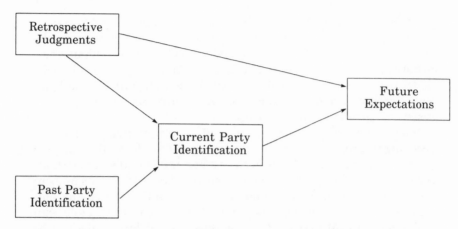

Fig. 7.2. Factors molding voters' expectations. Source: Morris Fiorina, *Retrospective Voting in American National Elections* (New Haven, Conn., 1981), p. 189.

a no to the party in control of the government and then as a series of yesses to the party that assumes control. In both the 1890's and the 1930's, the electorate first replaced the old majority in the House (1894 and 1930 elections, albeit by the illness or death of Republican members in 1930) and in the next election gave the "new majority party" control of the government by electing a President of the same party. Then for six consecutive congressional elections the voters maintained the same majority party in the House of Representatives. Thus if both the 1890's and 1930's critical periods are compatible with a retrospective theory of voting, we should expect to observe electoral results varying with the state of the economy. I cannot of course prove that voters made retrospective evaluations of economic performance because no one has surveys of individual voters. However, if I show that in each period the in-party's seat totals are directly related to the economy's well-being, I can claim compatibility. I need not, nor can I, claim that voters' choices were determined by economic issues. Clearly, the nature of the CPDs in the 1890's affected the electoral results, and foreign policy in both periods affected some voters' decisions. Why, then, one might ask, go through the exercise if compatibility is the most that can be shown?

The answer is straightforward. If we are to explain policy and events in certain historical periods, then more is required than precise descriptions of unique events. I have assumed throughout this book that by examining periods when policy changes dramatically, we can get a handle on how the system operates. Implicit in this assumption is the notion that in democracies voters are rational, and that they make

judgments about the performance of elected leaders. In critical periods issue sensitivity is heightened; people can observe and feel the
effects of changes in the economy, and if such changes result in a new
majority sustained in power while times get better, I consider that evidence that voters are rational, and that elections, institutions, and policy are related. I begin with the 1890's and 1930's eras because they are
easier to explain than the Civil War era.

The economic reversals of 1893 and 1929 were major; their far-
reaching effects have been well documented elsewhere. For our purposes, the assumption is that in the House and presidential elections
that followed the economic downturns, voters held the incumbent
party responsible for the economic malaise and rewarded the out-
party (Republicans in the 1890's and Democrats in the 1930's) with
majority status. Moreover, the new majority parties should also be
evaluated on the basis of economic improvement. The dependent
variable is the number of House seats lost or gained by the President's
party. Retrospective voting implies voters' judgments of the President's economic performance.[2] Since we already know that in both in-
stances the incumbent party at the time of the economic downturn
lost majority status, and that the new majority party was maintained in
office for sixteen consecutive years, we are seeking to measure the dependent variable in a more precise fashion—thus the use of the actual
gain or loss in seats to the incumbent party. Both series include pre-
and postcritical-period elections. For the purposes of this analysis I
have chosen to track both periods to the point where the new majority
party became the out-party—1886 to 1910 in the first case, 1920 to
1946 in the second. The major independent variable is the state of the
economy. The assumption is that voters feel and observe the effects of
the economy and hold incumbents responsible for them.

Measuring the state of the economy in a manner consistent to both
eras is somewhat problematic. The measure most often used in this
kind of analysis is the decline or rise in real income. Unfortunately,
this information is not available in a meaningful form for the entire
1890's period. I therefore collected data on variables measured in the
same fashion for both periods: the number of business and farm failures, the Frickey-Kendrick Index of Manufacturing Production, the
Consumer Price Index, Personal Income in Current Prices (for the
1930's), as given in the government's *Historical Statistics* volumes.[3] Since
these indexes are highly correlated with each other, the strategy was
to run each one separately against both the incumbent party's vote
gain or loss and its House seat gain or loss. In addition to the economic variable, the year was entered as an independent variable to

show that the results were not dependent on some unmeasured trend, and its identification as a presidential or nonpresidential election year was entered to provide for the surge and decline in voter interest associated with presidential elections.

The decision to use the incumbent party's seat gains or losses as one of the dependent variables was based on the concern for policy results. That is, in the words of Roderick Kiewiet and Douglas Rivers, "The subsequent composition of Congress, after all, is of more direct consequence for public policy than the national vote total."[4] Since I have argued that congressional turnover is an important component of changing policy, it follows that seat changes should be a dependent variable.[5]

The expectation is that the slopes (*B*s) for the economic variables will be significant, and that each regression will explain a high percentage of the vote and seat shifts. The Frickey-Kendrick Index of Manufacturing Production will be positively related to the incumbent party's fortunes (i.e., the higher the index, the more votes and seats gained by the incumbent party). The business and farm failures figures will be negatively related to the incumbent party's vote and seat swings, since as failures increase, the incumbent party's fortunes should decline. The economic variables are measures of change from the previous election.

The results of the analysis are consistent with the retrospective voting model (see note 5 for the full results). The Frickey-Kendrick, business, and farm failures measures are all related to the fortunes of the incumbent party. In the 1890's a rise of 1 point in the production index yields a positive gain of 0.45 percent of the vote for the incumbent party and a gain of 1.72 seats in the House of Representatives. Similar increases in the business and farm failures measures yield losses of 0.21 and 0.30 percent of the incumbent party's vote totals. The seat losses to the incumbent party in the House of Representatives are 0.79 for the business failure measure and 0.86 for the farm failures measure. In each case, it should be noted that the seat gain or loss is relatively higher than the corresponding vote gain or loss. This result is, of course, to be expected, given that when the CPD is peaked, the translation of votes to seats will yield a disproportionate number of seat switches for minor shifts in the vote. This is in contradiction to the contemporary situation, where the CPD is bimodal (few competitive seats and many safe seats) and vote swings yield very few seat changes.

In more concrete terms, the Index of Manufacturing Production rose from 47 in 1884 to 79 in 1892, then fell to 68 in 1894. From 1896 through 1904 the index rose to 121, and from 1904 through 1908 it rose to 172. Thus the Republicans' victory in 1894 coincided with a sharp fall in productivity. During their dominant period, the index rose steadily. The electoral losses of the Republicans in 1910 and 1912 coincided with a drop in the index. The business and farm failures indexes both behaved in the same fashion. The Republicans' critical victories are associated with rises in farm and business failures; their dominance was associated with steady decreases in failures. Thus, we conclude that the critical 1890's period is consistent with retrospective voting, during both the Republican takeover and the period of Republican dominance.

The results for the New Deal period are also consistent with the theory of retrospective voting. Each of the economic indicators has a significant B. A shift of 1 point in personal income resulted in a gain of 0.32 percent in the vote toward the incumbent party and a shift of 2.84 seats to the incumbent President's party. An increase of 1 point in the Manufacturing Production Index yielded a 0.77 increase in the incumbent party's vote totals and an increase of 1.91 in its seats. Increases in the business and farm failures measures yielded significant decreases in the incumbent party's vote and seat totals. Thus these results too are consistent with the notion that voters judge the economic performance of the incumbent party. The Democrats' takeover in the House was associated with the sharp decline in the economy; their period of dominance with increases in economic well-being. (These data were also run excluding the years 1941–45, and the results were essentially the same. That is, the results were not determined by the rise in productivity associated with World War II. In the 1920–40 analysis each of the economic variables was significantly related to the shift in the House seats of the President's party.)

In both the 1890's and the New Deal era, retrospective economic voting is strongly indicated. This result should not be surprising, given the sharp economic declines that dominated the issue content of these elections. The Democratic response to the Panic of 1893 was to nominate a candidate who promised to radically change America's industrial society; yet voters appear to have held the Democratic Party responsible for the state of the economy and rewarded the Republicans when the economy improved. The Republican response to the Depression was to defend the status quo, while the Democrats indicated a willingness to try to ameliorate the effects of the depression. Voters in 1930 and especially 1932 responded, à la Key, with a strong no to the Republicans and thus an implicit yes to the Democrats. Voters did not send Roosevelt and the Democrats directions to try the

NIRA, AAA, CCC, and other New Deal legislation. Rather, they created conditions under which political leadership could attempt innovation, or, in Key's words, "self-governmental leadership with the initiative and imagination necessary to meet the public problems that develop and with the courage to assume the political risks involved."[6]

The Civil War era is more difficult to explain by economic retrospective voting, in part because there are only sketchy economic data available. More important, to my mind, is the inability of retrospective economic voting to account for the birth of the Republican Party and its subsequent majority status. The economic downturn in 1857 may have boosted Republican fortunes, but economic conditions did not give rise to the Republican Party or account for its early successes. I believe that the results for the critical Civil War period were largely driven by the slavery issue and the economic consequences associated with slavery.

The fundamental turning point in the Civil War era was the introduction of the Kansas-Nebraska Bill in Congress. Prior to 1854, the antislavery movement had affected election results in some states, but Abolitionism could not have become the sole basis for a new party. The Compromise of 1850 had been a bipartisan effort, smoothing over differences between the Northern and Southern wings of both the Whigs and the Democrats. The introduction of the Kansas-Nebraska Bill and its subsequent passage gave rise to an immediate anti-Democratic swing in the vote (see Chaps. 2 and 6, and especially Tables 2.1–2.4). In the Midwestern states the newly formed Republican Party was the beneficiary; however, in the Northeastern states the American Party was the major beneficiary of the anti-Democratic vote. Thus there were two separate issues that had the potential to create a new majority party. One was the transformed slavery issue, now essentially converted to a free soil–free men–free labor issue. The other was an anti-Catholic, nativist issue. The argument subscribed to here is that the Republican Party attained majority status by successfully combining these issues. Ronald Formisano has put the claim this way: "Nativism, anti-Catholicism, anti-Southernism, anti-slavery and racism did not flow through the political universe in neatly separate streams. . . . Rather, one must understand how racial, ethnic, religious, economic, sectional and other groups were interwoven symbolically and how issues such as Popery, Slavery, Party, and Rum permeated one another with emotional resonance."[7]

If we consider these different issues as openings for political entrepreneurs, it is possible to understand the changes in the Civil War era. The Kansas-Nebraska Act changed the slavery issue forever by abol-

ishing the Mason-Dixon line and making Northern territories potential slave states. The immediate effect of Kansas-Nebraska was the call
for a new political party to combat the act, which had been passed on a
bipartisan vote.[8] In a very short time Republican parties were formed
in a number of states, and, as we have seen, they were victorious in the
Midwest. Thus the first stage in the process of Republican victory was
the sharp reaction to the Kansas-Nebraska Act.

Political scientists find it hard to believe that one congressional act
could generate the intensity of feeling necessary to shift partisan preferences so dramatically. Since I am contending that the act did exactly
that, let me document the phenomenon. First, the act broadened the
slavery issue in such a way that what was now at stake was not just slavery itself, but economic freedom and prosperity. Put in this light, the
intensity of feeling is more understandable. The evidence for intensity is in one sense obvious; from nonexistence in 1852 the Republicans became the largest party in the House of Representatives by
1855. A second way to demonstrate the intensity of the issue is to look
at voter turnout in House elections from 1852 to 1860. If, as I have
claimed, the introduction of the Kansas-Nebraska Act generated intense voter interest, then the electoral turnout figures for the 1852–56
elections should show the effects of that interest. Those effects were
indeed visible: first, in the off-year elections of 1854, voter turnout actually increased in Midwestern states over the turnout for the 1852
presidential election; second, in those Northern states that held elections in 1853 prior to Kansas-Nebraska, the turnout followed the normal pattern of decline from the presidential year.

The importance of these findings should not be underestimated.
In American politics presidential elections are high-salience elections,
and off-year elections normally low-salience. Voter turnout thus declines dramatically in off years. In the 1854 House elections the effect
of the Kansas-Nebraska Act was to create so intense a reaction against
the Democrats and Whigs for passing the bill as to increase voter turnout where a 14 percent decrease would normally have been expected.
(See the typical pattern of surge and decline in the 1856–60 elections,
Table 7.1.) The increase in turnout yielded a strong pro–Republican
Party vote, which was maintained throughout the Civil War era. In the
Northern states holding House elections in 1853 prior to Kansas-
Nebraska, turnout declined a predictable 13.25 percent. The turnout
figures for 1854 are unique in American political history. That the
issues raised by the Kansas-Nebraska Act intensified public opinion to
an unparalleled extent is attested both by the turnout and by the creation of a new American political party.

TABLE 7.1

Voter Turnout in House Elections in the Midwest and Northeast, 1852–1860

Election year	Midwest[a]		Northeast[b]	
	Total vote (hundreds)	Percent change	Total vote (hundreds)	Percent change
1852	7,533	—	10,160	—
1854	7,606	1.0%	10,014	−1.5%
1856	10,519	27.6	13,025	23.1
1858	9,945	−5.5	11,330	−14.9
1860	13,192	28.3	14,330	20.9

[a] Ill., Ind., Mich., Ohio, Wis.
[b] Maine, Mass., N.Y., Pa.

But having won the Midwest, the Republicans were still a long way from becoming a majority party. As noted above, the American, or Know-Nothing, Party was the primary beneficiary of the anti-Democratic turn of 1854 in the Northeast. The second part of the story of the Republicans' rise to dominance is their blending of the free men–free soil–free labor issue with the American Party's issue of nativism. This process was brought about at different rates in the various states, but at the heart of the merger was the question of registration laws.[9] The influx of Irish and German Catholic immigrants to the United States reached epic proportions after 1848. These immigrants settled in the Northeast and in general voted Democratic. The American Party was the result of a strong Protestant reaction to these immigrants. The American Party was anti-Catholic, anti-Democratic, and to a certain extent, anti-rum. It did not disappear from the scene once voters returned to the Democratic Party and elected a President in 1856. In fact, the American Party successfully competed in elections in at least New York through 1858. The gist of the story is that Republican Party leaders eventually adopted registration laws in state party platforms that would entice nativist voters to the Republican effort.

In the Northern states of Maine, Massachusetts, New York, and Pennsylvania, 40 of 75 House elections in 1854 were three-way contests; 37 of these contests involved American Party candidates in Massachusetts and New York. In 1856, 37 of 44 Massachusetts and New York elections were three-way contests; this number dropped to nineteen in 1858 and to eight in 1860. Republican House victories rose in proportion as the number of American Party candidates dropped. Joel Silbey's excellent study of New York politics during this period shows how, in spite of the influential William H. Seward's objections, New York Republicans came gradually to majority status by adding the registration issue to their free men–free labor–free soil issue.

I cannot and need not duplicate his careful analysis in detail; suffice it to say that he shows that Republican leaders recognized the need to bring American Party adherents into their coalition: "Therefore, to the 'two branches of the Opposition party' in the state the question of unifying the anti-Democratic groups became an important matter. Neither party 'can hope to achieve a victory single-handed' against the 'bogus Irish Democracy.'" [10] By 1858 the merger of issues and parties had been successfully achieved, to the benefit of the Republicans.

At least two things seem clear in New York state after 1857. First, the Republican establishment had come over to the registration issue even though some of them remained ambivalent about the matter. The Know-Nothings clearly gained. When the registry finally passed in 1859, it was an imperfect bill in the eyes of many, but one that was important nonetheless. But the Republicans gained as well: their tactics paid off electorally. Thus, both parties won something from their interaction. The relationship that developed, however, revolved around the question not of whether the Know-Nothings dominated the Republicans, but of how electorally useful they were and how much influence in shaping Republican behavior their realization of that usefulness gave them. [11]

The coalescing of nativism and Republicanism was not limited to the East. Formisano has shown how Michigan Republicans integrated attacks on Catholics with attacks on slave power and passed registry laws in an attempt to form a majority. [12] Michael Holt's work *Forging a Majority* also supports the notion of a deliberate Republican strategy to achieve power by making necessary policy concessions to the American Party. There are, of course, historians who disagree with this ethnocultural thesis. Fortunately, it is not my task to resolve this issue, but rather to show how the Republicans became the majority party in the 1850's. I have argued that this took place in two stages, the first being an increased opportunity structure available to political entrepreneurs after the Kansas-Nebraska Act. The passage of the act eliminated the Missouri Compromise and meant that Northern territories could "elect" to be slave states if majorities so voted. The intense and immediate reaction of many Midwestern political entrepreneurs was to call for a new party, and to that end the Republican Party was formed. In the process the new party's leaders transformed the slavery issue from the moralism of the abolitionists to one of economics; namely, the threat of slave power to the principle of free men—free labor—free soil. This appeal was most powerful in the newer Midwestern states, where farming interests were strongest.

The second stage in the Republicans' rise to majority status was the formation of a Republican–American Party coalition. This was a two-phase process, where first party leaders searching for majorities decided to make policy compromises, and then those compromises won electoral vindication. The results show that as concessions were made, the number of American Party candidates shrank and Republican House victories increased. Thus by 1860 the Republicans were dominant in Northern states, thanks in no small part to the highly competitive nature of the party system—that is, a very leptokurtic constituency party distribution allowing small vote swings to produce large seat swings.

None of this is to imply that party leaders had no other values besides winning majorities. In fact, the difficulties many leaders had in agreeing to electoral registry laws is proof that ideals mattered to them. The claim I have made is simply that in order to achieve their ends, they had to find and shape a set of issues that would enable them to create and maintain an anti-Democratic majority. The elements of such a majority had been present since the introduction of the Kansas-Nebraska Act, but the process of putting it together was, of necessity, a time-consuming and piecemeal process. The winning combination ultimately appealed to voters' *prospective* economic and ethnocultural well-being. The fact that the winning coalition was highly sectional rests in part on the fact that voters with these preferences were primarily distributed in the Northern states. The victory of Lincoln and the Republicans in 1860 proved for a number of different reasons to be so threatening to the Southern states that they seceded. Electoral results after 1860 follow the paths determined by the Civil War, Reconstruction, and the readmission of the Southern states.

The theory of retrospective economic voting holds that average citizens evaluate candidates and economic policies on the basis of their everyday effects. Moreover, it holds that most voters do not care much about the means used to bring about policy results. That is, voters notice that their paychecks buy more or less, and that some of their neighbors are either back to work or still laid off. The cumulation of voters' judgments about candidates and issues yields election results that can be said to be retrospective. The important point about the Civil War critical period is that voters' reactions were not triggered by this day-to-day process. Rather the passage of the Kansas-Nebraska Act was a signal from Washington that brought instant and dramatic electoral change.

The closest analogy in contemporary American politics is voter reaction to Watergate. That is, Republican losses in the 1974 midterm elections can be attributed to a combination of a recessionary economy *and* voter reactions to Watergate, especially President Gerald Ford's pardoning of Richard Nixon. A similar case is voter reactions in Arkansas' 5th District to Representative Brook Hays's pro–civil rights stance during the 1957 school-integration crisis in Little Rock. Fiorina describes these situations as "gut issue(s) for which constituents consider a vote with them as the very sine qua non of representation. A right vote merits no reward; . . . a wrong vote on such issues amounts to an abject betrayal of the representative's trust."[13] The vote on the Kansas-Nebraska Act can be considered such a "gut issue" where voters punished candidates and parties that supported passage. Voting against a candidate or a party that betrays such a fundamental trust is a form of retrospective voting, albeit not retrospective economic voting. It is retrospective voting in that voters are making judgments about representatives' past behavior rather than future promises. However, these voter judgments *do not* concern the outcomes of past policies. They are immediate and visceral reactions to the politician's actions and not to their observed consequences. The Watergate and Brook Hays examples are similar to Kansas-Nebraska to the extent that they reflected voters' visceral judgments. They differ dramatically in their consequences. Brook Hays's pro–civil rights stance cost him his seat, and the Watergate scandal almost certainly cost the Republican Party some congressional seats. Neither is comparable to the effects wrought by the reaction to Kansas-Nebraska.

Key has claimed that "only infrequently is a new program or a new course of action advocated with such force and the attention it receives so widespread that the polling may be regarded as [prospective voting approval]."[14] It seems clear that voters in 1854 were not giving prospective approval to Republican policies; rather, they were clearly and significantly saying no to the parties that passed the Kansas-Nebraska Act. It was up to the new Republican Party to build a majority party by proposing policies that would draw a majority of voters to it. In Fiorina's words, "Politicians are elected to maintain social harmony and economic prosperity. Sometimes this may require only administration of the status quo, but at other times it may require identification and solution of new problems—innovation and leadership."[15] The intense reaction to Kansas-Nebraska created the conditions under which Republican politicians could lead.

★ Implications of the Findings for Contemporary Politics

Observers of contemporary American politics continue to argue about whether certain elections were realignments. Various authors

have claimed that 1964, 1980, and 1984, among others, were realigning elections.[16] The findings reported in this book make it difficult
to believe that there have been any realignments in the House since
the New Deal. The most impressive evidence involves the shape of
the CPDs. In the twentieth century the CPDs over time have been
platykurtic (Fig. 7.1). That is, they have been characterized by large
numbers of safe seats at the left- and right-hand margins of the distributions, and a relatively few competitive seats in the middle, where
seats are normally won or lost. Under these conditions it is highly unlikely that enough seats can be shifted to bring about a true realignment. The effect of platykurtic party distributions on contemporary
American politics merits elaboration and clarification.

For a critical election to occur, one party must succeed electorally in
winning a lasting permanent majority that allows the party to hold
control of the House, Senate, and Presidency for at least a decade.
The question is, how does this occur, or what drives the change? In
terms of our variables, such change is driven by shifts in the mean
vote for a party or in the variance in the vote, or both. In the first two
critical periods, the mean vote in the Northern states shifted to the
Republicans, coupled with a shift to the Democrats in the South. Because of the highly competitive nature of the party system in the
North (a leptokurtic CPD), a slight shift in the mean vote brought a
significant shift in seats to the Republicans, resulting in fourteen years
of unified control of government. The New Deal critical period differed in that the CPD was noncompetitive (platykurtic), thus requir-
ing a major shift in the mean vote to drive the seat switch to the Democrats. Variance fell in the 1932 election, but remained twice as high as
it was in either of the two previous critical periods. In short, the 1930's
critical period was characterized by an across-the-board shift to the
Democrats that pushed the CPD curve toward the Democratic end of
the spectrum. The important point to remember is that the shape of
the CPD in each instance reveals the dynamics of the electoral change.

A party distribution characterized by a U-shaped platykurtic curve
can be realigned only if there is a major shift in the mean toward one
or the other of the parties. The more U-shaped the curve, the less
likely there are to be any presidential coattails. That is, if there are
very few competitive seats, a successful presidential candidate must
shift a large number of votes across many districts in order to bring in
a majority to govern with him. Since FDR, only Dwight Eisenhower
has managed to do that, and the Republicans lost control of Congress
in the next election. Three times, Republican candidates—Nixon in

1972 and Reagan in 1980 and 1984—have won landslide victories and not carried the House with them. No Democratic President, with the possible exception of Lyndon Johnson in 1964, has had presidential coattails, and the Democrats lost heavily in the 1966 elections.[17]

The analysis outlined above treats the platykurtic CPD as an exogenous variable. That is, I have simply claimed that such distributions exist, and have argued that no post-Roosevelt election meets the criteria for a realignment. Treating the CPD as exogenous allows me simply to specify the consequences of this type of distribution for the linkage between elections, institutions, and policy. I have already mentioned one important consequence—the decline of presidential coattails, which, as John Ferejohn and Randall Calvert have already shown, have all but disappeared. Given the U-shape of party distributions, it is easy to see why that has happened. One obviously important consequence of the decline of coattails is that Presidents elected with large personal margins of victory may be faced with opposite-party control of the House or the Senate, or both. And the policy consequences are straightforward. Lincoln, McKinley, and Franklin Roosevelt came to office with built-in majorities and were able to rely on them to pass their legislation. Eisenhower, Nixon, and Reagan faced the more difficult task of building bipartisan majorities, with the prospect of seeing their legislative programs watered down. Democratic Presidents elected in the post–New Deal era have all had Democratic majorities in both House and Senate, but with the exception of Lyndon Johnson in the 89th Congress, all have been faced with serious majority-building problems. In part, the majority-building problem is related to the decline of party voting in the twentieth century. As discussed earlier, today's congressmen have much more individual control over their electoral fate; plainly, members who have created their own campaign organizations, raised their own money, and withstood presidential electoral tides toward the other party are less likely to support their party and President than members who were aided by either the party or the President.

Another consequence of a U-shaped CPD is that with such a distribution it is more difficult to alternate party control of the House. From 1850 to 1900 there were 26 general House elections; the Democrats won eleven, the Republicans thirteen, and the Whigs two; and in nine of the 25 election pairs (e.g. 1850–52) a switch occurred. This clearly indicates a competitive party system. Now consider the 43 general House elections between 1900 and 1986: the Democrats won 30 times and the Republicans 13 times; in only seven of the pairs did the party majority in the House alternate. Since 1953 control of the

House has not alternated. This is clear evidence of an important effect of a U-shaped party distribution. David Mayhew's article on disappearing marginal districts points to the implications of this phenomenon for democratic theory: the swing in the mean party vote has to be enormous in order to change majority-party representation; thus an imperfect means of citizen control is rendered even more imperfect.[18]

A third consequence of the disjunction between electoral results and party control of the Presidency and the Congress is that politics becomes less responsible. During each of the critical periods examined in this book, there was a rough correspondence between party platforms, election results, and policy outputs. In each instance the parties offered distinct policy alternatives on the critical issues of the era, the electoral verdict was clear, and the will of the electorate was transformed into policy shifts via partisan voting. Moreover, the freshmen members of the majority party voted overwhelmingly for the policy changes.[19] Thus, in an important sense, these three critical periods were an American variant of responsible government. The linkage between elections, institutions, and policy was relatively straightforward, with political parties playing the key intermediary role. That is, voters choosing Republicans in the Civil War and 1890's eras and Democrats in the New Deal era signaled a preference for change, and in each case the newly elected majority party in Congress voted cohesively to enact that change. The "new" majority parties dominated elections for over a decade, time enough for their policy innovations to take root. In the post–New Deal period the conditions necessary to establish coherent and responsible policy changes have not obtained. Only Lyndon Johnson and the 89th Congress came close to meeting these conditions—clear-cut policy differences and policy shifts voted in by a cohesive majority party. However, the condition of longevity was not met. In the 1966 midterm election the Democrats suffered major losses in House elections, and in 1968 a Republican was elected President, owing largely to a bitter, divisive conflict within the Democratic Party. In short, a party system characterized, as the present system is, by a U-shaped distribution in which incumbents win reelection on the basis of personal rather than party organizations is not likely to yield sustained and coherent public policies. Rather, it will produce weak parties that cannot provide the linkage between elections, institutions, and policy that is a necessary condition for any variant of responsible government.

If this book were to continue, it would be necessary to treat the CPDs as endogenous. That is, we would ask what accounts for the

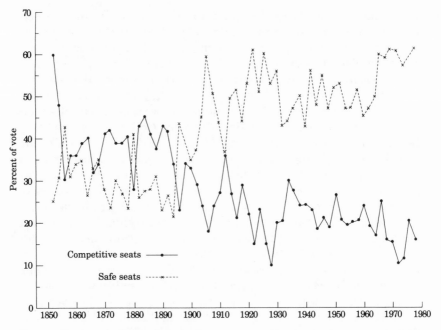

Fig. 7.3. Democratic CPDs, 1850–1976

shift from a highly competitive party system, in which the control of government is frequently altered, to a system characterized by competitive presidential races and noncompetitive House elections. If we plot the number of House races decided by plus or minus 5 percent (competitive seats) and the number of House races decided by margins greater than 25 percent (safe seats) from 1850 to 1976, the curves cross in 1894 and meet again only once, in 1910, where they are equal (Fig. 7.3). In the early twentieth century the safe-seat curve jumps dramatically and remains high, whereas the competitive-seat curve steadily trends downward. In the nineteenth century the kurtosis values are consistently positive (leptokurtic); in the twentieth century the same values are consistently negative (platykurtic). Moreover, the correlation between kurtosis and standard deviation is −.932, which shows that electoral variance was limited when the CPDs were competitive and high when the CPDs were U-shaped, or noncompetitive.

All of this indicates that sometime in the late nineteenth century, there were changes that shifted the distribution of party preferences to their present shape. The explanation must lie in the structural changes in both electoral laws and institutions that have weakened the strength of and sanctions available to political parties.[20] The endogenous quality of CPDs is, however, a topic for a future work. At this point all I can claim is that, given the noncompetitive nature of contemporary House elections, two conditions of responsible government are difficult to meet. Presidents will not carry majorities into office with them, and there will be little alternation of or undivided control of the government. Under these conditions American government will continue to be characterized by drift rather than mastery, and by fragmentation rather than coherence.

Reference Material

APPENDIX

Classifying the Issues

THE METHOD used to establish the issue dimensions shown in Chapters Two, Three, and Four is essentially the same as that used by Clausen (1973) and Sinclair (1977). Based on historical sources, newspapers, the *Congressional Record*, congressional biographies, and so forth, the researcher subjectively classifies roll calls by content. Thus, for example, in the pre–Civil War era, roll calls dealing with questions of slavery were classified in the slavery, secession, and civil rights dimension. The content of issues changes over time and, for example, questions of slavery pass away and the question of secession takes its turn, to be replaced by post–Civil War questions of civil rights for newly freed slaves. In each of the three eras examined in this book, the author's subjective classifications were checked by having others categorize the same roll calls. In each period, the correlation between observers' categorization was over r = .9. Thus, I feel confident that the subjective categorization was valid.

Once the relevant categories have been established, the question then becomes, do the roll calls in these categories form scalable issue dimensions? Within categories a Yule's Q analysis was run on all roll calls with at least 10 percent opposition. Then with a hierarchical clustering technique, a dimension was defined as consisting of a group of roll calls with a common content for which the minimum Yule's Q intercorrelation was .5. This criterion produced clusters with mean intercorrelations that average about .7 for each of the periods. Given the unidimensionality of these clusters, a simple scoring procedure was used. In each issue cluster one critical roll call was chosen to establish direction; thus, the direction of every other roll call is given by its sign of correlation with the chosen roll call. The roll call chosen in each cluster was in accord with the policy changes associated with the realignment. Thus, for example, on the slavery, secession, and civil rights dimension, the direction-determining roll call favored liberal policies toward blacks.

Every representative who voted on at least half the roll calls was then scored accordingly. The representatives' scores on each issue dimension are then correlated with the same representatives' scores on the same dimension in the following Congresses. If the scores of continuing members continues to correlate at a high level, over .8, then we can claim that these issue dimensions have the property of over-time reliability.

The high turnover of membership in the Civil War era creates some difficulty in establishing over-time reliability. The problem is that over the 1850–74 period, the number of representatives present across all Houses is small; thus a variation of the technique is used. Each consecutive pair of Houses is analyzed in terms of the representatives present in both Houses. These results were then compared to the results for the same analyses run over all representatives present in three, four, five, and so forth consecutive Houses. This method allows me to ascertain the historical validity of the issue dimensions without having the small-number-of-members problem casting doubt on the findings. In no case were there significant differences between the results, regardless of the length of the time span. That is, the representatives had the same position on the scale scores regardless of whether I looked at, for example, slavery, secession, and civil rights scores from two Houses or from five Houses.

The final product of this technique is the establishment of historically valid issue dimensions for each of the three critical periods examined in this book. Each representative has a scale score that measures his or her relative position in the various dimensions and this score is then correlated with the representatives' party identification to determine the extent to which party predicts voting scores.

Notes

Full authors' names, dates, and publication data for the Notes cited in short form are given in the Bibliography, pp. 196–205.

CHAPTER ONE

1. Charles O. Jones, lecture, University of Houston, March 1976; Sundquist, *Politics*, p. 513.
2. Alexander Hamilton, quoted in Farrand, p. 348.
3. De Tocqueville, p. 1204.
4. MacNeil, p. 8.
5. William Smith, p. 261.
6. Huntington, "Congressional Responses."
7. *Washington Post*, Jan. 9, 1966.
8. Rhode and Shepsle, p. 2. See also Shepsle, "Institutional Arrangements"; Shepsle and Weingast, "Structure-Induced Equilibrium"; and Riker, *Liberalism*, pp. 170–212.
9. The first to make this point was Marie-Jean de Condorcet, *Essai sur l'application de l'analyse à la probabilité des décisions rendues à la pluralité des voix* (Paris, 1785). A good review of the issues and relevant works can be found in Schwartz, "Meaning of Instability." See also McKelvey; Riker, "Implications"; Schofield; and Arrow.
10. Clausen, concluding chapter. Tullock, p. 189, points to the same phenomenon when he says: "If we look at the real world . . . we observe not only is there no endless cycling, but acts are passed and then remain unchanged for very long periods of time."
11. On this point, see among others Brady and Bullock; and Epstein.
12. Fiorina, *Congress*; Jacobson, *Politics*; Jacobson and Kernell.
13. Fiorina, "Case of the Vanishing Marginals"; Jacobson, "Congressional Elections"; Ferejohn, "On Decline."
14. Riker, *Liberalism*, pp. 189, 190. For a review of committee selection, see Eulau; Asher; Bullock, "Freshman"; Fowler et al.; and Ray.
15. Shepsle and Weingast, "Political Preferences."
16. Mayhew.

17. Sorauf.

18. The standard works on this era are Rossiter, *1787*; Rossiter, *Seedtime*; Brandt, *James Madison*; Madison, *Journal*; and Wood, *Creation of the American Republic*.

19. Most notably Frederick J. Turner.

20. Madison, Essays 10 and 51, in *The Federalist Papers*.

21. Bensel; John Reed.

22. Huntington, "Political Development."

23. Neustadt. See also, among others, Lowi, *End of Liberalism*.

24. Oppenheimer, "Policy Effects."

25. For an excellent general statement of the point, see Cooper, "Congress." For specific studies, see Oppenheimer, "Policy Effects"; Oleszek; Peabody; Oppenheimer, "Policy Implications"; and Dodd and Oppenheimer, *Congress Reconsidered*.

26. Fenno and Munger.

27. Key, *Politics*.

28. See Eulau; Bullock, "Freshman"; and especially Fenno, *Congressmen*.

29. Lowi; McConnell; Redford; Davidson.

30. Holcombe; Miller.

31. Sorauf.

32. Key, *Politics*.

33. See Neustadt, Chap. 1. A common interpretation of Carter's 1976 electoral victory was that the old Roosevelt coalition of 1940 and 1944 was back in business.

34. Burns, *Deadlock*, pp. 1–87; Key, *Politics*.

35. Mann. Fenno, *Home Style*, makes the point that members develop styles that increase trust among their constituents. Mayhew shows that members of the Congress emphasize advertising and credit claiming at the local level. Fiorina, *Congress*, shows that members engage in local constituency service in order to ensure reelection.

36. In the following section I rely on Cooper, "Strengthening the Congress"; and Cooper, "Congress in Organizational Perspective."

37. Cooper, *Origins*.

38. See also Bogue, *Earnest Men*; and Benedict.

39. Huitt, "Congressional Committee"; Huitt, "Morse Committee"; Huitt, "Outsider."

40. On the general point regarding how committee structure affects policy, see Ferejohn, *Pork Barrel Politics*; Shepsle, *Giant Jigsaw Puzzle*; and Riker, *Liberalism*.

41. Cooper, "Strengthening the Congress"; Cooper, "Congress."

42. Lowell; Brady, Cooper, and Hurley.

43. Cooper, "Congress"; Cooper and Brady, "Institutional Context."

44. Clausen; Sinclair, *Congressional Realignment*.

45. Key, *Politics*, p. 677.

46. Cooper, "Congress"; Polsby, "Institutionalization"; Polsby, *Congress*, Chap. 4.

47. Rhode and Shepsle.
48. Stevens et al.
49. Burnham, *Critical Elections*, Chap. 1.
50. Wilson, pp. 206−8; Galloway, *Congress*, p. 2; Burns, *Deadlock*, p. 2.
51. Wilson, p. 82.   52. Galloway, *Congress*, p. 334.
53. Burns, *Congress*, pp. 28−31.   54. Orfield, p. 18.
55. Mann; Mann and Wolfinger.
56. Burnham, *Critical Elections*; Key, "Theory"; Sundquist, *Dynamics*.
57. Sundquist, *Dynamics*, Chaps. 1, 2.
58. Huitt, "Congressional Committee."
59. On ideology and committee assignments, see Shepsle, *Giant Jigsaw Puzzle*; Fenno, *Congressmen*; and Murphy.
60. Orfield.
61. Sinclair, "Party Realignment"; Sinclair, *Congressional Realignment*. See also Brady and Stewart.
62. Sundquist, *Dynamics*.

CHAPTER TWO

1. For an interesting interpretation of how political thought, political institutions, and policy are related during and after realignments, see Huntington, *American Politics*.
2. R. P. McCormick, *Second*; McKitrick. Traditional analyses of the pre−Civil War period are Nevins, *Ordeal of the Union*; Nichols, *Disruption of the American Democracy*; Nichols, *Stakes of Power*; Fehrenbacher, *Prelude to Greatness*; Potter, *Impending Crisis*; and Stampp, *Imperiled Union*. Beginning in the 1960's the "new" political historians, led by Allan Bogue and Lee Benson, presented a distinct perspective concerning voters, parties, and issues. Silbey's *Partisan Imperative*, clearly elucidates the difference between the traditional and the new approach. In my opinion the best books in the new tradition are Bogue, *Earnest Men*; Silbey, *Shrine of Party*; Holt, *Political Crisis*; Benson, *Concept of Jacksonian Democracy*; Formisano, *Birth of Mass Political Parties*; and Kleppner, *Third Electoral System*. Although not in the new-history tradition, Foner, *Free Soil*, provides insights into how the Republicans created a majority party. For a more extensive bibliography of the new history, see Silbey, *Partisan Imperative*; and Bogue, "New Political History."
3. Formisano.
4. Litwack; Fredrickson; and Foner all make this point forcefully.
5. Pease and Pease.   6. Holt, *Political Crisis*, p. 177.
7. Sewall, p. 254.   8. Sundquist, *Dynamics*, p. 90.
9. Ginsberg, "Critical Elections"; Ginsberg, "Elections and Public Policy."
10. Ginsberg, "Critical Elections."
11. All quotations from the platforms are from Porter and Johnson.
12. Butler and Stokes, pp. 135−44.
13. See Clubb et al., Chap. 2, and Flanigan and Zingale, "Measures," for an elaboration of the reasons why the analysis should be run on both parties. Essentially, the reason is that because of third-party candidates, the vote for

one party will not always be the complement of the other party's vote. For most periods in American history, these differences will be very slight. Wherever possible, I will run the analysis on both parties (e.g., Republicans vs. Democrats after 1860).

14. Silbey, *Respectable Minority*.

15. See Flanigan and Zingale, "Measures," for an elaboration.

16. Holt, *Political Crisis*, Chap. 6.

17. For the clearest explication of this matter, see Silbey, *Partisan Imperative*, Chaps. 8, 9. Although the American Party did well in the 1856 election in the Northeast, the Republicans were the major anti-Democratic party elsewhere.

18. For an elaboration of their technique, see Flanigan and Zingale, "Measures." Especially important is their discussion of why correlational techniques will not pick up an across-the-board realignment. Also note their discussion of why region matters in ascertaining realignment change.

19. Clubb et al., pp. 109–10. "The North" excludes the Border states as well as the Southern states.

20. For an analysis of the Cube Law and the swing ratio, see Tufte.

21. Clubb et al., pp. 222–30.

22. Madison, Essay 62, in *The Federalist Papers*.

23. Clubb et al., Chap. 5.

24. On this point, see Fenno, *Congressmen*; Fenno, "House Appropriations Committee"; Hinckley, *Stability*, pp. 59ff; Swanson; Bullock, "Apprenticeship"; Masters; and Smith and Deering.

25. Fenno, *Power of the Purse*, pp. 226–27, for example, shows that high turnover on the Appropriations Committee as a result of the 1946 election affected committee norms and behavior. See also Polsby, "Institutionalization," for the mean average number of freshmen per House.

26. The techniques used to establish issue dimensions are drawn from Clausen; Clausen and Cheney; and Clausen and Van Horn. See the Appendix for a brief review of the technique.

27. Polsby, "Institutionalization."

28. Silbey, *Respectable Minority*.

29. Woodward.

CHAPTER THREE

1. Hacker, *Triumph*; Hacker, *Course*, Chaps. 9, 11.

2. Kirkland, *Industry*; Kirkland, *History*; Williamson.

3. Quoted in Taylor, p. 1.

4. On the Radical Republicans in Congress, see Bogue, *Earnest Men*; and Benedict. Studies of past Radical Congresses include Leech and Brown; Thompson; Blaine; and Gillette. See also Bryce, Chap. 15.

5. Woodward, *Reunion and Reaction*.

6. See also Brady and Stewart.

7. Ginsberg, "Elections and Public Policy," p. 48.

8. All quotes from the platforms are from Porter and Johnson.

9. Ginsberg, "Elections and Public Policy," p. 44.

10. Morgan, pp. 210–12.

11. Mayer, p. 251.

12. Glad, *Trumpet Soundeth*, p. 50.

13. Flanigan and Zingale, "Measurement."

14. Clubb et al., p. 94.

15. Ibid., p. 111.

16. On ideology and the 1896 election, see Glad, *McKinley*; Stanley Jones; and Taussig.

17. Polsby, "Institutionalization."

18. U.S. Congress, House, *Congressional Record*, 31: 764.

19. William McKinley, quoted in Morgan, p. 235.

20. Wilson, p. 58.

21. Fenno, *Power of the Purse*, pp. 226–27.

22. U.S. Congress, House, *Congressional Record*, 31: 5973.

23. Ibid., p. 5967.

24. Ibid., 30: 74.

25. Burnham, "Changing Shape."

26. The standard work on pork barrel politics is Ferejohn, *Pork Barrel Politics: Rivers and Harbors Legislation, 1947–1968*.

27. Polsby, "Institutionalization."

28. Burnham, "Changing Shape."

29. On the Speaker's powers, see McConachie, Chap. 5; and Alexander, Chap. 12. On the powers of the Rules Committee, see McConachie, p. 205; and Brady, *Congressional Voting*, Chap. 4. Summaries of Reed's ending of the disappearing quorum can be found in Alexander, pp. 158–72; and Galloway, *History of the House*, pp. 49–64.

CHAPTER FOUR

1. For two important studies of the party in this period, see Mayer, *Republican Party, 1854–1966*; and C. Jones, *Minority Party*.

2. C. Jones, *Minority Party*, pp. 67–72.

3. Soule.

4. U.S. Dept. of Commerce, Vol. 1, series G, pp. 319–36.

5. Galbraith, pp. 177–81.

6. Other general sources on the effects of the depression are Leuchtenburg; and Frank Freidel's four-volume study of FDR.

7. Leuchtenburg, p. 23.

8. All quotes from the platforms are from Porter and Johnson.

9. Ginsberg, "Critical Elections," p. 622. See also Ginsberg, "Elections and Public Policy."

10. Ginsberg, "Critical Elections," p. 623.

11. See Wills, Chap. 10, for a review of the argument that there was no difference.

12. Freidel, 3: Chap. 23.

13. Ibid., p. 337.

14. See the argument in Brady, "Re-evaluation."

15. Key, "Theory."

16. Sundquist, *Dynamics*, argues that the poor condition of the farm economy was a harbinger of the Great Depression.

17. Ibid. On the farm problem in the 1920's and 1930's, see Fite; and Shover.

18. See Leuchtenburg; and Frank Freidel, "Election of 1932," in Schlesinger, pp. 2741–2806.

19. Polsby, "Institutionalization"; Polsby, Gallagher, and Rundquist; Abram and Cooper.

20. See Polsby, "Institutionalization," Table 3, p. 148.

21. Taken from Polsby, Gallagher, and Rundquist; and Abram and Cooper.

22. Freidel, Vol. 4.

23. U.S. Congress, House, *Congressional Record*, 77.1: 76.

24. Ibid.	25. Ibid., p. 79.
26. Ibid.	27. Ibid., p. 141.

28. Cooper, *Origins*.

29. Clausen, *How Congressmen Decide*; Sinclair, *Congressional Realignment*.

30. See Sinclair, "Party Realignment"; and Brady and Stewart.

31. Sinclair, "Party Realignment."

32. Bailey.

33. U.S. Congress, House, *Congressional Record*, 79.9: 10316, 10319.

34. Ibid., p. 10358.	35. Ibid., p. 10327.
36. Ibid., p. 10331.	37. Ibid., 79.5: 5455.

38. Ibid., p. 5468.

39. Joseph P. Monaghan (R–Mont.) in ibid., p. 5461.

40. Ibid., pp. 5529–30.

41. Ibid., 77.1: 667, 669, 685.

42. Sinclair, "Party Realignment"; Sinclair, *Congressional Realignment*; Brady and Stewart.

43. Brady and Stewart.

44. Sinclair, "Party Realignment," p. 943. On the general point, see pp. 942–45.

45. Ibid., p. 952.

46. Key, *Politics*, pp. 741ff.

47. Caro, Chap. 2.

CHAPTER FIVE

1. For a good review featuring the development of committee studies over time, see Eulau and McCluggage, "Standing Committees." Two excellent studies featuring a social choice perspective are Ferejohn, *Pork Barrel Politics*; and Shepsle, *Giant Jigsaw Puzzle*.

2. On this point two works are particularly insightful: Fenno, *Congressmen in Committees*, and Huitt, "Congressional Committees."

3. Matthews uses theory from sociology to explain committees. Other studies making the point in the text are Masters; Bullock and Sprague; Bullock, "Committee Transfers"; Shepsle, *Giant Jigsaw Puzzle*; and Jewell and Chu.

4. Riker, *Liberalism.*

5. Smith and Deering, p. 119.

6. Fenno, *Congressmen,* Chap. 1.

7. Fenno, *Power of the Purse,* Chaps. 5, 9.

8. Fenno, *Congressmen,* Chap. 1.

9. Ibid., Chaps. 1, 2. See also Manley, *Politics.*

10. Manley, *Politics,* Chap. 7; Surrey.

11. Manley, *Politics,* pp. 354–75.

12. Shepsle, *Giant Jigsaw Puzzle*; Ferejohn, *Pork Barrel Politics.*

13. On the energy bill, see Oppenheimer, "Policy Effects." On the shift to floor activity in the post-1974 period, see Gilmore; and Rudder.

14. Fenno, *Power of the Purse,* pp. 226–27.

15. I do not use an example from the Civil War era because even though turnover increased, the data on committee decisions are not readily available. For example, the amounts appropriated by the Ways and Means Committee by department are not consistently available. Thus, I chose to illustrate the structural point with the examples cited above.

16. Fenno, *Power of the Purse,* Chap. 1.

17. C. Jones et al.; Cooper and Brady, "Institutional Context"; Polsby, "Institutionalization."

18. Brady, *Congressional Voting,* Chap. 4; Brady, "Congressional Leadership."

19. These are the same votes that Fenno uses to determine levels of integration; see his *Power of the Purse,* pp. 191–206 and 471–502.

20. I stick with the final House passage because we are studying the effects of committee structure on House decisions.

21. Shepsle, *Giant Jigsaw Puzzle,* Chaps. 3–5.

22. Ibid., p. 129.

23. Ibid., p. 130.

24. U.S. Congress, House, *Congressional Record,* 46.1: 680.

25. On McNary-Haugenism, see Fite; Shover; Kursman; and Sundquist, *Dynamics.*

26. C. Jones, "Representation."

27. Kursman, Chap. 3.

28. U.S. Congress, House, *Congressional Record,* 75.2: 1580.

29. The best brief review of the technique can be found in Judge et al., pp. 387–90. Kiewiet and McCubbin use the technique for similar reasons.

30. Quandt, "Estimation of the Parameters of a Linear Regression System." See also Goldfeld and Quandt.

31. Cochrane and Orcutt, "Applications of Least Squares Regressions."

CHAPTER SIX

1. Clubb et al., pp. 110, 111.

2. Gudgin and Taylor, p. 31. The formulas for skewness and kurtosis that follow are from pp. 68 and 71, respectively.

3. Ibid., pp. 71–73.

4. Ibid., p. 73.

CHAPTER SEVEN

1. Key, *Politics*, p. 544.
2. Fiorina, *Retrospective Voting*, pp. 37–43.
3. U.S. Dept. of Commerce, Part 1, E 135–66, pp. 210–11; F 163–85, p. 296; K 1–16, pp. 457–64; Part 2, P 17, p. 654.
4. Kiewiet and Rivers, p. 213.
5. Two further decisions warrant mention. All the results point to the same conclusion. However, I rely on the results for the Frickey-Kendrick, farm failures, and business failures indexes. I do not show the results for the

TABLES TO NOTE 5

Regression Analyses of Economic Indicators on Votes and Seats, 1886–1910

Indicator	Regression 1: Frickey-Kendrick	Regression 2: business failures	Regression 3: farm failures
	SEATS[a]		
Economic variable B	1.72	−0.79**	−0.86**
Presidential election B	78.10***	67.89***	73.21***
Year B	−0.03	0.56	0.84
R	0.69	0.65	0.67
	VOTES[b]		
Economic variable B	0.45*	−0.21*	−0.30*
Presidential election B	4.14***	3.72***	3.91***
Year B	−0.01	0.27	0.38
R	0.51	0.49	0.50

NOTE: * = significant at .10; ** = significant at .05; *** = significant at .01. Durbin-Watson's not significant.
[a] Constant range: −75.42 to −67.89.
[b] Constant range: −5.2 to −3.7.

Regression Analyses of Economic Indicators on Votes and Seats, 1920–1946

Indicator	Regression 1: Frickey-Kendrick	Regression 2: business failures	Regression 3: farm failures	Regression 4: personal income
	SEATS[a]			
Economic variable B	1.91**	−2.61**	−2.52**	2.84***
Presidential election B	25.27*	26.55*	24.36*	28.08*
Year B	−3.07	−2.93	−3.19	−3.48
R	0.75	0.80	0.78	0.77
	VOTES[b]			
Economic variable B	0.77***	−0.28**	−0.26**	0.32**
Presidential election B	0.79	0.26	0.29	0.35
Year B	−0.12	0.04	0.03	0.31
R	0.72	0.67	0.65	0.69

NOTE: See note to table for 1886–1910 for meaning of asterisks.
[a] Constant range: 20.22 to 22.73.
[b] Constant range: −8.1 to −3.5.

Consumer Price Index and some other indexes because they all show retrospective voting at about the same level as the indexes I do use. Further, when one uses regression techniques on small data sets, there are problems in assessing the B estimates. I used the Tukey jackknife technique to correct for small data sets (Tukey, "Problem of Multiple Comparisons"; David; Duesenberry and David). That is, after each regression was run, one year was eliminated and the regression rerun. Then that year was replaced in the sample, and the analysis rerun; the process was repeated until each year had been eliminated for one run. The results can then be used to determine how much individual data points affect the estimates. For both indexes the jackknife technique showed that the B estimates for the time series reported here were stable. That is, the dropping of single data points did not change the B estimates by more than 10 percent. This is especially convincing because the important House elections of 1894 and 1932 are outliers in the sense that a great number of seats changed hands. The accompanying tables show the results of the original regression of the economic variables against the incumbent party's vote and seat changes.

6. Key, *Politics*, p. 544.

7. Ronald Formisano, "To the Editor," *Civil War History*, 21: 188 (June 1975), cited in Silbey, *Partisan Imperative*, p. 172.

8. For an analysis of the actual House votes, see Wolff.

9. Silbey, *Partisan Imperative*, Chap. 8.

10. Ibid., p. 142.

11. Ibid.; Gienapp, "Origins"; Gienapp, "Nativism."

12. Formisano, "To the Editor" (as cited in note 7, above); Formisano, *Birth of Mass Political Parties*.

13. Fiorina, *Representatives*, p. 45.

14. Key, *Public Opinion*, p. 474.

15. Fiorina, *Retrospective Voting*, p. 201.

16. See, for example, Burnham, *Current Crisis*; and Chubb and Peterson, Chap. 1.

17. Ferejohn and Calvert.

18. Mayhew, p. 296; Tufte.

19. Brady and Lynn.

20. The first shift away from competition toward a U-shaped curve is clearly the result of decreased competition in the South because of electoral arrangements such as the poll tax. The continued decline of competition, especially in the North, remains an unanswered question, although it is quite clear that the decline in competitive seats is not a mid-1960's phenomenon but began very early in the century.

Bibliography

The following abbreviations are used in the Bibliography: *AJPS, American Journal of Political Science*, and *APSR, American Political Science Review.*

Abram, Michael, and Joseph Cooper. "The Rise of Seniority in the House of Representatives," *Polity*, Fall 1968, pp. 52–84.

Alexander, De Alva Stanwood. *History and Procedure of the House of Representatives*. Boston, 1916.

Anderson, James. *Public Policy Making*. New York, 1979.

Anderson, James, David W. Brady, and Charles Bullock. *Public Policy and Politics in the United States*. North Scituate, Mass., 1976.

Arrow, Kenneth. *Social Choice and Individual Values*. New Haven, Conn., 1963.

Asher, Herbert. "Committees and the Norm of Specialization," *Annals of the American Academy of Political and Social Science*, 411: 63–74 (1974).

Bailey, Stephen. *Congress Makes a Law*. New York, 1950.

Benedict, Michael. *A Compromise of Principle: Congressional Republicans and Reconstruction, 1863–1869*. New York, 1974.

Bensel, Richard. *Sectionalism and American Political Development, 1880–1980*. Madison, Wis., 1984.

Benson, Lee. *The Concept of Jacksonian Democracy: New York as a Test Case*. Princeton, N.J., 1961.

Blaine, James G. *Twenty Years of Congress: From Lincoln to Garfield*. Norwich, Conn., 1886.

Bogue, Allan. *The Earnest Men*. Ithaca, N.Y., 1981.

———. "The New Political History in the 1970's," in M. Kammen, ed., *The Past Before Us*. Ithaca, N.Y., 1980.

Bolling, Richard. *House Out of Order*. New York, 1964.

Brady, David W. "Congressional Leadership and Party Voting in the McKinley Era: A Comparison to the Modern House," *AJPS*, 16: 439–59 (Aug. 1972).

———. *Congressional Voting in a Partisan Era*. Lawrence, Kans., 1973.

———. "A Re-evaluation of Realignments in American Politics: Evidence from the House of Representatives," *APSR*, 77: 31–33 (March 1985).

Brady, David W., and Charles Bullock. "Party and Factions Within Legislatures," in Gerhard Loewenberg, Samuel Patterson, and Malcolm Jewell, eds., *Handbook of Legislative Research.* Cambridge, Mass., 1985.

———, and Naomi Lynn. "Switched Seat Congressional Districts: Their Effects on Party Voting and Public Policy," *AJPS*, 17: 528–43 (Nov. 1973).

———, and Joseph Stewart, "Congressional Party Realignment and Transformation of Public Policy in Three Realignment Eras," *AJPS*, 26: 333–60 (May 1982).

Brady, David W., Joseph Cooper, and Patricia Hurley. "The Decline of Party in the U.S. House of Representatives, 1877–1968," *Legislative Studies Quarterly*, 4: 381–407 (Aug. 1979).

Brandt, Irving. *James Madison.* Indianapolis, 1961.

Bryce, James M. *The American Commonwealth.* London, 1888.

Bullock, Charles. "Apprenticeship and Committee Assignments in the House of Representatives," *Journal of Politics*, 32: 717–30 (Nov. 1970).

———. "Committee Transfers in the United States House of Representatives," *Journal of Politics*, 35: 85–120 (Feb. 1973).

———. "Freshman Committee Assignments and Re-election in the U.S. House of Representatives," *APSR*, 66: 996–1007 (Sept. 1972).

Bullock, Charles, and David W. Brady. "Party, Constituency and Roll Call Voting in the U.S. Senate," *Legislative Studies Quarterly*, 8: 29–43 (Feb. 1982).

———, and John Sprague. "A Research Note on the Committee Reassignments of Southern Democratic Congressmen," *Journal of Politics*, 31: 493–512 (May 1969).

Burnham, Walter D. "The Changing Shape of the American Political Universe," *APSR*, 59: 7–29 (March 1965).

———. *Critical Elections and the Mainsprings of American Politics.* New York, 1970.

———. *The Current Crisis in American Politics.* Oxford, 1982.

Burns, James M. *Congress on Trial.* New York, 1949.

———. *The Deadlock of Democracy.* New York, 1963.

Butler, David, and Donald Stokes. *Political Change in Britain: Forces Shaping Electoral Choice.* New York, 1969.

Caro, Robert. *The Years of Lyndon Johnson.* New York, 1982.

Chubb, John, and Paul Peterson, eds. *New Directions in American Politics.* Washington, D.C., 1985.

Clark, Joseph. *Congress: The Sapless Branch.* New York, 1964.

Clausen, Aage. *How Congressmen Decide: A Policy Focus.* New York, 1973.

Clausen, Aage, and Richard Cheney. "A Comparative Analysis of Senate-House Voting on Economic and Welfare Policy: 1953–64," *APSR*, 64: 138–52 (March 1970).

———, and Carl Van Horn. "How to Analyze Too Many Roll Calls and Related Issues in Dimensional Analysis," *Political Methodology*, 4.3: 313–32 (1977).

Clubb, Jerome, William Flanigan, and Nancy Zingale. *Partisan Realignment: Voters, Parties, and Government in American History.* Beverly Hills, Calif., 1980.

Cochrane, D., and G. Orcutt. "Applications of Least Squares Regressions to Relationships Containing Auto-Correlated Error Terms," *Journal of the American Statistical Association*, 44: 32–61 (March 1949).

Cooper, Joseph. "Congress in Organizational Perspective," in Lawrence Dodd and Bruce Oppenheimer, eds., *Congress Reconsidered*. New York, 1977.

———. *The Origins of the Standing Committees and the Development of the Modern House*. Houston, 1970.

———. "Strengthening the Congress: An Organizational Analysis," *Harvard Journal on Legislation*, 12: 307–68 (April 1975).

———, and David W. Brady. "Institutional Context and Leadership Style: The House from Cannon to Rayburn," *APSR*, 75: 411–25 (June 1981).

Dahl, Robert. *A Preface to Democratic Theory*. Chicago, 1965.

David, H. A. "Multiple Decisions and Multiple Comparisons," in Ahmed Sarhan and Bernard Greenberg, eds., *Contributions to Order Statistics*. New York, 1962.

Davidson, Roger. "Subcommittee Government: New Channels for Policy Making," in Thomas Mann and Norman Ornstein, eds., *The New Congress*. Washington, D.C., 1981.

Duesenberry, C. P., and H. A. David. "Some Tests for Outliers," *Biometrika*, 43.3-4: 379–90 (1961).

Elezar, Daniel. *American Federalism: A View from the States*. New York, 1968.

Epstein, Leon. "What Happened to the British Party Model?," *APSR*, 74: 9–22 (March 1980).

Eulau, Heinz. "Committee Selection," in Gerhard Loewenberg, Samuel Patterson, and Malcolm Jewell, eds., *Handbook of Legislative Research*. Cambridge, Mass., 1985.

Eulau, Heinz, and Vera McCluggage. "Standing Committees," in Gerhard Loewenberg, Samuel Patterson, and Malcolm Jewell, eds., *Handbook of Legislative Research*. Cambridge, Mass., 1985.

Farrand, Max, ed. *The Records of the Federal Convention of 1787*, Vol. 1. New Haven, Conn., 1966.

Fehrenbacher, Don. *Prelude to Greatness: Lincoln in the 1850's*. Stanford, Calif., 1962.

Fenno, Richard. *Congressmen in Committees*. Boston, 1973.

———. *Home Style*. Boston, 1978.

———. "The House Appropriations Committee as a Political System," *APSR*, 56: 310–24 (June 1962).

———. *The Power of the Purse*. Boston, 1966.

Fenno, Richard, and Frank Munger. *National Politics and Federal Aid to Education*. Syracuse, N.Y., 1962.

Ferejohn, John. "On the Decline of Competition in Congressional Elections," *APSR*, 71: 166–76 (March 1977).

———. *Pork Barrel Politics: Rivers and Harbors Legislation, 1947–1968*. Stanford, Calif., 1974.

Ferejohn, John, and Randall Calvert. "Presidential Coattails in Historical Perspective," *AJPS*, 28: 127–46.

Fiorina, Morris. "The Case of the Vanishing Marginals: The Bureaucracy Did It," *APSR*, 71: 177–81 (March 1977).

———. *Congress: Keystone of the Washington Establishment*. New Haven, Conn., 1977.

———. *Representatives, Roll Calls and Constituencies*. Lexington, Mass., 1974.

———. *Retrospective Voting in American National Elections*. New Haven, Conn., 1981.

Fite, Gilbert. *American Agriculture and Farm Policy Since 1900*. New York, 1964.

Flanigan, William, and Nancy Zingale. "The Measurement of Electoral Change," *Political Methodology*, 1: 49–82 (Summer 1974).

———. "Measures of Electoral Competition," *Political Methodology*, 1: 31–48 (Summer 1974).

Foner, Eric. *Free Soil, Free Labor, Free Men: The Ideology of the Republican Party Before the Civil War*. New York, 1970.

Formisano, Ronald. *The Birth of Mass Political Parties: Michigan, 1827–1861*. Princeton, N.J., 1971.

Fowler, Linda, Scott Douglass, and Wesley Clark. "The Electoral Effects of House Committee Assignments," *Journal of Politics*, 42: 307–19 (Feb. 1980).

Fredrickson, George. *White Supremacy*. New York, 1981.

Freidel, Frank. *Franklin D. Roosevelt*. 4 vols. Boston, 1952. Vol. 3: *The Triumph*. Vol. 4: *Launching the New Deal*.

Galbraith, John K. *The Great Crash*. New York, 1955.

Galloway, George. *Congress at the Crossroads*. New York, 1946.

———. *History of the House of Representatives*. New York, 1962.

Gienapp, William. "Nativism and the Creation of a Republican Majority," paper presented at the annual meeting of the Organization of American Historians, Cincinnati, Ohio, 1984.

———. "The Origins of the Republican Party, 1852–1856," Ph.D. dissertation, University of California, Berkeley.

———. *The Origins of the Republican Party, 1852–1856*. New York, 1986.

Gillette, William. *Retreat from Reconstruction, 1869–1879*. Baton Rouge, La., 1979.

Gilmore, John. "Political Consequences of the Congressional Budget Process," unpublished manuscript, Berkeley, Calif., 1985.

Ginsberg, Benjamin. "Critical Elections and the Substance of Party Conflict: 1844–1968," *Midwest Journal of Political Science*, 16: 603–25 (Nov. 1972).

———. "Elections and Public Policy," *APSR*, 70: 41–49 (March 1976).

Glad, Paul. *McKinley, Bryan and the People*. Philadelphia, 1964.

———. *The Trumpet Soundeth: William Jennings Bryan and His Democracy, 1896–1912*. Lincoln, Neb., 1966.

Goldfeld, S., and R. Quandt. "The Estimation of Structural Shifts by Switching Regressions," *Annals of Economic and Social Measurement*, 2: 475–85 (Oct. 1973).

Goodwin, George. *The Little Legislatures: Committees in Congress*. Amherst, Mass., 1970.

Gudgin, G., and R. J. Taylor. *Seats, Votes, and the Spatial Organization of Elections.* London, 1979.
Hacker, Louis. *The Course of American Economic Growth and Development.* New York, 1970.
――――. *The Triumph of American Capitalism.* New York, 1947.
Hays, Samuel P. *The Response to Industrialism.* Chicago, 1957.
Hinckley, Barbara. *The Seniority System in Congress.* Bloomington, Ind., 1971.
――――. *Stability and Change in Congress.* Bloomington, Ind., 1978.
Holcombe, Arthur. *Our More Perfect Union: From Eighteenth Century Principles to Twentieth Century Practice.* Cambridge, Mass., 1950.
Holt, Michael. *Forging a Majority: The Formation of the Republican Party in Pittsburgh, 1848–1860.* New Haven, Conn., 1969.
――――. *The Political Crisis of the 1850's.* New York, 1978.
Huitt, Ralph. "The Congressional Committee: A Case Study," *APSR*, 48: 340–65 (June 1954).
――――. "The Morse Committee Assignment Controversy: A Case Study," *APSR*, 51: 313–29 (June 1957).
――――. "The Outsider in the Senate: An Alternative Role," *APSR*, 55: 566–75 (Sept. 1961).
Huntington, Samuel. *American Politics: The Promise of Disharmony.* Cambridge, Mass., 1981.
――――. "Congressional Responses to the Twentieth Century," in David Truman, ed., *Congress and America's Future.* Englewood Cliffs, N.J., 1965.
――――. "Political Development and Political Decay," *World Politics*, 17: 386–430 (April 1965).
Jacobson, Gary. "Congressional Elections, 1978: The Case of the Vanishing Challengers," in Louis Maisel and Joseph Cooper, eds., *Congressional Elections.* Beverly Hills, Calif., 1981.
――――. *The Politics of Congressional Elections.* Boston, 1983.
Jacobson, Gary, and Samuel Kernell. *Strategy and Choice in Congressional Elections.* New Haven, Conn., 1981.
Jewell, Malcolm, and Chu Chi-hung. "Membership Movement and Committee Attractiveness in the U.S. House of Representatives, 1963–1971," *Midwest Journal of Political Science*, 18: 433–41 (Aug. 1974).
Jones, Charles O. "Joseph Cannon and Howard Smith: An Essay on the Limits of Leadership in the House of Representatives," *Journal of Politics*, 30: 617–46 (Aug. 1968).
――――. *The Minority Party in Congress.* Boston, 1970.
――――. "Representation in Congress: The Case of the House Agriculture Committee," *APSR*, 55: 358–67 (June 1961).
Jones, Stanley. *The Presidential Election of 1896.* Madison, Wis., 1964.
Judge, George, William Griffiths, R. Carter Hill, and Tsoung-chao Lee. *The Theory and Practice of Econometrics.* New York, 1983.
Keller, Morton. *Affairs of State.* Cambridge, Mass., 1980.
Key, V. O., Jr. *Politics, Parties, and Pressure Groups.* New York, 1964.

————. *Public Opinion and American Democracy*. New York, 1961.

————. "A Theory of Critical Elections," *Journal of Politics*, 17: 3–18 (Feb. 1955).

Kiewiet, Roderick, and Douglas Rivers. "A Retrospective on Retrospective Voting," in Heinz Eulau and Michael Lewis-Beck, eds., *Economic Conditions and Electoral Outcomes*. New York, 1985.

————, and Matthew McCubbin. "Congressional Appropriations and the Electoral Connection," *Journal of Politics*, 47: 59–82 (Feb. 1985).

Kirkland, Edward C. *A History of American Economic Life*. New York, 1951.

————. *Industry Comes of Age*. New York, 1962.

Kleppner, Paul. *The Third Electoral System, 1853–1892: Parties, Voters, and Political Cultures*. Chapel Hill, N.C., 1979.

Kursman, Nancy. "The House Agricultural Committee, 1880 to 1950," Ph.D. dissertation, Rice University, 1985.

Leech, Margaret, and Harry Brown. *The Garfield Orbit: The Life of President James Garfield*. New York, 1978.

Leuchtenburg, William. *Franklin Delano Roosevelt and the New Deal*. New York, 1963.

Lichtman, Alan. "Critical Election Theory and the Reality of American Politics, 1916–1940," *American Historical Review*, 81: 317–48 (April 1976).

Litwack, Leon. *North of Slavery: The Negro in the Free States, 1790–1860*. Chicago, 1961.

Lowell, A. Lawrence. "The Influence of Party Upon Legislation in England and America," *American Historical Association Annual Report for the Year 1901*, 1: 319–550 (1901).

Lowi, Theodore. *The End of Liberalism*. New York, 1979.

McConachie, Lauros. *Congressional Committees*. New York, 1898.

McConnell, Grant. *Private Power and American Democracy*. New York, 1966.

McCormick, Richard L. *The Party Period and Public Policy: American Politics from the Age of Jackson to the Progressive Era*. Oxford, 1986.

McCormick, Richard P. *The Second American Party System: Party Formation in the Jacksonian Era*. Chapel Hill, N.C., 1966.

McKelvey, Richard. "Intransitivities in Multi-Dimensional Voting Models, and Some Implications for Agenda Control," *Journal of Economic Theory*, 2: 472–82 (Oct. 1976).

McKitrick, Eric. "Party Politics and the Union and Confederate War Efforts," pp. 117–51 in William Chambers and Walter Burnham, eds., *The American Party Systems*. London, 1975.

MacNeil, Neil. *Forge of Democracy*. New York, 1963.

MacRae, Duncan. Issues and Parties in Legislative Voting: Methods of Statistical Analysis. New York, 1970.

————. "Roll Call Votes and Leadership," Public Opinion Quarterly, 20: 543–58 (Fall 1956).

Madison, James. *The Federalist Papers*. Baltimore, 1981.

————. *Journal of the Federal Convention*. New York, 1893.

Manley, John. "The House Committee on Ways and Means: Conflict Management in a Congressional Committee," *APSR*, 59: 927–39 (Dec. 1965).

——. *The Politics of Finance: The House Committee on Ways and Means*. Boston, 1970.

Mann, Thomas. *Unsafe at Any Margin*. Washington, D.C., 1978.

Mann, Thomas, and Raymond Wolfinger. "Candidates and Parties in Congressional Elections," *APSR*, 74: 617–32 (Sept. 1980).

March, James. "Party Legislative Representation as a Function of Election Results," in Paul Lazarsfeld and Neil Henry, eds., *Readings in Mathematical Social Science*. Chicago, 1966.

Masters, Nicholas. "Committee Assignments in the House of Representatives," *APSR*, 55: 345–57 (June 1961).

Matthews, Donald. *U.S. Senators and Their World*. Chapel Hill, N.C., 1960.

Mayer, George E. *The Republican Party, 1854–1966*. New York, 1968.

Mayhew, David. *Congress: The Electoral Connection*. New Haven, Conn., 1974.

Miller, John. *Alexander Hamilton*. New York, 1959.

Morgan, H. Wayne. *William McKinley and His America*. Syracuse, N.Y., 1963.

Murphy, James. "Political Parties and the Pork Barrel: Party Conflict and Cooperation in House Public Works Committee Decision Making," *APSR*, 68: 169–85 (March 1974).

Neustadt, Richard. *Presidential Power*. New York, 1976.

Nevins, Allan. *The Ordeal of the Union*. London, 1947.

Nichols, Roy F. *The Disruption of the American Democracy*. New York, 1947.

——. *The Stakes of Power*. New York, 1961.

Oleszek, Walter. *Congressional Procedures and the Policy Process*. Washington, D.C., 1978.

Oppenheimer, Bruce. "Policy Effects of U.S. House Reform: Decentralization and the Capacity to Resolve Energy Issues," *Legislative Studies Quarterly*, 5: 5–30 (Feb. 1980).

——. "Policy Implications of Rule Committee Reforms," in Leroy Reiselbach, ed., *Legislative Reform: The Policy Impact*. Lexington, Mass., 1978.

Orfield, Gary. *Congressional Power: Congress and Social Change*. New York, 1975.

Peabody, Robert. "The Enlarged Rules Committee," in Robert Peabody and Nelson Polsby, eds., *New Perspectives on the House of Representatives*. Chicago, 1977.

Pease, William, and Jane Pease. *They Who Would Be Free*. New York, 1974.

Polsby, Nelson. *Congress and the Presidency*. New York, 1986.

——. "The Institutionalization of the House of Representatives," *APSR*, 62: 144–69 (March 1968).

Polsby, Nelson, Miriam Gallagher, and Barry Rundquist. "The Growth of the Seniority System in the U.S. House of Representatives," *APSR*, 63: 787–807 (Aug. 1969).

Porter, Kirk, and Donald Johnson, eds. *National Party Platforms, 1840–1972*. Urbana, Ill., 1973.

Potter, David. *The Impending Crisis*. New York, 1976.

Quandt, Richard. "The Estimation of the Parameters of a Linear Regression System Obeying Two Separate Regimes," *Journal of the American Statistical Association*, 53: 873–80 (Dec. 1958).

Ray, Bruce. "Federal Spending and the Selection of Committee Assignments in the U.S. House of Representatives," *AJPS*, 24: 494–510 (Aug. 1980).

Redford, Emmett. *American Government and the Economy*. New York, 1966.

Reed, John. *Southerners: The Social Psychology of Sectionalism*. Chapel Hill, N.C., 1983.

Reed, Thomas B. "Reform Needed in the House," *North American Review*, 150: 537–46 (May 1980).

Rhode, David, and Kenneth Shepsle. "The Ambiguous Role of Leadership in Woodrow Wilson's Congress," paper delivered at the annual meeting of the American Political Science Association, Washington, D.C., Sept. 1985.

Rice, Stuart. *Quantitative Methods in Politics*. New York, 1969. Originally published in 1928.

Riker, William. "Implications from the Disequilibrium of Majority Rule for the Study of Politics," *APSR*, 75: 432–58 (June 1980).

———. *Liberalism Against Populism*. San Francisco, 1982.

Rossiter, Clinton. *Seedtime of the Republic*. New York, 1953.

———. *1787: The Grand Convention*. New York, 1966.

Rudder, Catherine. "Committee Reform and the Revenue Process," in Lawrence Dodd and Bruce Oppenheimer, eds., *Congress Reconsidered*. New York, 1977.

———. "The Policy Impact of Reform of the Committee on Ways and Means," in Leroy Reiselbach, ed., *Legislative Reform: The Policy Impact*. Lexington, Mass., 1978.

Schattschneider, E. E. *Party Government*. New York, 1942.

Schlesinger, Arthur. *The History of American Presidential Elections, 1789–1984*. New York, 1984.

Schofield, Norman. "Instability of Simple Dynamic Games," *Review of Economic Studies*, 45: 575–90 (Oct. 1978).

Schwartz, Thomas. "The Meaning of Instability," paper delivered at the annual meeting of the American Political Science Association, Washington, D.C., Sept. 1985.

Sewall, Richard. *Ballots for Freedom*. New York, 1976.

Shepsle, Kenneth. *The Giant Jigsaw Puzzle*. Chicago, 1978.

———. "Institutional Arrangements and Equilibrium in Multi-Dimensional Voting Models," *AJPS*, 23: 27–59 (Feb. 1979).

Shepsle, Kenneth, and Barry Weingast. "Political Preferences for the Pork Barrel: A Generalization," *AJPS*, 25: 96–111 (Feb. 1981).

———. "Structure-Induced Equilibrium and Legislative Choice," *Public Choice*, 37.3: 503–19 (1981).

Shover, John. *First Majority, Last Minority*. DeKalb, Ill., 1976.

Silbey, Joel. *The Partisan Imperative: The Dynamics of American Politics Before the Civil War*. New York, 1985.

————. *A Respectable Minority: The Democratic Party in the Civil War Era, 1860–1868.* New York, 1977.

————. *The Shrine of Party.* Pittsburgh, Pa., 1967.

Sinclair, Barbara. *Congressional Realignment, 1925–1978.* Austin, Tex., 1982.

————. "Party Realignment and the Transformation of the Political Agenda: The House of Representatives, 1925–39," *APSR*, 71: 940–53 (Sept. 1977).

Smith, Steven, and Christopher Deering. *Committees in Congress.* Washington, D.C., 1984.

Smith, William. *Speakers of the House of Representatives of the United States.* Baltimore, 1928.

Sorauf, Frank. *Party Politics in America.* Boston, 1976.

Soule, George. *Prosperity Decade.* New York, 1962.

Stampp, Kenneth. *The Imperiled Union: Essays on the Background of the Civil War.* New York, 1980.

Stevens, Arthur, Arthur Miller, and Thomas Mann. "Mobilization of Liberal Strength in the House, 1950–1970: The Democratic Study Group," *APSR*, 68: 667–81 (June 1974).

Sundquist, James. *The Dynamics of the Party System: Alignment and Realignment of Political Parties in the United States.* Washington, D.C., 1973.

————. *Politics and Policy: The Eisenhower, Kennedy, and Johnson Years.* Washington, D.C., 1968.

Surrey, Stanley. "The Congress and the Tax Lobbyist; How Special Tax Provisions Get Enacted," *Harvard Law Review,* 70: 1145–82 (May 1957).

Swanson, Wayne. "Committee Assignments and the Nonconformist Legislator: Democrats in the U.S. Senate," *Midwest Journal of Political Science,* 13: 84–94 (Feb. 1969).

Taussig, Frank. *Tariff History of the United States.* New York, 1923.

Taylor, George Rogers. "The National Economy Before and After the Civil War," in David Gilchrist and W. David Lewis, eds., *Economic Change in the Civil War Era.* Greenville, Del., 1965.

Thompson, Margaret. *The Spider Web: Congress and Lobbying in the Age of Grant.* Ithaca, N.Y., 1985.

de Tocqueville, Alexis. *Democracy in America,* ed. Philips Bradley. New York, 1945.

Tufte, Edward. "The Relationship Between Seats and Votes in Two-Party Systems," *APSR,* 67: 540–54 (June 1973).

Tukey, John W. "The Problem of Multiple Comparisons," in *International Encyclopedia of the Social Sciences,* 9: 339–51. New York, 1968.

Tullock, Gordon. "Why So Much Stability?," *Public Choice,* 37.2 (1981).

Turner, Frederick J. *Essays in American History.* New York, 1910.

————. *The Significance of the Frontier in American History.* New York, 1968.

————. *The Significance of Sections in American History.* New York, 1932.

United States, Department of Commerce. *Historical Statistics of the United States: Colonial Times to 1970.* Washington, D.C., 1975.

Wiebe, Richard. *The Search for Order, 1877–1920.* New York, 1967.

Williamson, Harold. *The Growth of the American Economy.* New York, 1959.

Wills, Garry. *Confessions of a Conservative.* New York, 1979.

Wilson, Woodrow. *Congressional Government.* Cleveland, Ohio, 1973.

Wolff, Gerald. *The Kansas-Nebraska Bill: Party, Section and the Coming of the Civil War.* New York, 1977.

Wood, Gordon. *The Creation of the American Republic.* Chapel Hill, N.C., 1969.

Woodward, C. Vann. *Reunion and Reaction: The Compromise of 1876 and the End of Reconstruction.* Boston, 1966.

Index

Library of Congress Cataloging-in-Publication Data

Brady, David W.
  Critical elections and congressional policy making.

  (Stanford studies in the new political history)
  Bibliography: p.
  Includes index.
    1. Political planning—United States—History—
19th century. 2. Political planning—United States—
History—20th century. 3. United States. Congress.
House—History—19th century. 4. United States.
Congress. House—History—20th century. 5. Elections—
United States—History—19th century. 6. Elections—
United States—History—20th century. I. Title
II. Series.
  JK231.B73 1988   328.73'09   87-18068
  ISBN 0-8047-1442-8 (alk. paper)
  ISBN 0-8047-1840-7 (pbk.)